1,000,000 Books

are available to read at

Forgotten Books

www.ForgottenBooks.com

Read online
Download PDF
Purchase in print

ISBN 978-1-330-80951-8
PIBN 10108269

This book is a reproduction of an important historical work. Forgotten Books uses state-of-the-art technology to digitally reconstruct the work, preserving the original format whilst repairing imperfections present in the aged copy. In rare cases, an imperfection in the original, such as a blemish or missing page, may be replicated in our edition. We do, however, repair the vast majority of imperfections successfully; any imperfections that remain are intentionally left to preserve the state of such historical works.

Forgotten Books is a registered trademark of FB &c Ltd.
Copyright © 2018 FB &c Ltd.
FB &c Ltd, Dalton House, 60 Windsor Avenue, London, SW19 2RR.
Company number 08720141. Registered in England and Wales.

For support please visit www.forgottenbooks.com

1 MONTH OF
FREE
READING

at
www.ForgottenBooks.com

By purchasing this book you are eligible for one month membership to ForgottenBooks.com, giving you unlimited access to our entire collection of over 1,000,000 titles via our web site and mobile apps.

To claim your free month visit: www.forgottenbooks.com/free108269

* Offer is valid for 45 days from date of purchase. Terms and conditions apply.

English
Français
Deutsche
Italiano
Español
Português

www.forgottenbooks.com

Mythology Photography **Fiction**
Fishing Christianity **Art** Cooking
Essays Buddhism Freemasonry
Medicine **Biology** Music **Ancient Egypt** Evolution Carpentry Physics
Dance Geology **Mathematics** Fitness
Shakespeare **Folklore** Yoga Marketing
Confidence Immortality Biographies
Poetry **Psychology** Witchcraft
Electronics Chemistry History **Law**
Accounting **Philosophy** Anthropology
Alchemy Drama Quantum Mechanics
Atheism Sexual Health **Ancient History**
Entrepreneurship Languages Sport
Paleontology Needlework Islam
Metaphysics Investment Archaeology
Parenting Statistics Criminology
Motivational

Devon Notes and Queries:

a Quarterly Journal devoted to the LOCAL HISTORY BIOGRAPHY and ANTIQUITIES of the County of Devon edited by P F S AMERY JOHN S AMERY and J BROOKING ROWE FSA

VOLUME I.

From January 1900 to October 1901

JAMES G COMMIN
230 HIGH ST
EXETER
❖
1901

DA
670
D49D4
v. 1

872495

PREFACE.

The Editors upon the completion of the first volume of *Devon Notes & Queries*—the publication of which has extended over two years—beg to thank very sincerely all those contributors, well wishers and subscribers, whose assistance has made the effort to establish this magazine a success.

It is very clear that the periodical meets a want, and as a medium of communication between those interested in the history and antiquities of the County, it has to a great extent realized the hopes of its promoters. That it has in some respects fallen short of what was aimed at may be true, and the Editors are well aware of sundry shortcomings, but in the establishment of a Magazine of this kind, difficulties necessarily present themselves which only time and experience can remove. A wish has been expressed by many that the issue should be more frequent, but the quarterly publication must continue, at all events for the present.

The Editors ask for continued and frequent contributions relating to the history and antiquities of the County of Devon, Notes on the Discovery of the Remains of pre-historic and later ages, its Records, Manuscripts, and Ecclesiology, Biography, Folk Lore, Dialects, and Legends, which will find a warm welcome in our pages. The Editors will also be glad to receive portraits, paintings, drawings and engravings of local persons, places, and things for illustrations.

During the coming year the Supplemental part will be a new and revised edition, fully illustrated, of the Crosses of Dartmoor, by Mr. William Crossing, to be completed in 1902. Following this will be a very interesting and complete series of Churchwarden's Accounts of a Devon Parish, the transcripts of which has been placed at the disposal of the Editors.

> P. F. S. AMERY,
> J. S. AMERY,
> J. BROOKING ROWE,
> *Editors.*

Dated, 21st Sept., 1901.

LIST OF PLATES.

Great Fulford ... . *page*	1
Doorway of Great Fulford House	1
Sir Thomas Fulford's Monument in Dunsford Church	5
Totnes Guildhall: Interior	33
Totnes Guildhall: Entrance with Old Pillars ...	33
Totnes: The Old Church Walk ...	41
Sir Humphrey Gilbert	49
Monumental Brass to John Bowthe, Bp. of Exeter	57
Week Down Cross	65
Shorter Cross, Week Down ...	65
Hele Cross	65
North Bovey Cross	65
Antique Tazza in Colaton Raleigh Church ...	73
Thomas, First Lord Clifford of Chudleigh	81
Peasants Gathering Moss ...	89
Sandy Park Bridge on the Teign	89
Drewsteignton Cromlech ...	93
Millais' Studio at Budleigh Salterton ...	97
Cottage at North Bovey	105
The Steen, 1790	105
Carved Oak Screen in Lustleigh Church ...	113
Okehampton Castle	121
Monument of Thomas Chafe	129
Screen in Bridford Church ...	137
Exeter Guildhall Front: City Arms ...	153
Exeter Guildhall Front: Corbelled Treatment ...	155
Samuel Cook—Artist, 1806-1859 ...	161

Ancient Clock, Exeter Cathedral ...	179
John Cranch ...	193
Brass in Sidbury Church	201
Torbryan Church Altar	208
Churchyard Cross, Plympton St. Maurice	209
Tablet in Farringdon Church ...	216
Cadhay House	225
"Court of the Kings," Cadhay ...	233
Grant by Eva de Cantilupe, circa 1265	245

IN CAREW'S SCROLL OF ARMS.

George Carew, Earl of Totnes	1
Arms of Andrew Holland, A.D. 1350	5

Great Fulford.

Doorway of Great Fulford House.

Devon Notes and Queries.

1. NOTES ON GREAT FULFORD.—The following account is based on notes kindly supplied by F. D. Fulford, Esq., the present owner. That a house existed at Great Fulford many years ago there is no doubt, for we find that on 8th July, 1402, Bishop Stafford granted a license to Henry Fulford and Wilhelmina, his wife, to have Divine Service performed, "*infra mansiones suas de Ffoleford et Morton.*" This Henry Fulford was King Henry the Fifth's escheator for Devon and Cornwall in 1413, and four years later was appointed Sheriff of Cornwall. In 22nd and 23rd Henry VIII, the sum of £8 10s. 1d. was spent in repairs about Fulford House. Sir John Fulford purchased the Manor of Dunsford at the Reformation; it had previously belonged to the Priory of Canonsleigh. The lords of the Manor formerly had the power of inflicting capital punishment. Sir John Fulford, Kt., Sheriff of Devon, 5th Mary and 19th Elizabeth, was the builder of the present Fulford House. He married the daughter of Sir Thomas Dennys, of Holcombe Burnell, Kt., Chancellor to Queen Ann of Cleves, fourth wife of Henry VIII.

Prince says, "Fulford House is a large stately pile, standing pleasantly on a gentle ascent in an open but somewhat coarse country. It suffered much in the late unhappy wars, when it was garrisoned on behalf of King Charles I, of blessed memory, but it hath since been repaired by the care and cost of the present inhabitant, Col. Francis Fulford, to that degree of neatness and curiosity that it is now become the most beautiful and stately structure in all those parts.

Without doors it is well accommodated with gardens, fish ponds, park, etc.; within with a fine oratory, neatly wainscotted and seated, richly paved with white polished marble, as in the great hall, chequer-wise with white and black marble, whose staircase is a piece of great cost as well as cunning, being diversified with sundry pieces of parti-coloured timber, very artificially inlaid, which leads you up to a noble dining room, very sumptuously furnished, as is the whole throughout, so that it would require a considerable time but to repeat the great variety in carving, landskip paintings and the like, which art and cost there offer to your view." (*Vide* "Prince's Worthies," p. 392).

In a note to 2nd Edition, p. 395, it is stated by the Editors "that the mansion of Great Fulford is probably the most ancient in the county, and is remarkable for having continued by descent in uninterrupted succession in the name of Fulford during the long period of more than 600 years, from the reign of King Richard I. to the present hour, perhaps during a still longer period, as there is no record of its having a previous possessor of another name; and as tradition assigns to the family an earlier date, we may admit the probability of its earlier residence at this place."

Tradition assigns one of the rooms as the habitation of King Charles II. when Prince of Wales, and to this day it, and the staircase adjoining, are called by that monarch's name. At the same time there is no direct evidence of the king ever having rested here;. but, on the other hand, we have the gift of the portrait of King Charles I., and the appearance of Col. Francis Fulford's name on the roll of those to be appointed Knights of the Royal Oak—an Order which was contemplated but never founded—and the inn in the adjoining village still bears the sign of the Royal Oak. Colonel Francis Fulford, afterwards Sir Francis, garrisoned the house for the king, and his son Thomas was slain in his service. The House was afterwards taken by Sir Thomas Fairfax, in the month of December, 1645, and the command given to Colonel Okey, who was afterwards one of the King's Judges. The following is a copy of a pass granted by General Fairfax to Sir Francis Fulford:—

"These are to require you on sight hereoff to forbear to prejudice Sir F. Fulford, of Fulford, in the County of Devon, either by plundering his houses there, or at Toller or Whitchurch, in the County of Dorset; or rifling his goods, or taking away any of his horses, sheepe, or any catele whatsoever, or doing any violence to his person or family, as you or every of you will answer the contrary at your peril; and you are likewise to permitt and suffer him, with his two servants, and three horses, arms and necessaries, to pass the guards to Devon and Dorset, and from time to time to pass in the said Counties about his lawful affairs without let or interruption. Given under my hand and seal this 16th of March, at Truro, 1645-6. T. FAIRFAX."

Francis Fulford, Sheriff of Devon, in 17th year of the reign of George II, 1744, was the last member of the family who held that important office.

The present arrangements of the house were made by the grandfather of the present owner, the late Colonel Fulford, shortly after he came of age, at which time the reception rooms were on the other side of the quadrangle, with the windows facing inwards. These apartments were occupied by his predecessor, but, owing to his long minority, and the neglect of his trustees, they required repair, which the Colonel undertook and made some progress with, when unfortunately one day, whilst the workmen were at dinner, the ceiling in the ante-hall gave way, destroying a part of the grand staircase, upon which he closed the works in progress and laid out the present reception rooms, which had formerly been bed-chambers, entering one upon another. At that period he threw out the bays at the four corners of the house, removed the gables, and erected the present battlements. The other portion of the house was then dismantled, and has remained so ever since, as was the chapel, till about 20 years ago, when the marble was relaid in the chapel and the panelling repaired and a door made into the dining room. It is used for Divine Service on Sunday evenings in the summer months, during the owner's residence. The date 1534 may be observed on the panelling in the hall. The figures represent Sir Baldwin Fulford and two Saracens he fought and slew.

The carving in the hall is of three periods, the linen pattern many think is by Grinling Gibbons.

The stag's head is said to be the last hunted red deer killed on Dartmoor.

The ceilings in the bedrooms are supposed to be by an Italian artist who was working in this country. This was the opinion of the late Mr. R. Dymond, in whose office in Bedford Street, Exeter, may be seen similar work.

On the landing outside the smoking room stands an Armada chest. The outside of the pantry door contains brass-work of the time of Charles II, judging by the lock and hinges. A tracing was sent to South Kensington Museum, and this was their report.

In the park and at the entrance to the avenue from the house, are still to be seen the redoubts thrown up by the Parliamentary Army, when the house was beseiged by Fairfax.

The most ancient part of the house is the gateway in the back quadrangle, while the supporters to the arms over the front entrance are in the costume of the age of Queen Elizabeth or James I.

The house contains many interesting and valuable pictures, which are described in Fifth Report of Works of Art Committee in Vol. XVI, p. 168 (1884), Trans. Devonshire Association. P.F.S.A.

2. THE SHIELD OF ARMS OVER THE GATEWAY OF GREAT FULFORD HOUSE.

There are nine quarterings in this shield, being the arms of (1) Fulford (2) Fitzurse (3) Moreton (4) Belston (5) Bozom (6) St. George (7) Dennis (8) St. Aubyn (9) Challons

They are blazoned thus :—

1 Gu. a chev. arg. (Fulford).
2 Arg. on a bend sable, 3 bears' heads erased of the first, muzzled of the second (Fitzurse, co. Somerset).
3 Arg. a chev. sa. between 3 moorcocks of the second (Moreton).
4 Or. on a bend gu. 3 crosses molines (or formée) [Belston.]
5 Az. 3 birdbolts arg. (Bozum, of Bozom's Zeal).
6 Arg. a lion rampant gu. a chief az. (St. George).
7 Gu. a bend engrailed az. between 3 leopards' heads or, jessant de lis of the second (Dennis).

8   Arg. on a cross gu. 5 bezants (St. Aubyn).
9   Gu. 2 bars arg. and an orle of martlets of the second (Challons).

Above the shield is the crest of the Fulfords, a bear's head erased arg. muzzled or, and on each side 2 saracens as supporters.   MAXWELL ADAMS.

3. SIR THOMAS FULFORD'S MONUMENT IN DUNSFORD CHURCH.—This monument is in the north aisle of Dunsford Church, and is a good example of highly decorated Jacobean Art. On the base, which is panelled in rich relief and gilded, are the full length effigies of Sir Thomas Fulford and of Ursula, his wife. Sir Thomas is in steel armour picked out in gold, wearing a red velvet tunic and pantaloons and Elizabethan ruffle and wrist-bands, but ungauntleted and without helmet. His wife is in a dress of Elizabethan period, ornamented down the front with a trimming of gild quatrefoils. She also wears a ruffle and flat-topped head-dress. Over these figures is a canopy supported by three fluted Corinthian columns in front, and two pilasters at the rear, with gilt bases and capitals. The ceiling of the canopy is divided into panels, enriched with gilded bosses. The entablature is decorated with cupids' heads, shells, and a series of shields of arms, and above is a billeted cornice. At the back of, and raised slightly above the effigies of their parents, are the kneeling figures of the seven children of Sir Thomas and Lady Ursula Fulford. In front of the first is a desk, facing which is a shield of the arms of Fulford impaling Bampfield.

On the flat surface between the front columns is the following inscription:—

> Heare lyethe Sir Thomas Fulforde
> Who died last day of July, an° do 1610.
> Also his wife Ursula, who died 1639,
> daughter of Richd Bampfield, of Poltimore, Esqr

Their Children.

1st. Sir Francis, who married Ann, heir of Bernard Samways, Esqr, of Toller, Dorset;
2nd. William; 3rd. Thomas; 4th. Bridget, married to Arthur Champernown, Esq., of Dartington;
5th. Elizabeth, married to John Berriman, Esq.;
6th. Ann, married to John Sydenham, of Somerset.

There are eleven shields of arms on the entablature of this monument, which are as follows, beginning on the west side:

1. Gu. a chev. arg. (Fulford).

The remainder (2 to 11) are impaled with the arms of Fulford.

2. Or. on a bend gu. 3 mullets arg. (Bampfield).
3. Arg. on a bend sa. 3 bears' heads erased of the first, muzzled of the second (Fitzurse, co. Somerset).
4. Or. 3 torteaux (Courtenay).
5. Arg. a chev. sa. between 3 moorcocks of the second (Moreton).
6. Or. on a bend gu. 3 crosses molines (or formée) arg. [Belston]
7. Az. 3 birdbolts arg. (Bozom, of Bozom's Zeal).
8. Arg. a lion rampant gu. a chief az. (St. George).
9. Gu. a bend engrailed az. between 3 leopards' heads or, jessant de lis of the second (Dennis).
10. Arg. on a cross gu. 5 bezants (St. Aubyn).
11. Gu. 2 bars arg. and an orle of martlets of the second (Challons).

Over the monument hang an old helmet and sword.

MAXWELL ADAMS.

4. S. PETROC.—The man who has left a deeper impress on the West of England than any other Saint. The man who should be regarded in the West with the same affection with which S. David is looked up to in Wales.

Petroc is really Peterkin, that is to say Pedr with the diminutive *oc* added to the name. According to the "Life of S. Cadoc," he was the son of Glwys of Gwent. His elder brother was Gwynllyw the Warrior. He left Gwent "rejecting the vanities and transient allurements of the world, despising worldly for heavenly things, he began to adhere firmly to God, and gave up his country, his kindred, and at last all the things of this world. Leaving home, he reached Cornwall, in the district called Bormenei (Bodmin), where, throughout his life he served God most devoutly, and erected a very large monastery in His honour."

On the other hand the Welsh Genealogies say that he was a son of Clement, a Cornish prince. It is possible to reconcile these statements if we suppose Clement to have been brother or cousin of Gwynllyn, and to have headed the Gwentian-

Brecknock invasion of North Cornwall. Petroc had no choice, probably, but to adopt the ecclesiastical profession.

John of Tynemouth says he was "*natione Cumber*," a mistake or misprint for *Camber*, and he was followed by William of Worcester, who says, "*Sanctus Petrocus, rex patriæ Cumbrorum, id est partis borialis regni Angliæ reliquit regnum 'fratis suo junioris; jacet in pulchro scrinio apud Bodmun ecclesiam coram capella Beatæ Mariæ.*"

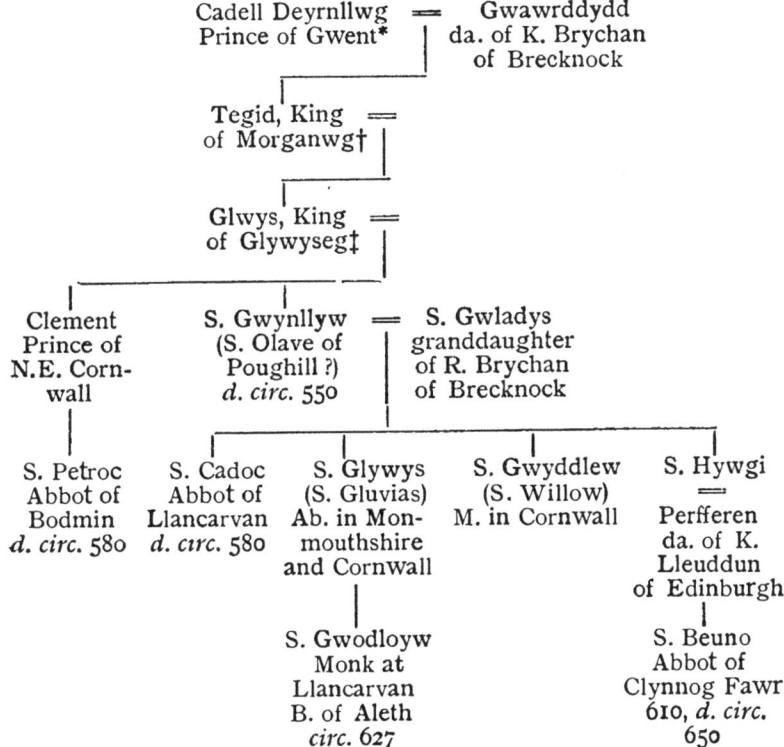

A hermit named Guron had a cell at Bodmin, and this he surrendered to Petroc.

After some years Petroc went to Ireland, where he studied for twenty years, reading profane and sacred literature. He was probably a disciple of S. Eoghain or Eugenius, of Kilnamanach, for S. Coemgen, when a child of seven, was entrusted to him by his parents to be reared for the monastic life, and he was with him for five years. Coemgen was a kinsman of Eoghain, and was educated by him as well as by Petroc.

---

* *Gwent* is Monmouthshire.   † *Morganwg* is Glamorganshire.
‡ *Glwyseg* is a portion of Monmouthshire.

Eoghain had been himself trained by S. **Mancen or Ninidh** of Ty Gwyn.*

Leland gives but a meagre outline of the legend.

> "Ex Vita Petroci.
> Petrocus gener Camber,
> Petrocus 20 annos studuit in Hibernia.
> Petrocus reversus est ad suum monasterium in Cornubia.
> Petrocus obiit prid. non. Junii." (Itin. iii., p. 52).

He probably had before his eyes the same legend that we have in Capgrave, from John of Tynemouth.

As soon as Petroc considered that he had become ripe in religious knowledge, that is after twenty years spent in Ireland, he resolved on returning to Cornwall, and he went back in the same wickerwork boat in which he had made the voyage to Ireland: but of course he had it fresh coated with hides.

Petroc and his companions, after a prosperous course, came into the Hayle or Camelmouth (Duffr) at Padstow, then called Laffenac. Mr. Adams says that the Saxons had made a descent there, and had established themselves at Padstow. He refers to Alford (Annales Eccl. ii, 10) who cites Capgrave as his authority; but Capgrave says nothing of the sort, only that Petroc was ill-received on his arrival by a party of harvesters, who churlishly denied him fresh water, but bade him find a spring for himself.

This could not have happened had these harvesters been Celts, *therefore* they were Saxons who had settled there. Such is Alford's conclusion, and Mr. Adam docilely follows him.

But the harvesters were in haste to carry their corn, fearing rain, and would not be delayed by a party of travellers just arrived. There were plenty of springs accessible. Let these men go find water for themselves.

But the story is introduced merely as an excuse for giving Petroc an occasion to elicit a spring miraculously, which he did at once with the end of his staff.

On landing at Padstow, Petroc enquired whether there were any servants of God there, and was informed that S. Samson lodged near. When Samson heard of the arrival of the party from Ireland, he wanted to depart, but was

---

* This is the Cornish Mawgan.

paralysed, so that he could not stir, till Petroc had kissed him and talked with him.

S. Samson's Chapel stood on the height now occupied by Place House.

At Padstow, Petroc remained with his disciples for thirty years, and he was wont daily to stand from cockcrow to dawn in the water chanting psalms. He ate nothing but bread, except on Sundays when he had a good bowl of porridge.

If we suppose that he was fifteen when he went to Ireland, and thirty-five when he returned to Cornwall, then he was aged sixty-five when he resolved on a pilgrimage to Rome. The occasion was this.

There had been an unusually rainy season. His disciples, and the people of the country round had recourse to him, and, he prophesied that on the morrow the rain would cease. But next day it poured as before, and his credit as a saint was so damaged that he deemed it advisable to disappear for awhile. He accordingly resolved on visiting the holy places.

The story of his travels is purely mythical. He visited Rome first, and then Jerusalem. From Jerusalem he started for India, and reached the ocean. There, he fell asleep on the shore. On awaking, he saw a large silver boat like a bowl swimming towards him on the waves. It was large enough to contain him, so casting down his sheepskin and planting his staff by it in the sands, he boldly entered the silver vessel. It was at once wafted over the blue sea without sail or oar, till he reached a certain island, on which he landed. There he spent seven years, living all the while on a single fish which he caught daily, and which, however often it was eaten, always returned sound to be eaten again.

At the end of the seven years the shining bowl again appeared. He took his place in it, and was carried back to the spot where he had left his sheepskin and staff; and lo! a wolf had kept guard over them all the time he had been away. Then he returned to Cornwall, and the wolf, perfectly docile, accompanied him.

It is abundantly clear that into the legend has been introduced a pagan myth of a divinity sailing in the silver bowl of the moon over the heavenly ocean.

When he returned to Cornwall, he found that his misadventure in prophecy had been forgotten.

At this time Tewdrig ruled in Cornwall, the notorious tyrant who figures in the legends of S. Fingar and S. Kea. Tewdrig had a tank into which he cast all the vipers that were found and brought to him; and into this tank he threw thieves and all such criminals as were sentenced to death. On the decease of Tewdrig, his son put an end to this method of execution; however, one serpent had grown to such a size on human flesh, that no one dared approach and destroy it. Thereupon, when an appeal was made to S. Petroc, the abbot promptly went to the monster and banished it beyond the seas.

Tewdrig does not seem to have been quite so bad as he has been represented, for Leland informs us that he made grants of land to Petroc, as did also Constantine, who was his contemporary.

"Regnabant eo in Cornubiâ sæculo, duo reguli, fama celebres, Theodorus et Constantinus; quorum cum libertate tum pictate adjutus, locum condendo aptissimum monasterio accepit; cui nomen patria lingua Bosmanach a monachis inditum." (*De Script, Britcen,* 61).

The spot chosen was Bodmin, where he had been in former times in the cell of Guron. Here again he elicited a spring. That by the Church is S. Guron's Well, but there is another Holy Well near "The Bery."

Bodmin became Petroc's most famous foundatur. But he must have travelled much and consecrated many souls in Devon, and there is reason for supposing that Buckfast was a Petrocian foundatur.

Whilst Petroc was at Bodmin, his interview took place with Constantine, which led to the conversion of that prince. Constantine was hunting a fawn, and it fled for refuge, and hid under the mantle of Petroc, who kept the hounds at bay till the king came up. This led to conferences and to Constantine's conversion from a disorderly life.

It is related in his legend that Petroc remained long in prayer, and that even when rain fell heavily it did not seem to moisten him whilst engaged in his devotions. This is a miracle developed out of the simple fact that he did not intermit his prayers for a passing shower.

One day when he and a certain unnamed holy bishop were in converse, a richly coloured mantle floated down from

Heaven, and fell between them. At once ensued a holy contention betwixt them, each asserting that the cloak was sent to the other. As neither would yield, a waft of wind carried up the mantle again, and, shortly after, down came two in its place, and thus was each gratified. This story has been transferred bodily to the Legend of S. Patrick.

A poor dragon got a splinter in its eye, and hastened to Petroc, who cured it. A woman had drunk water in which was newt spawn, and a salamander was hatched in her stomach, and greatly tormented her. Petroc extracted the beast when it had grown to the length of three feet.

Petroc died at an advanced age on June 4th.

The relics of S. Petroc were preserved in an ivory shrine. The story of the theft of the relics and their recovery in 1177 has been often told. The ivory reliquary is still extant at Bodmin. S. Petroc's date is difficult to fix. We know only that he belonged to a certain period, as he was brought in contact with certain princes and saints. But we have no fixed dates on which to base a chronology.

The initial difficulty begins at his birth, as we do not know who his father, Clement, was, whether a brother or a son of Gwynllyw. He was certainly at school in Ireland along with Coemgen who is believed to have been born in 498. It is quite impossible to hold that Petroc was tutor of Coemgen in 505, and also a means of the conversion of Constantine, in 589. But then we can not be sure that the date given to the conversion in the "Annales Cambriae" is correct.

Petroc on his return to Cornwall, after twenty years in Ireland, met S. Samson at Padstow. Samson was in Cornwall between 520 and 555, but he certainly left Padstow at an early period, say in 530. If, however, as has been supposed, Samson left Wales because of the ravages of the Yellow Death, then he did not arrive there before 547.

Petroc received grants from Tewdrig, whom we can not bring down later than 530. Then again, he had as his pupil Dagan, for five years, and Dagan died in 640. Dagan can have been with Petroc only when very young.

Under these circumstances it is hazardous to fix a date, even approximately, for his death.

If we may suppose that Coemgen was Petroc's "fag" at school rather than his pupil, we get over some of the difficulty, but Constantine's conversion must have taken place nearer 559 than 589. That is to say if the Constantine who was converted is the Constantine who was scolded by Gildas in or about 540. We may roughly assume the death of Petroc to have taken place about 580, some five years before that of Coemgen.

The days on which S. Petroc was commemorated were that of his death, June 4th. On this day Whytford in his Martyrologe, says "The deposicyon of Saynt Patryke a confessore," which is a blunder for Petrocke.

So also the York Missal, the Exeter Calendar, and 11th Cent. Calendar of Hyde or Newminster, the Wells Ordinal, the Reading Calendar, 1220-46, the Evesham Calendar, etc.

In the Bodmin Antiphonary as well, his Exaltation on Sept. 14th, and his Translation on October 8th.

At S. Meen, in Brittany, he was venerated on June 4th, and Sept. 4th. There he is called Saint Perreux, and the cult there is due to the theft of his relics which were conveyed to S. Meen.

Under the name of Pirric he has a church at Plouguin, in the diocese of Quimper. A church and chapel under his invocation are at S. Vincent-sur-Oult, in the diocese of Vannes; it is named in the Cartulary of Redon, in or about 862. The dedication there is quite independent of the theft of his relics in 1177.

In Art S. Petroc should be represented as an abbot with a silver bowl in his hand, and a wolf at his side, or else with a dragon.

Dedications to S. Petroc are :—

    The Church and Priory of Bodmin.
    The Parish Church of Padstow.
        ,,   ,,   Little Petherick.
                    Trevalga.
        ,,   ,,   Harford, Devon.
        ,,   ,,   Clanaborough, Devon.
    A Holy Well just outside the parish bounds in Colebrook.
    The Parish Church of Tor Mohun (Will of one Bartlett, 1517, C.C.C.)
    The Parish Church of South Brent.
        ,,   ,,   Newton Petrock

The Parish Church of Lydford.
The Church attached to the Castle at Dartmouth.
A Parish Church in Exeter.
A Chapel in the Cathedral at Exeter.
The Parish Church of Hollacombe.

Both Hollacombe and South Brent belonged to the Abbey of Buckfast. This is of extremely early foundation, before the Conquest. These dedications afford a presumptive evidence that the original abbey was a foundation of S. Petroc, as donations of land for cells and churches were made to saints personally, and the *daltha* or daughter churches of a Celtic collegiate establishment bore the name of the saint who was head of and founder of that establishment.

At Dunkeswell there is a Holy Well called S. Patrick's, but probably S. Petrock's Well. In the 13th century the parish church was re-dedicated to S. Nicolas. Previously we can hardly doubt it looked to S. Petrock.

Polwhele says that the earlier dedication of Kenton was to S. Petroc; it is now dedicated to All Saints, but S. Petroc has been introduced on the pulpit, in commemoration of the earlier dedication. We do not know what was Polwhele's authority.

The Legend of S. Petroc is unhappily late. We have no earlier version than that of John of Tynemouth, who flourished about 1366. He made use of earlier materials, but blended all kinds of floating mythological traditions with the genuine biographical facts.   S. BARING GOULD.

5. A DOMESTIC SERVANT'S INDENTURE OF APPRENTICESHIP IN 1732.—This Indenture made the twelfth day of September in the Sixth | year of the reign of our Sovereign Lord George the Second by the Grace of God of Great Britain | France and Ireland King Defender of the Faith, etc., Annoq. Dom. 1732 Witnesseth That James Knighton and Jacob Lawrence Churchwardens of the Parish of | St. Budeaux in the County of Devon And Mary Ffortescue | Widow and Thomas Pollard Overseers of the Poor of | the said Parish by and with the consent of His Majesty's Justices of the Peace for the said County whose | Names are hereunto subscribed, have put and placed, and by these Presents do put and place Ruth Knight a poor | Child of the said Parish,

Apprentice to Edmund Boger of St. Budeaux aforesaid Yeoman with him to dwell and | serve from the Day of the Date of these Presents until the said Apprentice shall accomplish her full Age of twenty one years | or be marryed according to the Statute in that Case made and provided During all which term, the said | Apprentice her said Master faithfully shall serve in all lawful Business, according to her Power, Wit, and Ability; and honestly, | orderly and obediently in all Things demean and behave herself towards her said Master and all his during the said term | And the said Edmund Boger for himself his Executors and Administrators doth Covenant and Grant to and with the said | Churchwardens and Overseers and every of them their and every of their Executors and Administrators, and their and every of their | Successors for the time being, by these Presents, That the said Edmund Boger the said Apprentice in House-wifery | shall teach and instruct or cause to be taught and instructed And shall and will, during all | the term aforesaid, find, provide and allow unto the said Apprentice, meet competent, and sufficient Meat, Drink, and Apparel, Lodging, Wash | ing, and all other things necessary and fit for an Apprentice And also shall and will so provide for the said Apprentice, that she be not | any way a Charge to the said Parish, or Parishioners of the same; but of and from all Charge shall and will save the said Parish and Parishio | ners harmless and indemnified during the said term. And at the end of the said term, shall and will make, provide, allow and deliver | unto the said Apprentice double Apparel of all sorts, good and new (that is to say) a good new Suit for the Holy-days, and another for the | Working-days. IN WITNESS whereof, the Parties abovesaid to these present Indentures interchangeably have put their Hands and Seals | the Day and Year above-written.   Sealed and Delivered in the presence of

     THOMAS STEPHENS } EDMOND BOGER.
     GEORGE VOISAY   𝕷.𝕾.

We whose names are subscribed Justices of the Peace of the County aforesaid do (Quor: unum) consent to the putting forth of the abovesaid Ruth Knight, Apprentice, according to the Intent and Meaning of the Indenture abovesaid.

     JOHN ELFORD.
     THO. PYNE.   J.B.R.

6. LICENSE GRANTED BY THE CROWN TO GEORGE PARKER, ESQ., TO INCLOSE FOR A DEER PARK TWO HUNDRED AND TWENTY ACRES OF LAND IN THE PARISH OF PLYMPTON SAINT MARY, DEVON.—The King, etc., To all, etc., Greeting. Whereas by a certain Indenture of Enquiry taken at Plympton St. Mary, in our county of Devon, on the seventh day of November, in the twelfth year of our reign, before John Davie, Sheriff of the aforesaid county, pursuant to our Writ addressed to the said Sheriff by the oath of good and lawful men of the aforesaid county, it has been found That it will be in no way to the hurt or prejudice of ourselves or others for us to grant to George Parker, Esquire, liberty, license and power to enclose divers closes (*clausa*) and parcels of arable land, meadow, pasture, furze, and underwood, containing in all by estimation two hundred and twenty acres or thereabouts lying in a ring fence within the parish of Plympton St. Mary aforesaid, now in possession of the said George, situate on the East side of the King's highway leading from Plymbridge to Ridgeway and thereon abutting, and along the same King's highway extending as far as the Crossways called Norther Cross, and from thence abutting and lying on the north side of a certain lane or way leading from the aforesaid spot called Norther Cross and extending along the said lane to a certain spot known as Broomhill Gate, and from thence extending along and abutting on the West side of a certain lane leading from Broomhill Gate aforesaid to a certain spot known as Mare Park Gate, and from thence extending along and abutting on the south side of a certain lane leading from Mare Park Gate aforesaid to a certain spot known as Canndowne, and so extending to a certain spot called Plymbridge Lane Gate, and from thence abutting on the south side of a lane leading from Plymbridge Lane Gate aforesaid into the King's highway leading to Norther Cross aforesaid; and to hold to himself and his heirs for ever the same closes and parcels of arable land, meadow pasture, scrub and brushwood so enclosed, and to make of the same closes and parcels of land aforesaid a park, and in the same park to preserve stags and game, as is more fully set forth and appears in the aforesaid Enquiry lodged in the court of our Chancery of Record. Now know ye that at the humble petition of the aforesaid George Parker, and for divers good causes and considerations

specially moving us at present, we of our special grace and of
full knowledge and our own mere motion, have given and
granted and by these presents for ourselves [our] heirs and
successors, do give and grant unto the said George Parker,
his heirs and assigns, special license and liberty and lawful
authority and power to enclose all those several closes and
parcels of arable land, meadow, pasture, scrub and underwood
already referred to in the afore-recited Writ and Enquiry and
in these letters several times mentioned, containing in the
whole by estimation two hundred and twenty acres or thereabouts lying in a ring fence within the parish of Plympton St.
Mary aforesaid, now in the possession of George himself, and
so abutting and described as is more particularly mentioned
and set forth in the afore-recited Writ and Enquiry, to hold to
himself and his heirs the same closes or (*sive*) parcels of arable
land, meadow, pasture, scrub and underwood so enclosed, or
to be enclosed, and to make of the same closes or parcels of
land a park, and in the same park to keep, depasture and
sustain stags, does, and game. And further for ourselves and
our successors we do grant to the aforesaid George Parker,
his heirs and assigns, that the aforesaid closes or parcels of
land so enclosed, or to be enclosed, shall in future for ever be
a free and lawful park for depasturing, sustaining, and preserving stags, does, and other game, and that the said George
Parker, his heirs and assigns, shall have free warren in the
park and land aforesaid, or in whatever parcel thereof.
Wherefore we will and by these presents for ourselves, our
heirs and successors, do grant that the aforesaid George
Parker, his heirs and assigns, shall each and all of them have
and hold and shall each and all of them be able and competent
to have, hold, use and enjoy the aforesaid park and free
warren freely, lawfully, well and peacefully, together with all
and irregular liberties, privileges and advantages which belong
or in any way may belong to such a park and warren. We
also will and by these presents for ourselves and our successors
do command and enjoin that no one shall enter or shall presume to enter the said park or warren for the purpose of
driving, hunting or fowling or therein taking, chasing or
disturbing stags, does or game or other wild animals or birds,
or taking anything there which belongs or ought or may
belong to a park or warren of this kind, nor for the purpose of

doing or committing anything in the said park or warren which is or may be to the hurt, harm or prejudice of the said park or warren, without the will and license of the said George Parker, his heirs or assigns, under the pains and penalties enacted and provided by the statutes and ordinances for preserving parks and warrens. We will further and by these presents for ourselves, our heirs and successors, do grant to the aforesaid George Parker, his heirs and assigns, that these our letters patent, or the enrolments of the same, shall be in all respects and in all points firm, valid, good, sufficient and effectual in law as well in all our courts as elsewhere within our kingdom of England without the procuring or obtaining any confirmations or other license toleration from ourselves, our heirs or successors, in any way, notwithstanding bad description or incorrect or untrue recital of the Writ or Enquiry aforesaid, or bad description or want of description, bad recital or want of recital of the aforesaid parcels of land and premises or any parcel thereof, or any tenant, farmer or occupier of the premises, or of any one parcel thereof, or any township, hamlet, parish or place where or in which the aforesaid premises lie or any one of them lies, in respect of nature, genus, species, quantity or quality of the premises or of any one [*being*] parcel thereof, or any thing, cause or matter whatsoever to the contrary notwithstanding. In testimony, etc., Patent Roll 12 Will. III., p. 2, No. 8. (Translation). J.B.R.

7. Chapple, in his Review of Risdon, 1785, refers to the North and South Hams as being ancient names, and states that Devon had originally a threefold division anciently known by the names of East, South and North Hams, p. 116. Can any of your readers inform me where I can find any reference to these divisions of the County? When were such names first given, and what are the boundaries of the localities?

J.M.R.

8. The term "Emmanuel Baptism" is occasionally found in church registers in some counties. Can any reader of *D.N.&Q.* throw any light on the meaning, or if such entries are found in the Devonshire Parish Registers?

P.F.S.A.

9. AN EIGHTEENTH CENTURY EXETER BOOKSELLER'S BOOK LABEL.—The following is printed on a label, about 3 inches by 2½ inches, pasted within the cover of a copy of William Nelson's Lex Maneriorum, fol. 1726:—

Margery Yeo, bookseller, over against St. | Martin's-Lane Exon, Sells all sorts of | bibles Common-Prayers books of Devotion | School-books Law-books History-books and all | other sorts of books: paper books of all sorts as | well Royal as Demy for Merchants Accompts | painted Papers for Hanging of Rooms: Maps | and Pictures of all sorts: Mathematical In | struments of all sorts and blank Warrants for | Justices' Clerks writing paper sealing Wax | Wafers Japan Inks and Pens gilt paper Ivory | Pocket-books and others of all sorts Letter | cases Standishes Japan Ink and Ink Powder and | all other sorts of Stationary Wares sold at | reasonable Rates. |

N.B. She likewise binds all sorts of books | very Reasonable.   J.B.R.

10. RINGING BELLS DURING A THUNDERSTORM.—The *Torquay Directory* for August 9th, 1899, contains the following paragraph:—

"It transpires that in conformity with an old usage, the bells in Dawlish Parish Church were rung during the recent thunderstorms, in the belief that 'the Spirit of the Bells would overcome the Spirit of the Lightning.' This superstitious belief in the efficacy of bell ringing in thunderstorms is very old. The surprise is that it should have survived to this day, and that the practice should still obtain at the pretty little South Devon resort of Dawlish."

I have searched every authority known to me in the hope of finding a record of the practice having obtained in other towns in Devonshire, but without success.

The custom of ringing church bells in storms is of very high antiquity in Christian times, and its origin may, perhaps, be found in a still more ancient belief of heathen nations.

The Roman herdsmen, in the days of Strabo, were accustomed to attach a bell to the necks of their flock, and it was believed noxious wild beasts were kept away by their sound. It was also believed that evil spirits would flee from the sound of bronze instruments. Hence the custom of beating bronzed vessels during an eclipse mentioned by Ovid and others. Beating bronze vessels and ringing bells on a person's death were thought to frighten away demons and spectres, as the sounds were very obnoxious to evil spirits.

In the time of St. Augustine, storms were attributed to the spirits of the air, and it was believed they were driven away by the sound of church bells. Hence probably the ordinance of blessing church bells has existed from a very early time.

Aubrey, in his "Miscellanies," says: "When it thundered and lightened they did ring St. Adehn's Bells at Malmesbury Abbey. The curious do say that the ringing of bells exceedingly disturbs spirits."

"If that the thunder chaunce to rore, and stormie tempest shake,
A wonder is it for to see the wretches how they quake ;
Howe that no faith at all they have, nor trust in anything,
The Clarke doth all the Bells forthwith at once in Steeple ring,
With wondrous sound and deeper farre than he was wont before,
Till in the loftie heavens darke, the thunder bray no more.
For in these christened Belles they think doth lie such powre and might
As able is the Tempest great, and storms to vanquish quight.
I saw myself at Nurnberg, once a Towne in Foring Coast,
A Belle that with this title bold hirself did proudly boast:
' By name I Mary called am, with sound I put to flight
The Thunder crackes and hurtful Storms, and every wicked Spright.' "
From Googe's version of "Nasgeorgus."

In support of the representation in the Churchwardens' Accounts of Sandwich, for 1464, occurs a charge for bread and drink for "ryngers in the great Thunderyng;" and in the burning of St. Paul's Church in London (1561) we find among other superstitions, " ringinge the hallowed bell in the great Tempestes or Lightninges."

The only other record of the custom in England, as far as I can find, is that of the Church of Oxney, in Kent. Fuller says of bells:—

"Man's death I tell, by doleful knell,
Lightning and thunder, I break asunder,
On Sabbath all, to Church I call,
The sleepy head, I raise from bed,
The winds so fierce, I do disperse,
Man's cruel rage, I do assuage."

The practice of blessing bells has prevailed in Christian countries from the earliest times. In *Notes and Queries* for March 24th, 1855, I find: " The Roman Catholic Bishop of

New Jersey blessed a chime of Bells for the 'Church of the Most Holy Redeemer,' of New York City, so that whensoever they shall sound hereafter, the power of devils, the shades of phantasms, the attacks of mobs, the striking of lightnings, the shock of thunder, the ruin of tempests, and every spirit of the storms may be driven back."—*Freeman's Journal*.

As Devonshire appears to have possessed a very fair share of most superstitions, one can scarcely be satisfied that the Dawlish case is the only one known in the county. Perhaps some reader of *D.N.&Q.* may know of other cases, and if so, it would be interesting to have a record of them in these pages. A. J. DAVY.

[*Voce mea viva depello cunta nociua* is, the Rev. H. T. Ellacombe tells us in his " Church Bells of Devon " (Trans. Exeter Dioc. Arch. Soc., 2nd ser., Vol. I., pp. 240-242) to be found on twenty-two bells in our county. " A visible and lasting proof," he adds, " that demons, storms and tempests were frightened away and dissipated by the sound of bells. . . . Whether there be scientifically any virtue in the noise of bells or cannons to dissipate storms impending, I will not venture to say, but it may be interesting to introduce here an event which is related in the *Teatro Critico* to have occurred in France in the year 1718. On Good Friday there arose a most violent tempest on a part of the coast of Brittany. Twenty-four churches were struck by lightening, and what is very remarkable is that the lightening fell only on the churches in which the bells were ringing, without touching many others in the neighbourhood in which the custom of not ringing on Good Friday was observed." See also " A Book about Bells," Tyacke, chap. xii., pp. 210-214.—EDS.]

11. THE OLD CHURCH WALK OR EXCHANGE, TOTNES.— The Church Walk or Exchange, formerly known as the Seed Fruit Market, stood on the south side of the Parish Church of St. Mary, which it entirely hid from view.

It appears to have been erected in 1611 by Richard Lee, a merchant of Totnes, of some standing, who held the office of Mayor in 1603, 1616, and 1619, dying during his mayoralty.

In 1611 he gave this building to the town of Totnes, " to be used for ever as an Exchange or place of resort for the transaction of mercantile and other business." This was at a time when the trade of Totnes with France was in a flourishing condition.

Among the Corporation Papers is a letter to the Mayor of Totnes, dated 28th April, 1609, signed R. Salisbury (the Lord

Treasurer). He states that "great loss and trouble hath divers times heretofore, and especially of late, happened to the merchants trading (in) Fraunce, by reason of the deceipt and disloyalty of English cloth which hath been transported thither by way of merchandise." His Majesty, therefore, " out of his princely care to his subjects in generall, and particularly for the setlinge of the said trade, hath passed a treatie of late with the French King." The Mayor is to make the same known, and is to send to his Lordship " the names of all such meer merchants inhabitange here, as are willing to be conjoined in that trade," by 30th June next ensuing.

In former times the trade between Totnes and France was very great in cloth, serge, yarn, leather, and shoes, and in the British Museum is a memorial to the Privy Council, respecting the goods of certain inhabitants of Totnes which had been stopped at Lyons, in France.

The building consisted of a large room fronting the street, supported by handsome granite pillars, on which were carved in raised letters, "Rychard Lee, 1611."

Underneath was an open space, or colonnade, for the merchants, and at the back an entrance through iron gates to the Church.

In token of gratitude for this gift, the Corporation of Totnes presented to Catherine Luscombe, widow, the daughter and co-heiress of Richard Lee, a gold enamelled ring, on which was represented the Church Walk, with the columns supporting the building, and the people of all nations in their respective habits transacting business there.

Mrs. Luscombe, in 1642, married Servington Savery, Esq., of Shilston, and the ring was formerly in the possession of Servington Savery, Esq., of Fowlescombe, but afterwards in the possession of Mr. Savery, of Modbury, and subsequently of his widow. It is inscribed with the letters " R.L. to T." and " T. to C.L.," viz., Richard Lee to Totnes, and Totnes to Catherine Luscombe.

In the Corporation Accounts is the following entry relating to the rings, from which it appears that two rings were given to the daughters of Mr. Lee. The other daughter besides Mrs. Luscombe was Christian Lee. The entry is as follows :—

" 1652. 6th January. Pd. to Mr. Eveleigh, to make up £4

due to him for 2 rings given to the daughters of Mr. Richard Lee, 6s., who had also £3 14s., out of the arrearages of Harker's house, 6s." This entry is in a book of accounts, bound in leather, and extending from 1643 to 1683.

There is extant a lease entered into the 20th September, 1655, between the Corporation and Richard Punchard, of Totnes, goldsmith, by which this Market or Exchange was leased to Punchard for five years at a rental of £8 per annum, and the following is the description of the building and its uses as a market:—"All the parts of the Market commonly called or known by the name of the Girse* Market, Pease Market, and the Apple Market, and the Customs dutie, and tollage thereunto belonginge now and heretofore kept in and before the place commonly called the walke before the Church in Totnes aforesaid; and also the use and benefit of one and forty Buckets and Tubs, commonly used for the unloading and lyeing girse and pease therein, for exposing the same to sale in the said markett, and also leave, liberty, licence and authority to house, keep, and place the said bucketts and tubs in the chamber over the said walke, commonly called the Lottery, and the ground room next adjoining on the west side of the said walke."

Punchard covenanted with the Corporation that he would place a candle-light with lanthorne to stand in the said walk on every evening from 1st November to 2nd February during the term of his lease.

There are in the accounts frequent entries of payments for rent of this market, and also of payments for ringing the market bell and setting the tubs in the walk in which the peas, corn, fruit, etc., would be placed.

In 1719 the upper part of this building was taken down and rebuilt, as appears by the following curious entry in the Court Book, dated 7th July, 1719:—"It is this day ordered and agreed that forasmuch as the Lottery or Church Walk, and the Chamber and roof over the same is now in a very ruinous and shattered condition, and in great danger of falling to the ground, and hath been often presented as a public nuisance by the Leet jury of this Borough, and the Right Worshipful the Mayor of this Borough having generously

---

* In Halliwell's Archaic Dictionary, Girse is said to mean Grass ; here it perhaps means grist or corn.

offered to give brick enough, which is computed to be between 20 and 30 thousand, to make and new build the same with a handsome brick front towards the street with arches over the pilars, that the same should be so rebuilt." It was accordingly left to the discretion and management of the Mayor (Nicholas Trist of Bowden, Totnes, Sheriff of Devon, 1708) and he was authorised if any stone or timber should be required for the work to pull down two of the poor-houses at Maudlin, " the same being a public nuisance and a nursery of thieves, and idle dissolute people," and use the material in new building the said Lottery.

It was accordingly rebuilt, the large room over the Church Walk being afterwards used as a Public Ball Room. In the wall facing the Church porch was a representation of the Town Arms, one of the best in the Borough, which is now placed in the wall of the Guildhall inside the smaller entrance door.

In 1878 the building was, by order of the Borough Justices, taken down, it being in a dangerous state. The granite pillars were stored away.

In November, 1884, the ground on which the Exchange had stood was thrown into the street, and levelled to improve the entrance to the Church, and in the levelling remains of human bodies were found a few inches below the paving, so that it would appear that the site of the Church Walk must have formed part of the churchyard.

In June, 1897, to commemorate the Diamond Jubilee of Queen Victoria, the old granite pillars were put up outside the Guildhall to support the canopy at the entrance.

Mr. Baring-Gould, in "A Book of the West: Devon," p. 317, says: "There existed in front of the Churchyard, and in continuation of the piazza, a butter market, which consisted of an enlarged piazza supported on granite pillars of the beginning of the seventeenth century. The vulgar craving to show off the parish church when so many pounds, shillings, and pence had been spent on its restoration: the fear lest visitors should fail to see that the shopkeepers of Totnes had put their hands into their pockets to do up the Church, made them destroy this picturesque and unique feature." The case, however, is not fairly or correctly stated.

The building was taken down by order of the Justices because dangerous. The Church was not restored until after the building was pulled down, and not by the shopkeepers, but by a native of Totnes, Mrs. Roberts, who restored the exterior wholly at her own cost. It is very probable that but for the exposure of the Church to view by the taking down of the Church Walk, it would not have been restored. It was not a continuation of the piazza, nor was it the butter market.

EDWARD WINDEATT.

12. WARRANT FOR MANNING THE FLEET, 1770.—In these days of mobilization of our reserves for both the Army and Navy, it may be interesting to know how our Navy was manned a century ago.

In 1770 we appear to have been in a bad state in regard to sailors. The great American War was looming in the near future, a series of irritating enactments was alienating the loyalty of our most valuable colonies. Pitt, who had resigned office in 1768, again appeared in his place and denounced in severe terms both the foreign and American policy of the Ministers. In this medley the Duke of Grafton resigned, and the King prevailed on Lord North to accept office and become Prime Minister. The Navy appears to have received early attention, and the following warrant was received by the Duke of Bedford, the Lord Lieutenant of Devon:—

"After our very hearty Commendations to your Grace. Whereas His Majesty's Service doth at this time require a speedy supply of seamen and seafaring men, to man His Majesty's Fleet which is now fitting out; We do therefore, by his Majesty's Command, hereby pray and require your Grace to call upon the Justices of the Peace within the County of Devon, whereof your Grace is Custos Rotulorum, and strictly enjoin and require them to cause all straggling seamen who are fit to serve on Board his Majesty's Ships, to be taken up and sent by proper persons from place to place, until they shall be brought to the Clerks of the Checque of his Majesty's yards at Deptford, Woolwich, Chatham, Sheerness, Portsmouth, Plymouth, or Harwich or to any of His Majesty's Ships or Vessels appointed to procure men at any other ports according as those places shall be nearest to where such straggling seamen shall be taken up, that so they may be put on Board such of His Majesty's Ships or Vessels as shall be appointed to receive them, and that there be paid to the Persons who shall be intrusted with the conducting them, by the aforesaid Clerks of the Checque, Twenty shillings for each seaman fit for His Majesty's Service and sixpence a mile for every mile they respectively travel not exceeding Twenty miles; But that if the men so taken up shall be sent to any place where no such Clerk of the Cheque doth reside, that then the same allowance be paid to the Conductors by the Collectors or proper Officers of the Customs residing at or nearest to the Place whereunto they shall be brought (out of money to be furnished them for that purpose by the Lords of His Majesty's Treasury as heretofore), upon Certificates from the Captain or Commander of the ship or vessel whereinto they shall be put, or from a Regulating Captain of his having received them; which allowance is to be reimbursed to the said Officers of the Customs, by the principal Officers and Commissioners of His Majesty's Navy, upon their transmitting to the said principal Officers and Commissioners. authentick accounts of what moneys they shall expend—and so not doubting of your Grace's Zeal and Vigour in the Performance of this service, we bid your Grace very hearty Farewell.

From the Council Chamber at St. James's, the 12th Day of October, 1770.

Your Grace's very loving Friends,

To our very good Lord John Duke of Bedford, Custos Rotulorum of the County of Devon. In his Grace's absence to the Justices of the Peace of the said County."

WEYMOUTH.
ROCHFORD.
NORTH.
HILLSBOROUGH.
SPENCER.
GEVONSTON.

13. THE PRINCE OF ORANGE'S FLAG.—It was stated at a Lecture in the Torquay Museum, that the Flag under which William, Prince of Orange, landed at Brixham, was flown from the leading barge in the ceremonial of opening the Exeter Canal. Bluett states that this Flag belonged to one of the Watsons, and that a Watson was with the Great Deliverer.

Is that precious banner in existence? If so, where?

S.G.

14. WISHING TREES.—At Berry Castle there is a large wide-spreading beech tree; it is believed that if a person walk three times backwards round it with the sun, in silence, thinking of the wish all the time, and not tell anyone the wish, it is sure to be fulfilled. In "Bygone Days in Devon and Cornwall," the author, writing of Berry Pomeroy, remarks: "The prettiest superstition of the place is the 'Wishing Tree.' If you whisper your wish softly against its trunk it will be sure to come true." The late Mr. E. Parfitt, of Exeter, remarks on this subject: "It is somewhat curious, but so far as I can discover, this is the only 'Wishing Tree' in England; I can find nothing of the kind in Notes and Queries, or in any Antiquarian or Legendary books I have at hand." The legend of the Wishing Tree is of Eastern origin and of ancient date, and had its birth among the Aryan nations; and, although it was probably imported here from the East, it does not appear to have flourished, but to have lingered only in the woods on the banks of the Dart. Major Cuningham, in Vol. X. of the Archæological Survey of India, gives a plate of a Kalpa-drûm, or Wishing Tree, and states that the Wishing Tree of the common people is a smooth-barked tree, and consequently would correspond with the beech at Berry Pomeroy. This coincidence seems to strengthen the bond of relationship between the Aryan legend and the one naturalised on British soil. It may only be a coincidence, but if only so, it is a happy one. Can any reader of D.N.&Q. record other Wishing Trees in Devon, or throw further light on the pretty superstition?   P.F.S.A.

15. BULL-RING AT ASHBURTON.— In the alterations recently carried out in the Ashburton Market the workmen found, whilst excavating in the fish market, a block of stone with a massive iron ring securely fixed to it. Old people well remember such a ring existing in the open space, between the old Market and the house where the Capital and Counties Bank now stands. It disappeared in 1850, when the old Market was demolished, and the roadway levelled, and as it now appears, was used in filling in the foundation of the new building, then in course of erection.

This relic, then, is the veritable "Bull-ring," from which the central open space takes its time-honoured name, and brings up a host of memories, among them those of the brutal and gross sports of our ancestors, with which it was so intimately associated in the good old times. The sport of Bull and Bear-baiting is very old, and is mentioned in 1174 by Fitz-Stephen, in his description of London, where he says: "in the forenoon of every holiday in the winter the young men amused themselves by baiting bulls and bears with dogs." For bull-baiting there was this excuse, that the flesh of that animal is naturally tough and unsuited for food. The baiting made his flesh tender and digestible and, therefore, enhanced its value to the butcher; moreover, a Statute ordered old bull's flesh might not be exposed in the shambles unless baited. In reality, the excited state of the animal just before death disposed it for putrefaction, and like a hunted hare, it must be cooked in time or be soon unfit. Here, then, almost to the time of living memory, was a stout iron ring, securely leaded into a granite stone, about mid-way between the end of the Market house and the houses opposite. To this ring the bull was secured by a rope three or four yards long, fastened to a collar round his neck. By means of the length of the rope the bull could turn round to watch his enemies, which were low strong mastiff dogs, with short noses and great power of jaw, still known as bull dogs. The sporting community of those days bred and trained numbers of these dogs, on the endurance and pluck of which heavy wagers were made.

The situation of the Ashburton Bull-ring was well adapted to permit a large number of persons to enjoy the sight free from danger; and we can picture to ourselves the windows of the old gabled houses being packed with eager faces of women and children. The Rose and Crown Inn, we may be sure, reaped a rich harvest at such times. The wide opening of the Corn Market Chamber in the tower, just under the face of the clock, would be crowded with those privileged persons who liked to see all from a safe place   A ring of excited men and youths, holding dogs still more excited, and women too, would form around the bull, now secured to the ring and perhaps vainly testing the strength of the rope, but at a distance clear of his horns. At the appointed time a well trained mastiff would be let loose, and would advance creeping upon its belly, that he might if possible seize the bull by the nose, which he as carefully endeavoured to defend by laying it close to the ground, while with his horns he attempted to toss the dog. In this way the two manœuvred amid breathless silence until the dog made a jump to seize the bull's nose; if the bull was quick he caught the dog on his horns and tossed him away many feet in the air, sometimes to the height of twenty or thirty: then with a rush men and women jumped forward to catch the dog and break its fall on the ground, for which purpose the women wore stout aprons which they held spread before them. In doing this the bull, if his attention was not instantly diverted by the onslaught of another dog, might toss or gore a person, which frequently happened. The second dog would then try his powers, perhaps be tossed, or, if fortunate, succeed in fastening to the bull's nose, in which case the dog's backer would run in and seize a fore leg of the bull; if he could hold it up for two minutes, the dog still keeping his grip, he was declared victor. Dog after dog came on, and as the baited bull expended its strength in furious wrath and vain attempts to charge his enemies, it became weaker and wilder, giving an opportunity for younger dogs to taste his blood, to the admiration of the assembly. When at last, he had no more strength to resist, a butcher appeared and gave the *coup de grace*. The carcase was dressed and sold in the Market.

Such, then, with many variations, were the brutal scenes the now quiet and respectable Bull-ring has witnessed. The barbarous pastime was encouraged by the rank and fashion of of the age, but, happily, after a time public opinion turned against it, and the sport was removed from the town to a distant field where only the lowest class of the sporting community followed it, and in 1835 was totally abolished by Act of Parliament. The last Bull-baiting was held in a field at the end of Carrion Pit Lane, on which occasion the bull broke loose, creating a panic and stampede.

It is said the first stage coaches between Exeter and Plymouth, about 1755, so arranged their time on occasions of a Bull-baiting at Ashburton, that passengers could witness the sport. The creating of the direct road through Ashburton the Royal Mail Road early in the century necessitated the discontinuing the sport in the public highway and led to its removal to a field. I am not aware that the owners of house property around the Bull-ring were compensated for their loss of privilege and consequent injury to their property. P.F.S.A.

16. "DEVON GLEE CLUB."—From a copy of the quaint "Rules and Regulations" which I possess, it appears this Club was established Nov. 2nd, 1821, with its rendezvous to be "at some convenient place in Exeter." The number of members was restricted to fifty. Monthly meetings were to be held in the winter, with a dinner at each, to last from 5 to 9 o'clock. No instrumental music or songs were allowed. "The object of this Society being to promote Harmony, no Politics or Arguments will be allowed." The Club was in existence on 5th Feb., 1830, with Charles Brutton as Treasurer. Can any subscriber to *D.N.&Q.* give us fuller particulars about this Club? Who were the first and last presidents and other officers and members? Where did it meet? When did it cease? Was it merged into any other Club or local Musical Society (*e.g.*, the Exeter Oratorio Society was formed in 1846) or did it disappear altogether? And why? J. ISAAC PENGELLY.

❖ ❖ ❖

NOTICES OF BOOKS.

17. FEUDAL AIDS.*—This Volume of "Inquisitions and Assessments relating to Feudal Aids" contains matter referring to the counties of Bedford, Berks, Buckingham, Cambridge, Cornwall, Derby and Devon. The materials included are: (1) The Survey known as Kirby's Quest; (2) The Aid for marrying the King's daughter, 31 Edward I. (3) The names of the Townships, 9 Edward II. (4) The Aid for Knighting the King's eldest son, 20 Edward III. (5) The Aid for marrying the King's eldest daughter, 3 Henry IV. (6) Subsidy of 6 Henry VI. (7) Subsidy of 9 Henry VI. These documents are printed *in extenso* without note or comment, the text having been prepared by Mr. A. S. Maskelyne, Mr. C. Johnson, and Mr. A. E. Stamp, of the Public Record Office. A preface by Sir H. C. Maxwell Lyte explains the nature of the documents, and

---

* Inquisitions and Assessments relating to Feudal Aids with other analogous Documents preserved in the Record Office, A.D. 1284-1431, prepared under the superintendence of the Deputy Keeper of the Records. 15/-. London. Her Majesty's Stationery Office, 1899.

an Index by Mr. J. V. Lyle gives some assistance to the student for the identification of names and places.

Sir Maxwell Lyte seems to be satisfied that the date of the returns commonly known as Kirby's Quest is 12 Edward I. So far as Devonshire is concerned, we should like to ask how this date can be reconciled with the fact that Robert de Dynan and Emma his wife are mentioned as middle-lords in a large number of fees, and the *After Death Inquest*, No. 23, p. 62, shews that Robert de Dynan died 5 Edward I.? Sir Maxwell states that several of these returns are printed among the Hundred Rolls of Somerset and Dorset. May we add that the return for Wonford among the Hundred Rolls of Devon appears also to belong to Kirby?

Mr. Lyle's Index is some help towards the identification of places named amid the variant spellings. Although the fact is not mentioned, Mr. Lyle seems to be much indebted in its compilation to the Rev. T. Whale's papers in the Transactions of the Devonshire Association. At any rate, besides Mr. Whale's correct identifications, he reproduces some of Mr. Whale's earlier errors and is silent upon identifications when Mr. Whale is silent. It is to be regretted that more care was not devoted to this part of the work, since the Index is likely to stereotype errors at a time when much local attention is being given to the work of correct identification. It is also to be regretted that Mr. Lyle, like Mr. Whale, connects estates with the civil parishes with which they have been recently grouped, instead of with the old ecclesiastical parishes with which their history is connected. For instance, Lovecot is described as being in Harwood, but the old Hundred Rolls of 3 Edward I. tell us that Lovecot was the name of the inland Hundred coterminous with the manor of Fremington. We see, therefore, that the place intended was Lovecot in Fremington, where the Hundred Court was held. If Mr. Lyle is correct, this place appears to have been recently included in Harwood.

It would take too long to give a complete list of some of the errors which we have detected in this Index. Confining observation strictly to the County of Devon, we notice the following among those most obvious :—

Aleborn is not Allabear in Totnes, but Yalberton in Stoke Gabriel. It was held of the bishop, not of the Honour of

Totton. Aereston, Alriggeston, Alrycheston, and other *aliases*, the Ailricheston of the Pipe Rolls, is Easton in Cheriton Bishop, together with Trebbles and Partridge, both held of the Honour of Gloucester; it represents the Lamford, an estate of 1,272 acres, which Godwin held in Domesday. Burgh is not Borrough in Drewsteignton, but Borough in Stoke Canon, also held of the Honour of Gloucester. It appears in Risdon as Comberew, and is represented in Domesday by Combe, another estate held by Godwin. Alycheston and Alleston can hardly be Ashcombe, which Testa de Nevil shews was held in fee-farm as part of Berry Pomeroy; it is no doubt Oxton in Kenton. Ammyngescote Mr. Lyle does not attempt to identify; it represents Duningeston or Duningescote, now Denson in Clayhanger, which was held by Torre Abbey by gift of Brewer. Aysford Peverel, next Mamhead, now Ash Farm in Kenton, appears to be the Mammaheved held by Saulf in Domesday. Wodemanston is not Bearcombe; it appears in Domesday as Bocland, and is an estate in Buckland Toutsaints. Beare, held with Rowdon and Grindon, is not Beare in Roseash, but Ashbear in Witheridge, adjacent to Rowdon and Grindon. Beare 365 can hardly be Beare in Branscombe, but is most probably Traysbeare in Honiton Clist, one of the earliest possessions of the See. Nether Blatchford is the Glebe of Cornwood Vicarage, as MS. 28649 in Brit. Mus. shews. Borcomb is not Branscomb, but a separate estate, an outlier of the parish of Colyton. Bullworthy is in Rakenford, not in Alverdiscott; the Hundred being Witheridge proves this; Alverdiscott is in Shebbear Hundred. Burdon is in Highamton, not in Sampford Courtney. Childon (382) is not Chaldon, but Chilton in Thorverton. Down Umfravil is not Charton; Charton appears in Domesday as Cheletone, held by the Bishop of Coutances and, therefore, belonged to the Honour of Barnstaple, whereas Down Umfravil appears in Domesday among Godwin's estates and was held, therefore, of the Honour of Gloucester. Clyst Moys is not Poltimore, but West Clist in Broad Clist. The Rolls mention the two as quite distinct: Clyst Moys being held in Frankalmoign under the patronage of Okhamton Honour's lord, Poltimore held as a fee with Hyll in Witheridge of the Honour of Plymston. Crook Burnell is in North Tawton, not in Down St. Mary. Cutton is in Poltimore, not in Rew.

Dotton was a parish by itself till four years ago, when it was annexed to Colaton Raleigh, but it is not in Rockbear. The Dunsland held with Westacot and Rokworthy is in Jacobstow, not in Cookbury. Fidelesworthy is Pidsley in East Worlington. Fremancote is West Yeo in Witheridge, as the ownership of William Vassal proves. Thureslegh is East Leigh in Harberton, not in Buckfastleigh. Goodrington is in Woodland, not in Paignton; Godrington in Paignton belonged to the bishop's estate of Paignton. Rappingheyes in Gittisham is not Hayes Poer in Budleigh. Rappingheyes appears in Domesday under the name of Otri. Hayes Poer or Hayes Barton is a post-Domesday creation out of the royal estate of Budleigh. Hill, which lies in Faringdon, held with Exton in Woodbury, is a different place from Hill next Exmouth in Withycombe Raleigh, which was the endowment of the bailiffship of Budleigh Hundred. The latter, an estate of some 30 acres only, appears in last century deeds as Rill, otherwise Hill next Exmouth. Stockley is not in Crediton, but Priorton in Sandford. It was so called because it was held by the Prior of Plymston. Lidewicheston is Liverton in Woodland.

Why does Mr. Lyle invariably write St. Mary Tedburne? Everybody living in the county knows it as Tedburn St. Mary.

Why does he simply index Nitherton as being in Devon? His own references might have shewn him that there are two Nitherton fees, both in Exminster Hundred. One of them is in Exminster, and is connected with Towsington and Shellingford Abbots, being a portion of the Domesday Selingeforde held by William Capra. The other is in the parish of Combe in Teignhead, portions of which parish are in no less than three different Hundreds.

Why is no assistance given towards identifying Combe Olleston? Testa Nevil, under the Barony of Braneys, makes it quite clear that this is Combe in Witheridge Hundred, with Yalderstan in Budleigh Hundred, which latter is situated in the southern extremity of Tiverton parish.

We wish we could speak more satisfactorily of this Index, as it is the only assistance given to the student of the subject. But we must regretfully own that in several cases it is absolutely misleading.   OSWALD J. REICHEL.

George Carew, Baron Carew of Clopton, and Earl of Totnes, 1555-1629.

Totnes Guildhall. Interior.

Totnes Guildhall. Entrance with Old Pillars.

18. RALEIGH, WALTER v. SLADE, ROGER.—(Chan. Proc. B. & A., Series II, 1558-1579, P.R.O.) Bill of Walter Raleigh: Whereas Walter Raleigh, of Budleigh, in the countie of Devon, Esq., sued Roger Slade, of Sidmouth, co. Devon, yoman, for right title and interest of tything ffysche, they not only submitted to award of Robert Denys, Kt., Chris. Chudleigh, Richd. Duke and Elys Haccombe, Esquires, but also were bound to each other in the obligacion of £60 for the performance of said award, which the said arbitrators did by their award indented ready to be shewed yor honble. courte, Award that the said complainant should have and enjoy during the life of the said Roger Slade, the said tything ffysche aforesaid and in consideration thereof the said complaynant and one George Raleigh his sonne and heir should pay the said Roger Slade during his life a yearly rent of £3 6s. 8d. at Christmas, Lady day, Midsommer and Michalmasse in the parish church of Sydmouth aforesaid between the hours of eight and nine of the forenoon and before the feast of St. John the Baptist. Complainants (Walter and George) to make graunte of said annuitie from the rents and profits of their said manor of Withycombe Ralegh. All of which complainants have not only done but at the feast of Christmas in the fifth yeare of the Quene's Majesties Reign the said complaynant at the houres and tymes said award specified by the said George his son tendered and offered payment of the parte and porcion of the sayd annuitie then dewe to the sayd Roger Slade yn the mancion howse of the sayd Roger who longe did dalye and talke with said orator's sonne as thoughe he wolde receyve the said monie protracting the time until ye said houre of payment to be mayde yn ye pysshe churche aforesayd were expired and ended having in the mean season, secretly craftily and cautelouselye sent one of hys assygns or attorneys to demand ye money at ye pysshe churche aforesayd mynding onlie to trap and endanger yor orator in forfayting of hys saide obligation and at last the tyme expired he utterly refused to receyve ye same abusyng ye ignorance of orator's sayd sonne, &c. Prays for Her Majestie's most gracious writ to stay this most unjuste and cautelouse sute.

Answer of Roger Slade (to the Bill of Complaynt of Walter Ralegh complaynante). He says it is true the arbitrators were Sir Robt. Denys, Kt., Chris. Chidley, Richd. Duke and Elis Holcombe, etc. He states complainant was behind in rent some two years, to the great damage of defendant, and that he not only refused payment, but declared he owed nothing, " whereupon this defendante hath comenced his accon for debt at comon law and myndeth to procede wth the same." Denies complaynant payd the yerly rent save at Christmas 5th Elizth. or that it was offered to him in his " mancion howse."

" I put Bill in Chy. 5 day term.   Pole."

REYNELL UPHAM.

The foregoing extract from a Chancery Suit between Walter Ralegh, the elder, and Roger Slade, is of much interest, especially as it partly serves to explain why some deeds relating to it found their way into, and are still preserved, in the parish chest of Sidmouth Church. It is undated, but as it is included in the Chancery Proceedings between 1558 and 1579, we may take it for granted it was not later than the latter year.

In explanation we must go back to 1560, when a deed was entered into between Thomas Baron and John Leigh, of the Manor of Sidmouth, and Walter Ralegh with his two sons, Carew and Walter, both minors, for " all the tythe ffyshe in Sidmouth comenly called the halfe share fyshe and also the the tythe of larkes wch Roger Slade before held," to be let to the latter on payment of a fine of £7 10s., and the annual sum of £5, to be paid " at the Feaste of seynt mychaell therch^{a}ungell and the fyrste daye of maye in the prishe of Sidmouth." Then in 1578, the Raleghs sold their interest in these tithes to William Peryam (subsequently Baron of the Exchequer) for £60. These two deeds are amongst the contents of the Sidmouth Chest. (Vide *Trans. Dev. Assoc., vi.* 227; xv. 173).

The record of the Chancery Suit holds an intermediate position to these, and the proceedings probably led to the Raleghs disposing of their interest in the tithes to W. Peryam, for the same amount as that of their obligation stated in the suit, which, according to the statement, was due to the Raleghs having violated the award of the arbitrators; but of the issue of this suit we know nothing.

Neither of the two deeds quoted contain any reference to Roger Slade having anything to do with the tithe of fish, and only a single allusion to him, and that for "the tythe of larkes" alone, so that we can only surmise that he purchased the interest of Baron and Leigh, and for the Raleghs to pay annually £3 6s. 8d. instead of £5 according to the original agreement.

It is singular the names of Carew and (Sir) Walter disappear from the suit, and that of their elder step-brother, George, should be substituted. Again, Walter and his son George are entered in the proceedings as possessing the manor of Withycombe Ralegh; but Walter had no direct interest in it, and although his son probably resided there at the time of the action, the manor belonged entirely to his step-brother Carew.

A good illustration is afforded of the mode formerly in vogue, of payments being made within the domain of the church (sometimes a particular tomb being named as the place where it was to be effected), and of the quibbling that arose on any attempt to conclude it elsewhere.

As the deeds related to Sidmouth, where Roger Slade resided, they were deposited in the parish chest, as being considered the safest place for important documents of that kind, and where they remained long after all the conclusion of any legal transaction relating to them. The late Mr. P. O. Hutchinson informed me that after an examination of the contents of the same chest he found some deeds of importance belonging to several families, and which were subsequently restored to their proper owners. T. N. BRUSHFIELD.

19. THE CUCKOO.—What is the latest date upon which the cuckoo has been heard in Devonshire? Though "in August fly he must," he has not infrequently been seen in the county in September. According to a cutting in one of my commonplace books, a young bird was shot somewhere in the county on September 12th, 1851. In his gizzard were found about twenty half-digested caterpillars. BUSY B.

The following notes by Mr. E. A. S. Elliot, M.B., Ornith. Union, relating to the Cuckoo, will not only answer the above query, but be of general interest in view of its expected arrival shortly. EDS.

In Messrs. D'Urban and Mathew's "Birds of Devon," we find it stated, "We have, after late springs, heard the cuckoo on 1st or 2nd July, but it is very rare to hear the bird cry after Midsummer Day, and in some years we have listened in vain for it after 10th June. Again, in a paper read by me in 1899, we find "his (cuckoo) note has not cracked this month, and is still heard up to the time of writing (June 25th)." The parent cuckoos usually retire south in July, but young birds often linger as late as October. The couplet runs—

> In April he comes,
> In May he sings all the day,
> In June he changes his tune,
> In July away he do fly.

Several points of interest relating to this bird have recently come to light mainly due to the observations of a German naturalist, Dr. Ray, and may be briefly summarised here:—

1. The egg of the cuckoo has been found in the nests of no less than 120 different species of birds.

2. The eggs of the cuckoo vary more in colour and markings than those of any other bird.

3. The most important characters of the eggs of the cuckoo are their form, the weight of their shells, and above all their thickness and hardness.

4. The majority of the eggs of the cuckoo resemble in colour and markings the type of one of our common Passerine birds, while some show a kind of mixed type, and some do not exactly resemble any known eggs.

5. Most cuckoos are in the habit of placing their eggs in nests of one species of bird, and take to other nests only if they cannot find their habitual nests.

6. They use, as a rule, one and the same district (mostly very limited) for depositing their eggs year after year.

7. The female cuckoo lays about twenty eggs every year, and these are laid on alternate days.

8. Each female cuckoo lays similar eggs during its life.

9. Cuckoos are polyandrous.

10. Each female places only one egg in one nest. If more than one be found they invariably belong to different females.

11. The time when the females lay varies greatly.

12. The female removes, in most cases (but not always), some of the eggs of the nest owners.

13. The female almost invariably lays its egg on the ground, and conveys it to the selected foster parent's nest, in her bill.

14. The young cuckoo commences to eject the other tenants of the nest as soon as it is hatched, and should there be two cuckoos in the same nest, the stronger ejects the weaker.

These particulars throw a strong light on the reasons which led to the adoption of a parasitic habit in these birds, for it would be obviously impossible for a bird laying the extraordinary number of twenty eggs to feed the progeny, especially birds with the appetite of a young cuckoo, whose voracity may be compared to that of a cormorant. We ourselves can personally corroborate many of these particulars, especially Nos. 5, 6, 9, 10, and 13. E.A.S.E.

20. PIXIES IN THE PRESENT DAY.—To those who take a delight in searching after folk-lore a bit of *fresh* evidence of the pixies must always be a rare treasure. Pixy evidence is never very forthcoming, and, when offered, too often resolves itself, under close scrutiny, into legends or sayings that have been written down twenty times already. Therefore, the information that the pixies had lately been active in our neighbourhood was exceedingly interesting. In December, 1898, they tied three knots in the mane of a cart-horse, living on a farm a few miles away. The owner knew from the way the knots were tied that no hands but the pixies could have twisted them, nor could they be unloosed by mortal fingers. The mane looked just as usual, excepting where the three knots made it "all of a twuzzle," and the mistress of the house explained the reason of them. It is, that the pixies ride the horses night-times, and because "they'm little fellows, not much bigger than clothes-pins," they tie themselves stirrups in the manes to keep themselves steady. She also gave it as her opinion that they must be like "dwarfies in shows." Another horse near by has recently been pressed in the same service, but the bare fact is alone recorded.

This is the only piece of the pixies' handiwork that has come actually within my own experience, but the following notes have been contributed by various speakers at odd times during the last two or three years, and may be of interest, as showing what is still said of the "little fellows" by, alas! the passing generation.

The pixies used to change the babies in the cradles. At Bishop's Teignton most of the women used to be very small, and folks said it was because they had been changed when they were babies. For all that, they would do many a poor soul a good turn, and would come into the house night-times and help with the work—get on with a bit of knitting, perhaps, or do some of the washing. Sometimes they would bring a load of hay or straw to a man's door in the night, a practice they seem, unfortunately, to have dropped. The pixies are fond of streams and pools, and haunt some marshes, not very far away, where on misty evenings they may be heard "laughing and playing the fiddle, beautiful." It is following the sound of their laughter that often enough leads folks astray and causes them to be pixy-led. Tales of such ill-fortune everywhere abound, and are too common even to be worth writing down.

The well-known remedy is, as everyone knows, to turn a coat or a pocket inside out, but a less spoken of way of breaking the spell is for some bystander to call the bewildered one by his name. A successful case was quoted the other day. Probably it is unusual to be pixy-led within hail of one's fellows, which would explain why the simplest remedy is not the popular one.

As to stories, I have heard "The Nurse and the Pixy," as given in English Fairy Tales, and, still more prettily told, in Mrs. Bray's "Borders of the Tamar and Tavy," but my version has a charming little ending omitted in both these books. *Their* tales close on the nurse being struck blind by the pixy; *mine* continues: "But she never knew in old age what want was, for her house was always filled with the things she wanted, though how they came there no one ever knew." So much charity should in justice be set to the credit of the Pixy, or Pixy-king, as the English Fairy Tales call him.

I have met with several instances of the "Farmer and the Pixies'"—a story, which in its different forms, bears a greater or less resemblance to Grimm's Shoemaker and the Brownies,

and here is a little pixy-tale less widely known. In the course
of ploughing a field a pixie's oven was once discovered,
and the man told the plough-boy to pick it up. But the boy
broke it (it was wooden) saying that "They old pixies
should'nt bake no more bread. Immediately he was set upon
by invisible enemies, and so severely pinched, that he was
obliged to go home to bed; his bruises being so bad that
he could not open his eyes for days. Another version tells
that the oven, already broken for want of a nail was put in
sight of the ploughman, and that he mended it. Afterwards
he found a mug of cider put out for him in the field by
the pixies. He offered a drink to the boy, who spoke
disrespectfully of them and their gift, and was thereupon
attacked.

It would indeed be lamentable that these tales should slide
into oblivion. Will any reader, gathering current intelligence
of the pixies, record it without delay?

ROSALIND NORTHCOTE.

21. CHURCH RIGHT AND CHURCH CHARTERS IN DEVON-
SHIRE.—In the *Cartularium Saxonicum*, published by Walter de
Gray Birch, I., 225, under the date 736, occurs the following
Charter relating to Worcestershire. (*Translation*):—

"The most glorious King of the Marchland (*Mercia*)
Aeðelred, with Earl Oshere, his associate, under-King of the
Wickmen, by request of the latter for the forgiveness of his
evil deeds, made a free grant in Church Right of an estate of
20 barton-lands (*cassati*) next the river Tillath to two holy
women, Dunne and her daughter Bucge, to set up there a
religious house, and confirmed the grant to them by under-
writing it with his own hand. The aforesaid handmaid of
God, Dunne, having set up a religious house on the said
estate, when about to join the Lord, being then alone in
charge of it, bestowed the same, together with its lands and
title-deed, upon her daughter's daughter [Hrotwari.] But
because the latter was still a mere child, she entrusted the
title-deed and the whole charge of the religious house, until
she should reach years of maturity, to [Bucge] her mother,
who was then married. When the grand-daughter demanded
the title-deed, the mother, not wishing to give it up, made
answer that it had been stolen. Upon the whole matter being

referred to the Holy Synod of Episcopal Councillors, the Venerable Council assembled together with the most Reverend Archbishop Nothelm [A.D. 735-741] decreed that the deed of gift both of the [two] Kings and of the aforesaid handmaid of God, Dunne, should be clearly made out afresh (*describi*) and restored to the aforesaid abbess, Hrotwari, and that she should be secured in fullest possession of the religious house, the Anathema being by decree of the Holy Synod pronounced on him who presumed by theft or in any other fraudulent manner to make away with the original deed of grant. This, too, the Holy Synod decreed, that after her [Hrotwari's] decease, this deed and land should revert to the Episcopal See in Worcester Castle in accordance with the regulations (*statuta*) previously made by the elder brethren (*seniores*).

The instrument is signed by Nothelm, who describes himself as " by the grace of God canonically archbishop," and by Daniel, Wor, Incgwald, Wilfrid, and Cudbert, each of whom describes himself simply as " bishop." This charter throws light on several obscure points.

1. A grant is made of land to a lady and her daughter to hold *by Church right*. The daughter appears to have forfeited her interest by marrying. The surviving holder then bestows it on her grand-daughter, and it may be presumed that the grand-daughter could have done the same but for the regulations (*statuta*) of the elder brethren. As a rule, the earlier Saxon monks appear to have preferred monasteries owned and administered by ladies, but the elder brethren in this case thought otherwise. We gather that land held by Church right was land vested in some one or more persons, but that these persons held it subject to the regulations made by the elder members of the community, in other words, in trust.

2. Another point is noteworthy. A charter is lost, and a Council orders it to be made out afresh. This was no forgery, because by old English rule a deed was not evidence in itself, but had to be proved by witnesses. Witnesses who could prove it, could reproduce its contents. No doubt witnesses who could, and did in all good faith, reproduce the contents of a charter might, and did sometimes, make mistakes in the names of signatories. A reproduced charter, if honestly made, is nevertheless substantially genuine, and we cannot pronounce a charter to be a forgery, because there are

The Old Church Walk, Totnes.
From a photograph by Messrs. Brindley & Son, Totnes

difficulties connected with the signatories. Mr. J. H. Round (Feudal England, p. 485) owns to this difficulty in dealing with Henry I.'s charter to Laund Priory, and yet does not venture to call it a forgery.

3. Among lands held by English thanes in the Devonshire Domesday is Jacobscherche (p. 1,191 in the reprint; Exchequer D. 118, 3; Exon D. 487, 450;) a small estate of 100 acres held by a lady called Alveva, who had also held it in the Confessor's time. This estate cannot be Jacobstow (1) because Jacobstow until the 14th century formed part of, and was included in Hatherleigh, and (2) because the sequence in the Exeter Domesday requires Jacobscherche to be looked for in Wonford or Hairidge Hundreds. It is no doubt the township of St. James, or St. Jacob as it is called in the Hundred Rolls of Edward I., otherwise known as Tre or Trew St. Jacob, lying on the Exe, in the parish of Heavitree, by Salmon pool and Trew Wear, on the site afterwards occupied by St. James' Priory. It may be concluded that St. James' Priory was not originally founded in 1143 as stated by Oliver (Mon. 190) but was only a refoundation in that year of an earlier existing monastery with an increased endowment. Alveva who held it at the time of the Conquest no doubt held it by Church right, which will account for its name Jacob's Church, and will also explain her not being dispossessed.   OSWALD J. REICHEL.

22. THE OLD CHURCH WALK HOUSE, TOTNES.—We now give a view from a photograph by Brimley and Son, Totnes, taken in 1868, of the Church Walk, Totnes, as it was before its removal, an account of which appeared in the last number; also of the old granite pillars now supporting the canopy at the entrance to the ancient Guildhall on the north of the Parish Church. The Guildhall is part of the Priory of St. Mary, Totnes, and was granted to the Corporation of Edward VI. In 1572, Queen Elizabeth made a grant under her great seal annexing the Guildhall to the Borough. In the hall, over the Mayor's chair, are the Royal Arms and the date 1553. Good specimens of linen pattern wood carving are to be found in the hall, in the gallery wall are the arms of the Earl of Bedford, and on the walls portraits of various Totnes worthies.   E.W.

23. THE VOICE OF THE WATERS.—The late Mr. R. J. King, in an article on Devonshire Folk-Lore, observed that the rivers that have their sources on Dartmoor, still retain something of the reverence with which they were anciently regarded. They are spoken of, as Sir Walter Scott has remarked of the great rivers of Scotland, with a certain respect, and an almost personal character is attributed to them. "Dart" especially—*the* Dart is seldom heard—bears traces of his former distinction. The "cry of Dart," as the moormen call that louder sound which rises from all mountain streams toward nightfall, is ominous, and a sure warning of approaching evil when heard at an unusual distance. The local rhyme runs thus:—

"River of Dart, O river of Dart,
Every year thou claim'st a heart."

Answering curiously to the German saying, "the river spirit (flussgeist) claims his yearly offering."

A German paper gave an account recently of observations on the tone of waterfalls made by Herren A. and E. Heine, who remarked that a mass of falling water gives the chord of C sharp (C, E, D), and below these notes the non-accordant F. When C and D sound louder than the middle note, F is heard very fully. It smothers the pure chord of C sharp, so that it is no longer heard as a concord, but as a clear rushing noise. The F is a deep dull humming far-resounding tone, strong in proportion to the mass of falling water. It can be heard round rocky corners or through thick woods, and at a distance at which the others are imperceptible.

Besides F, C and G are also heard. E is always weak, and the ear scarcely recognises it in small falls. The notes C, E, G, F belong to all rushing water, and in great falls often in different octaves. Small falls often give the same tones one, two, or three octaves higher. No other tones can be found. In strong falls F is the easiest to hear; in weak ones, C. On first attempts to distinguish the notes, C is usually the most readily recognised, and as each note is accompanied by its octave, it is often difficult to decide which—C, G or F—is heard. Persons with musical ears attempting to sing near rushing water spontaneously use the key C sharp, or of F sharp if near a heavy thundering fall. Other keys give an ugly discord.

The late Charles Kingsley, during a day's fishing on Dartmoor, composed the following lines :—

> "I cannot tell what you say, green leaves,
> I cannot tell what you say ;
> But I know there is a spirit in you,
> And a word in you this day.
>
> I cannot tell what you say, rosy rocks,
> I cannot tell what you say ;
> But I know there is a spirit in you,
> And a word in you this day.
>
> I cannot tell what you say, brown streams,
> I cannot tell what you say ;
> But I know there is a spirit in you,
> And a word in you this day."

* * *

THE REPLY.

> "O, rose is the colour of love and youth,
> And green is the colour of faith and truth,
> And brown of the fruitful clay.
> The Earth is fruitful and faithful and young,
> And her bridal morn shall rise ere long,
> And you shall know what the rocks and the streams
> And the laughing green woods say !"

If the musician and the poet have found a spirit of song in the wild moorland streams, we must not think our ancestors superstitious if they, too, found Nicors, or water spirits, in each black pool or hissing waterfall. P.F.S.A.

24. DEVONSHIRE DIALECT.—It is much to be wished that a good vocabulary of the Devon dialect could be compiled before the School Boards and modern civilisation have rendered the task impossible. Much has been done by Mr. Elworthy and Miss Hewitt for our Devon dialect, and by Mr. Jago and Mr. Quiller Couch for that of Cornwall; but there seems room for a vocabulary which shall be drawn up upon more scientific principles. The new Dialect Dictionary seems to me singularly disappointing. A grammar of the dialect should precede the vocabulary, and the pronunciation of the words should be given according to Mr. Sweet's notation. The intonation of the dialect should be thoroughly described and discussed, and the possibility of Celtic influence should not be left out of consideration. The words should be carefully classified, according to the sources

whence they spring, Saxon, French, Celtic, Cornish, or from other languages. Where possible the derivations should be given. It is plain that to carry out successfully such an undertaking several agencies are absolutely necessary. First and foremost, it would be necessary to get a complete list of the words peculiar to Devonshire, and to carefully distinguish between those which are obsolete and those yet in use. For this purpose, the services of a judicious scholar would be required, who should be competent to judge of evidence, and perfectly familiar with the Devonian dialect. It would be his business to ransack old vocabularies, and to gather up from whatever quarter they may come words actually in use. But, besides this, it would be requisite to enlist the services of several specialists, whose task it would be to refer the words to their source, and to trace their history. The most important of these specialists would be the Anglo-Saxon scholar, for most of our vocabulary comes from West Saxon sources. But a good Scandinavian scholar might throw light upon many words, and a good Celtic scholar with a knowledge of Welsh in all its stages, and of the Cornish language, would find his services invaluable. More words than is commonly thought owe their origin to a Celtic source. Such are crowder, muxy, pillum, linhay (?), tallack, basam, akether, and I venture to think the word "berth," whose derivation has been so much disputed. Barth is simply a mutation of *parth*, itself a loan word from *pars*, as in *partibus infidelium*. Then there are a certain number of French words, some, no doubt, of late entry into the dialect, such as rendezvous, cuchy (left-handed), keels (jeu de quilles), and suant, which may be older. Of course there are numerous words whose genealogy seems hardly to have been explained with sufficient certainty; such are "daps," "frauzy" (afternoon refreshment), etc. Unless this work be speedily taken in hand it will be too late.

Univ. Coll., Liverpool. HERBERT A. STRONG.

25. ELECTION DAY TREATING IN THE LAST CENTURY.—
I have in my possession a bill for the entertainment of voters at the Golden Lion Hotel during the Election of Mr. Walter Palk, of Marley, to represent the Borough of Ashburton in the House of Commons in 1796. The number of voters at

that time was about two hundred; they were all freeholders holding burgages within the Borough. The returning officer was the Portreeve, who also scrutinised the validity of each holding, and whose decision was final, subject to appeal to the House of Commons.

Nov., 1796. Walter Palk, Esq., Dr. to James Lloyd.

	£	s.	d.
Entertainment of certain votes the day before election and morning of election	18	5	8
Dinner	36	10	0
Beer, Porter, Cyder and Pop	4	5	0
Wine—612 Bottles Red Port @ 3/6	107	2	0
14 Bottles of Sherry @ 4/-	2	16	0
12 Bottles Madeira @ 6/-	3	12	0
2 Bottles Claret @ 6/-		12	0
Spirits—12 Bottles of Brandy @ 6/-	3	12	0
7 Ditto of Rum @ 6/-	2	2	0
15 Ditto of Gin @ 6/-	4	10	0
Fruite	1	10	0
Sugar	1	15	0
Tea and Coffee	4	0	0
Cards		10	6
Supper Porter and Cyder	3	0	0
Pipes and Tobacco		10	6
Store house shut up at half past 6 o'clock, after wich (*sic*) the following Liquor was consumed—			
Grog and Punch	3	12	6
55 Bottles of Port Wine	9	11	6
Negus	2	12	0
3 Bottles of Brandy		18	0
Hay and Corn	1	15	0
Damage for sundry Articles broken	5	19	0
	£219	0	8
Deduct breakages	5	19	6
	£213	1	2

Paid 13th Feby., 1797, the contents, By cheque on Bank
£213 1 2   JAMES LLOYD.

P.F.S.A.

26. EMMANUEL REGISTERS (par. 8, page 17).—The Rev. Francis Thomas, of Werrington Vicarage, Launceston, writes: "I may say I have tried to gather information from every quarter with regard to 'Emmanuel' entries. I find the word 'Emmanuel' used as an equivalent for Manuel in the fourteenth century.* But Emmanuel, the name of the Second Person in the Holy Trinity, was used by the Puritans much as the cross was used. It was, in fact, the Puritan "sign of the cross," and was prefixed to letters-missive, and other public deeds. In 'the famous play of Henry V' I am inclined to think Emanuel stands for sign'd Manual, not the Holy Name.

The quotation is, 'I beseech your grace to deliver me your safe conduct under your brad seal, Emanuel.' See Nare's Glossary, 1822, N.&Q. VII, 351 and 396 for quotation from 2 Henry VI, IV, 7, where I think Emmanuel is an anachronism.

There are letters headed as follows: 'Emmanuel, dated from London, 1584.' 'Immanuel dated from Cobm., in parish of Wem, Salop, 1593,' and 'Inn I dated from Preston Gubbals, near Shrewsbury, 1576.'

The following passage written in 1773 is from the Register of Emm. Coll., Camb., p. 88: 'It was customary with the Puritans, about 1584, when the college was founded, to begin their familiar letters with this word, 'Immanuel,' 'God with us,' and this was the case with many known to be intimate with the founder. Some of them begin, 'Our Father which art,' etc., many are directed to 'Our Father' or 'God,' but by far the greater number have 'Emmanuel.' It was the watchword of the party. Our founder, therefore, intending his college for a nursery of Puritans, was led to give us this name.'

In the archives of the Borough of Dorchester is a book begun at both ends with these headings: 'Emanuel, the second day of August, 1619,' 'Emanuel, the 30th daye of Januarie, 1622.' (N.&Q. VIII, Series viii, 351).

North Petherwyn Register has 'Emmanuel Christninge. Thomas the sonne of Rowe and Sarah his wife was baptized the eleventh day of October 1653.'

---

* See Peter's Launceston in reference to service book.

Werrington Register has 'Emanuel Burialls. Joane Dawe was buried the 4th of December 1653.'

There is no reference to such entries in books on Parish Registers. Mr. Tancock, the brother-in-law of the late Vicar of Tavistock, saw my register lately, and he had not come across anything like it in the Eastern Counties, and the Vicar of S. Breward, who knows Cornish Registers better than any man, has not met the word elsewhere.

By Forster's Alum., Oxon, we find Hancock, Vicar of N. Petherwyn, was a strong Puritan; speaks of himself as a minister of God's Word, and his son-in-law as minister of God's Word, in publication of banns.

Karslake (*vide* Brook's Puritans) was Chaplain at Werrington, which was a donative."

F.T.

27. ABBOTSKERSWELL, KINGSKERSWELL.—What is the origin of these names? The prefix Abbot and King is easily settled, but the remainder, Kerswell, is not so soon disposed of. I saw over a shop in Budleigh Salterton last summer, "Kersbrook." Isaac Taylor says that Ker is the same as Car and Caer in Welsh and Cornish, viz., a fortified place or castle. It may be in some cases, but I don't think it applies in this.

The suffix *well*, I feel sure, does not mean a spring of water. The whole neighbourhood is full of water, and a well can be had at very little trouble; so there is no necessity to bring habitations to some few favoured spots. In addition to Abbotskerswell and Kingskerswell, there are Ogwell, Coffinswell, Edginswell, and perhaps others. Isaac Taylor has a valuable note in his "Names and their Histories."

"*Weil* or *Wyl* is the name of several places in Germany, and *weiler*, *weil*, or *wyl* forms the suffix of 271 German names. The word *willa*, now *weil* or *wyl*, denoted a single house, while *wilare*, now *weiler*, signified a hamlet or collection of houses, etc., etc."

It would thus seem that a settlement of Saxons took place along the Valley of the Aller, and called their homesteads *weil* or *wyl*, with a special prefix. Must we then assume that *Ker* or *Kers* was a prefix like Edgin, Coffin, and Og, etc.

I should like to know what other readers of the *D.N.&Q.* think on the subject.

P.Q.K.

28. HAMS (par. 7, page 17.)—For the derivation of this word, the difference of its meaning in places other than in Devon and Somerset, where a plot of meadow land near a river is so called, see *N.&Q.* 7, 8, I, 427, II, 11, 12.

The *Antiquarian Magazine and Bibliographer*, for December, 1888, contains a paper on the suffix "Ham." "Notes on the name of Ham, in reference to its occurrence more especially in Devonshire," by J. H. Pring, M.D., will be found especially in the *Western Antiquary*, Vol. V, p. 13.

EVERARD HORNE COLEMAN.

29. WISHING TREES (14, part I.)—I am not acquainted with any articles on this interesting subject, other than some song notes in the *Western Antiquary*, Vol. II, p. 9, 58, 61, 88, to which your correspondent is referred.

EVERARD HORNE COLEMAN.

30. BULL-RING (15, page 26.)—Referring to the article on the Bull-ring at Ashburton in the first number of *D.N.&Q.*, it may, perhaps, be interesting for me to state that the name of the Bull-ring is still kept alive at Great Torrington, a tannery near its site being called the "Bull-ring Tannery."

I well remember hearing an old inhabitant of this place, who has now been dead for some years, give a graphic description of the "bull baitings" which he had seen. Instead of catching the tossed dog in aprons, as at Ashburton, the spectators in the vicinity of the falling dog would, as he came down, simultaneously stoop forward so as to receive him on their backs and break his fall.

At the close of the performance, the bull was generally let loose and ran through the streets, scattering the terrified women and children in all directions in his headlong career.

GEORGE M. DOE.

31. TORRINGTON.—The following paragraph appeared in a Magazine (not the *Gentleman's*, but probably the *European*), of February, 1760; is anything known of the occurrence beyond this report?

"A huntsman, near Torrington, in Devonshire, has been devoured by his own hounds." T.N.B.

Sir Humphrey Gilbert, 1539-1583.
From a print in the Fisher Library, Royal Albert Museum, Exeter.

32. BRANSCOMBE FOLK-LORE.—The late Mr. Henry Howe, son of the well-known actor of the same name, and himself for many years on the staff of the *Morning Advertiser*, informed me that during a visit he paid to Branscombe in 1853, he saw an old woman, reputed to be a witch, who was followed by a number of boys pelting stones at her. On speaking to one of the inhabitants about it, he was informed, " Oh, she's a witch." She had a blind husband.

T.N.B.

33. BENJAMIN ROBERT HAYDON, the painter, in his autobiography [Vol. I., p. 4] states that his mother was a Miss Cobley, the daughter of a clergyman, who had the living of Ide, near Exeter, who was killed, Haydon says, " by the fall of the sounding-board on his head while preaching"—*early in life*. What Haydon means by early in life is difficult to say, for he tells us that his unfortunate grandfather left a widow and eight children, and that a daughter was married. Is there any account of this accident anywhere?

J.B.R.

34. DEVON MUSTER ROLL, TIME OF ARMADA.—It may be interesting at this time, when our Volunteers are being so largely represented at the front in S. Africa, and Parliament is seriously discussing a scheme for the future defence of our coasts, to know what steps were taken three centuries ago in Devon to repel the threatened invasion by Spain. We must not think the country was so unprepared as some historians lead us to suppose. Nor were our Devonshire forces wanting in experienced captains, for it must be remembered that young Gawen Champernoune, of Dartington, had, by the permission of Queen Elizabeth, raised a body of one hundred Volunteers among the Western gentlemen, in which his cousin, Walter Ralegh, served, to assist the Huguenots in France, the autumn after the death of Condé in 1569. Champernoune afterwards married the daughter of Count de Montgomerie, the leader of the Anglo-French Huguenots. The departure of those Volunteers must have stirred the military spirit in Devon as much as the sending off our Imperial Yeomanry and Volunteers of to-day.

The following returns relating to Devon I have extracted from the State Papers in the Record Office. (State Papers Domestic, Vol. CXXII.)

11th Jany 157$\frac{7}{8}$. "The certificate of the vewe and muster as well of able men as the furniture of the weapons in the County of Devon taken by the Justices of the Peace in the same County in the several divisions in the month of October ano. Regni Domine nostro Eliz. Reg. 19 by virtue of Her Maj. commission in that behalf directed as hereafter followeth."

The return is a table in which all the items are given for each of the 33 Hundreds, of which the following is a summary:*

Total "able men," 10,000.
- Furnished (armed) - 2,974.
- Trained - 490.
- Selected to serve - 2,974.
- Unfurnished - 6,827.

Arms and Furniture in the County:

Pikemen.		Archers.		Bills.
Corsletts - 841		Long Bows with Sheafs of arrows } 651		
Pikes - 830				1160
Sallets and Steel Caps } 862		Calyvers - 647		
		Murryans - 647		

To act as Artificers (Engineers):

Wheelwrights, 340. Symths, 337. Pioneers, 1074.

There is endorsed on this return a note in another hand:— "Only six coats of plate armour are returned, no halberts and partisans or semi-launces, no harquebusses, handgons (guns) or curvieus or fully equipped light horse, as are in returns of some other counties."

Attached to the return is the following:—

Devon, 24th Jan^y, 157$\frac{7}{8}$.

A Schedule of the nomber of Alehouses, Innes and Tavernes wthin the said Countie as well in not exempt places as places so relevaged as hereafter followeth:

Towns and places not relieved.
- Inholders - 60
- Vintners - 30
- Alehouses - 100
} 190

Towns and places relieved.
- Inholders - 20
- Vintners - 10
- Alehouses - 100
} 130

---

* (For Details vide Trans. Devon Assoc. Vol. XXVI., 1894, pp. 97, 98, 99).

In State Papers (Domestic) Elizabeth, Vol. XXI, 1588: 1st March. Abstract of return from Devon of trained men with names of captains, and how they are sorted with weapons:—

Captains.	Men.	Shotte Firearms.	Corsletts Pikemen.	Bows Archers.	Bills.
Sir Wm. Courtney Sir Rt. Dennys	1753	533 cal. 67 musk.	333	300	500
Hugh Fortescue Anty. Pollard Wm. Monk	1734	533 cal. 66 musk.	334	300	500
Sir J. Gilbert Rd. Champernoun Thos. Fulford	1733	534 cal. 67 musk.	333	300	500
	5220	200 musk. 1600 cal.	1000	900	1500
Untrayned	1000	400 1800 50 musk. 350 cal.	200	200	200
Summa Totalier	6220	2200	1200	1100	1700

Launces none, for the County hath no keeping for them; Light Horse, 200; Gawin Champernoun, Captain.

18th March, Exeter. From Lord Lieutenant, Earl of Bath, to the Council—"Divers gentlemen claim protection of the stauneries and refuse to attend the general muster."

It is interesting to note that between the dates of the two musters, viz. 1578 and 1588, firearms were introduced. The late Mr. G. W. Ormerod finds the first mention of firearms at Chagford, under date of 1587, when two cullivers—large horse pistols or blunderbluss—were bought (Trans. Devon. Assoc., Vol. XVII., 1885, p. 339). In comparing the details of the two returns, it will be observed that during the ten years between them a great advance had been made in organization as well as in weapons. In 1588, we find the forces placed under experienced and responsible captains, and great method shown in the arrangement of the proportion of men, armed with the various weapons in each force. The thousand untrained men, it will be observed, were all armed in their true proportions, and were most likely the recruits of the year under training, who, in a short time, would join their respective companies.

It may be interesting also to identify the commanders, and how they were connected with each other in true Devonshire cousinship.

William Bourchier, 3rd Earl of Bath, as Lord Lieutenant of Devon, would be in supreme command of the County Forces. He had seen service in the Netherlands as a Volunteer, under the Earl of Leicester, in 1585, and was created Vice-Admiral of Devon in 1586.

Gawen Champernoun, of Dartington, who commanded the Light Horse, we have previously stated had commanded the West Country Volunteers in the Huguenot Wars in France, and had seen service in the best school of arms under experienced leaders. He had married into a distinguished French Protestant family.

The three bodies of infantry—which appear to represent East, North, and South Devon—were of equal strength, and similarly armed, and, with the recruits, amounted to over 2,000 men each, probably a brigade.

The East Devon Force was under the command of Sir Wm. Courtenay, Knt., of Powderham, possibly also of Colcombe Castle, Colyton, he had served as Sheriff of Devon in 1581. With him was associated in the command Robert Dennys, of Holcombe Burnell, son of Sir Thomas Dennys, who had been seven times High Sheriff of Devon; Prince (*Worthies of Devon*, p. 291) says Sir Robert Dennys "New built the houses (Bicton), made a park for deer, with the addition of drives, commodities both for use and pleasure."

The North was commanded by Hugh Fortescue, of Wear Giffard, who had been Sheriff of Devon in 1583, and had married Elizabeth, sister of Sir Arthur Chichester, and with him was his son-in-law, Anthony Pollard, of Way, in the parish of Fremington, who had married his daughter Joan, and also William Monk, doubtless of Potheridge, and of the family of General Monk, created Duke of Albemarle.

The officers of South Devon were all in a way connected. Sir John Gilbert of Greenaway and Compton Castle was the elder brother of Sir Humphrey and Adrian Gilbert, the celebrated navigators, and half brother of Sir Walter Ralegh, their mother being a Champernoun of Modbury, and so he was a first cousin to Gawen, who commanded the Light Horse. Sir Humphrey, whose portrait is given as an illustration in this number, was the first to carry into effect the project for the colonisation of North America by England, and so became the father of Greater Britain. Sir John Gilbert was held in great esteem by Queen Elizabeth, from whom he had received knighthood in 1570. He married Elizabeth, daughter of Sir Richard Chudleigh, of Ashton, and was one of the most influential men of his time. With Sir John Gilbert was associated in the command Richard Champernoun, of Modbury, his first cousin once removed, whose mother was a daughter of Sir Richard Edgcombe, of Cotehele, and he himself had married a daughter of Lord Chief Justice Popham, he was also first cousin to Gawen Champernoun. With these was also a Thomas Fulford, of Great Fulford and Bosenzeal, who was a grand nephew to the Lord Lieutenant the Earl of Bath, his grandfather, Sir John Fulford, having màrried Lady Joan Bourchier, the Earl's aunt.

To complete this labyrinth of relationships, a few years subsequently, Arthur Champernoun, son of Gawen, married Bridget, daughter of Sir Thomas Fulford.

Thus the officers commanding the Devon levy at the time of the Spanish Armada were nearly all in some way connected with each other, and were *off relations* if not Devonshire cousins.

To compare with the foregoing returns, we add a summary of the strength of the Volunteer forces as returned for the County of Devon, 31st October, 1899:—

Cavalry.	Royal 1st Devon Yeomanry - 295		
	North Devon Hussars - 339		
		634	
Artillery.	1st Devon V.A. (Exeter) - 785		
	2nd Devon V.A. (Devonport) - 489		
			1,274
Engineers.	1st Devon & Somerset Volunteers		
	Torquay - 94		
	Exeter - - 193		
		287	
	Carried forward		2,195

                                    Brought forward   2,195

Rifles and Infantry.
1st (Exeter and S. Devon) V.B.D.R.	872
2nd (Prince of Wales) V.B.D.R. (Plymouth)	885
3rd V.B.D.R. (East Devon)	672
4th ,, (Barnstaple)	819
5th (The Haytor) V.B.D.R. (Newton Abbot)	677
	3,925
Making a grand total of	6,120

                                                                                               P.F.S.A.

35. POOR LAW ADMINISTRATION AT HONEYCHURCH DURING THE EIGHTEENTH CENTURY.—Among the Parish Records of Honeychurch, there is a curious old book containing the original accounts, in manuscript, of the Overseers of the Poor during the greater part of the Eighteenth Century. For many years of the period covered by these accounts, one Andrew Snell, a name still honourably connected with the district—was the overseer elected from year to year. John Dunning was also the overseer for many years—the Dunning family having also had a lengthened connection with the parish, being doubtless an offshoot of the Ashburton family, and related to many families still resident in the district.

John Dunning was Overseer of the Poor of Honeychurch Parish in the year 1719, and during that year he carried out a notable scheme he had formed for relieving the Poor Rate of the charge for the maintenance of a young woman named Elizabeth Bartlet. This lady was an out-pauper, and the burden of her maintenance may be gathered from this entry in the account for 1719:—

    Pd. Richard ffrost for keeping Eliz. Bartlet
        seaven weekes -   -   -   0 6 0

Master Richard Ffrost's charges for the board and lodging of the young woman, something under a shilling a week, does not seem exorbitant, but Mr. John Dunning, the Overseer, was evidently a man of resource, and by a payment to one William Soper of a sum of £1 10s.—only 35 weeks' keep of Elizabeth Bartlet—together with expenses, he transferred the entire responsibility for Elizabeth for life to Mr. Soper. The latter was a prisoner in the Bridewell, so it is evident that the wooing of Soper and Bartlet must have been done by proxy—in other words, the match was arranged by Mr. John Dunning, Overseer, on a purely commercial basis. The whole romance of this *mariage de convenance* is told in the Overseer's account rendered to the Parish at the close of the year, which I quote *in extenso* :—

	£	s.	d.
Imprimis, Pd. for a Warrant, and Mittimus ag^t Willm Soper	0	4	6
Pd. Richard Ffrost for keeping Eliz. Bartlett seaven weekes	0	6	0
Pd. Richard Ffrost 3 dayes labour at Exon about the marriage of Wm. Soper and Eliz. Bartlet	0	4	0
Expence at the wedding	0	12	0
Paid for lichence *(sic)* to marry them	1	0	0
Paid Wm. Soper in money	1	10	0

[Poor Soper seems to have only got 5 times as much for undertaking to keep Bartlet for life, as Ffrost had received for "seaven weekes" keep]

	£	s.	d.
Pd. Mr. Swetin to mary Soper and Bartlet	0	9	0

[This gives the Parson's fee, very nearly a third of that of the Bridegroom.]

	£	s.	d.
Pd. for a Deliberate to fetch Soper out of the Bridewell to be maried	0	14	6
Paid for 4 Sumons ag^t Jacobstow, Lampford and Exborne about Soper's settlement	0	2	0

[Honeychurch Parish wishes to charge the adjacent Parishes with some or all of the £1 10s. paid to Soper.]

	£	s.	d.
Pd. for an Order on Jacobstow	0	4	6
Pd. two witnesses to attend at Crockernwell	0	4	0
Expences the same time	0	2	6

[Here we lose sight of Mr. and Mrs Soper of Honeychurch; but there are many Sopers still in Devonshire.]

In 1759, Mr. Andrew Snell was overseer; and the summary that he gives of his disbursements for that year is almost tragic in its brevity. Here it is :—

	£	s.	d.
Dis Busted	6	3	6

This gentleman's peculiar notions of orthography come out again in the following year, 1760, on the Coronation of good King George III : —

	£	s.	d.
Y^e 22 day (September) Pd. for Alle & Caks Crowneation day	0	10	6

And in the year 1763 he again enters his disbursements:—
Dis Busted - - - - 6 11 4
And here are one or two more entries in the account for that year (1763):—

May 6. Pd. William Huxtable for Jorney to
    Bytheford [Bideford] about the **Millety**
    [Militia] - - - 0 2 6
Laid out for Ale yͤ Thankesgiven Day - 0 7 7
Pd. for a Chang [change of clothing] and Iner
    Wastcoat for Jane Ratenbery - - 0 6 3½
Again, in 1764, Mr. Snell charges:—
Pd. for two Journeys at Exeter - - 0 5 0
Dis Bustid All is - - - - 7 7 2½
Charged on yͤ Parish 24 Poore Rats which when
    collected is - - - - 7 9 0
Which with - 0 0 8
    last yeare due to yͤ Parish is - 7 9 8
Dis Busted . - - - 7 7 2½

Remens due to yͤ Parish . - - - 0 2 5½
Paid for farmer Huckstable going to Tavistock
    about yͤ Millity - - - 0 2 6

In 1767, Mr. John Dunning (perhaps the son or grandson of the Overseer of 50 years before) was Overseer, and an entry shows that he had learnt how to spell " militia," but not " journey " :—

Paid Richard Westlake for a Jorney to Tavis-
    tock about the Militia - - 0 2 6

I will transcribe a few more entries made during the overseership of this Mr. John Dunning between 1767 and 1787:—

                In 1768.
Paid for a Shift for Eliz. Haywood - - 0 3 6
                1769.
Paid for Directions concerning the Clubb Act - 0 1 0
June the 11th—Paid Elizabeth Haywood a months
    pay - - - - - 0 6 0
Given the Sacrament Money 1s. 10d. and 8d.
    beside to buy Elizabeth Haywood a shift - 0 0 8
July the 9. Paid for a shirt for Hugh Rattenbury 0 3 6

John Bowthe, Bishop of Exeter, 1465-1476.

From his Monumental Brass in St. Martin's, East Horsley, Surrey

1787.

Paid for a Summons to place apprentices	0	0	6
The Churchwardens and Overseers to North-Tawton to Bind Apprentices	0	2	0
Paid for two paire of Indentures	0	8	4
Paid with two Apprentices	1	0	0
Oct. ye 23. Paid for summonses served on Horn and Jones being Intruders in our Parish	0	1	0
For a jorney to North Tawton to have them examined to their respective settlement	0	1	0
Paid for two examinations	0	2	0
Paid for a Summons to summon Exburn Parish to Oakhampton	0	0	6
November ye 5. Appear'd agst Horn and Jones at Oakhampton	0	1	0
Paid for two orders for Removal of Horn and Jones	0	14	0
For caring Elizth Jones a Popper with an Order to the Parish of Exburn	0	2	6
For Caring Robert Horn a Popper and his family with an Order to ye Parish of Sampford Courtney	0	2	6

These Overseers' Accounts are full of curious information illustrating the manners and customs of the age. There is one preserved among the Parish Records of Exbourne for a much longer period, I believe, than that of the adjacent parish of Honeychurch. I think that these—and doubtless there are many more in various parts of Devon—might prove to be worthy of being transcribed and printed *in extenso*.

ROPER LETHBRIDGE.

36. BISHOP JOHN BOWTHE.—We give an illustration, from a rubbing, of the monumental brass of this Bishop of Exeter, which is in the parish church of St. Martin, East Horsley, Surrey, where, no doubt, he was buried. He belonged to a family, members of which held high office from time to time in Church and State. There has been some doubt as to what his relationship to the two Bothes, Archbishops of York, really was. William was thought to have been an uncle, and Lawrence either a brother or an uncle. Professor Tout, however [Dictionary of National Biography, Vol. V.,

p. 387] says positively that both these prelates were his half brothers, being the sons of John Bothe by his first wife Joane, daughter of Henry Trafford; John, our Bishop, being his son by Maud, the daughter of Sir John Savage, his second wife. Oliver's pedigree [Lives of the Bishops of Exeter, p. 106] seems altogether wrong. The Dictionary of National Biography contains no account of John Bothe; of his more distinguished relatives, the two Archbishops, there are memoirs. John Bothe, or Bowthe—the surname is spelt in at least six different ways— Prebendary of Strensall in the Cathedral of York; Rector of Barnack, Northamptonshire; Prebendary of Wistow, in the Cathedral of Durham; Treasurer of the Diocese of York; Archdeacon of Richmond; and Warden of the Collegiate Church of Manchester;—was consecrated Bishop of Exeter 7th July, 1465. The cares of his episcopate apparently did not sit heavily upon him. It was nearly two years before he thought it well to come into his diocese, which he did, it would seem, for the first time in February, 1467, and he remained in it for two years only. He was then absent until August, 1474, when he returned, remaining five months. Early in 1476 he was in Exeter again, and was moving about the diocese for three months, and then left it altogether.

Notwithstanding these frequent absences, Hooker says, he served the diocese wondrous well. Wearied with the troubles of the times—he and his family were Lancastrians—he retired to the Episcopal Manor at East Horsley, the gift of Henry I to the See, which Oliver says was his favourite residence. Here he died 5th April, 1478. He left his mark on the Cathedral. In the bosses of the vaulting of the Chapter House is the oft-repeated shield of Bowthe, a boar's head, and tradition says, probably truthfully, that the very fine bishop's throne was the gift of John Bowthe. It is apparently a little earlier in date, but it may be that its carver was a workman of a passing period, and followed the style to which he had been accustomed; and that he was no 'prentice hand is certain. The brass is a very interesting one, the inscription commonplace :—

  Quisquis eris, qui transieris, sta, perlege, plora.
  Sum quod eris, fueramque quod es; pro me precor, ora.
  Hic jacet Johannes Bowthe, quondam episcopus Exoniensis, qui Obiit vº die mensis Aprilis, Aº Domini mcccclxxviij.

The bishop is represented in pontificals, vested for celebrating the Holy Communion, with mitre and pastoral staff. Oliver says, "*what is unusual, with the chasuble appearing on one side of the cope.*" What we are to understand by this observation of our dear old doctor, we cannot imagine. There is, of course, no cope. If the remark refers to the position, he is right, for a figure thus vested, and kneeling, is very unusual, and there are only two other brasses in England in which so much of the back is displayed. Profile brasses are not numerous, a very good one is that of William Langton, Canon of Exeter, in the Cathedral, but he is wearing a cope. This figure is in profile, slightly turning to the right, thus showing the apparel of the chasuble; below is the damatic, and then the flowing alb, plain, the tunicle is not visible, or any other part of the vestment. The bishop wears a low mitre, ornamented with gems, and having the hanging infulæ, and he holds in his left hand his richly carved pastoral staff. The prelate's arms are in the shield at the top of the brass, on the right hand. They are those of his family, which Guillim gives as: Topaz (*i.e.*, *or.*) 3 boars' heads erased, diamond (*i.e.*, *sa.*) armed topaz. The shield has a label for difference. J.B.R.

37. THE PARISHE, OF, HEVITREE, IN THE, COUNTYE, OF, DEVON.

Articles for the observation and contynuance of due and and necessarie Orders in Churche matters for the Parishe of Hevytree | newly concluded and agreed on by us John Isack, John Leigh of Wonforde, Richard Duck, and John Leigh Meere the younger | now bynge Sidemen or ffower men of the same Parishe, with the consent and assent of the whole Parishioners, or the moste | honest Inhabitants of the same Parishe assembled and gathered together within the saide Parishe Churche of·Hevytree upon Sonday | the sixe and twentith day of June in the yere of owre lorde god One thousand ffyve hundred Eightie Sixe, and in the Eight | and twentith yere of the Raigne of o^{ur} Sovraigne Ladye Elizabeth by the grace of god of England, Praunce and Ireland Queene | defendor of the faithe &c. To be observed and kepte (by us the foresaide ffower men, or any of the Parishioners wch hereafter is or shall be | elected one of the ffower men of the same Parishe) in churche matters, and other necessaries concernynge the comon utilitye of the | same Parishe. To the wch orders folowynge they all did agree and subscribe unto.

Inprimis whereas there is a stronge chest bounden with Iron wch hath three locks and three kayes wherein is alwaies to be kept the Parishe stock with all such | wrytynge and Evidence as belongeth to the said Paryshe. It is decreed the said chest shall remayne alwaies in the custody of one of the Sidemen. |

Item that the other three of the Sidemen shall have eache of them one of the saide kayes of the foresaid chest in keepinge and that the said chest be not at any time opened untill | they all fower come together, or three at the least.

Item that the churche wardens shall yerely the Sondaye after St. Andrewes daye make their accompte to the sidemen or to as many of them as be then psent in the | Parishe Churche theire after Mornynge prayer, and shall bringe in the Churche Store remayning in theire handes and delyv^r the same to the Sidemen aforesaide. And | in not so doynge shall forfeit to the Fowermen of the said Parishe for the tyme beynge the some of Tenne Poundes of good and lawfull mouye of England, to be leavyed | of them to the use and mayntenance of the said churche. And the said Sidemen are to delyver some reasonable some of money to the nexte wardens that are chosen yearly | to remayne in their handes that shalbe thought needefull for usuall repãcons in their owne handes.

Item that they which deale for the houses of Saynct Loye in the behalfe of the Parishe shall likewise yerely make theire Accompt the Sondaye before | All Saynctes in the saide Parishe Churche psently after Morning Prayer to the fower men of the same Paryshe or to as many of them as be then | present, and to bring in and delyver upp all such money as shall remayne in their handes to the saide fower men then present. And in not so doynge shall | forfeyte unto the fower men of the saide Paryshe for the tyme beynge the some of Tenne Poundes of good and lawfull mony of England, to be levyed of them to the | use of the poore or mayntenaunce of the saide Churche.

Item that all wrytynges, deedes, leases and other convayaunces whatsoever that belonge to the Parishe Howse, and

Saynct Loye, shalbe brought in w^{th}in | tenne dayes after the date above written to be kepte in the saide cheste.

Item that yf upon conference had amongest the Sidemen nowe beynge, or those that shalbe appoynted any time hereafter concernynge the Church matters or comon | utilitye of the Parish, Three of theym doe agree and the fowerth douth refuse, That then the Churche wardens for the tyme beynge wth the advise and condisent | of the saide three men shall displace the same One, disagreeynge, and in his steede nomynate and place one other, thought worthye of the office by theire discretions. |

Item that wee the fower men of the Parishe above named and they that any tyme hereafter shalbe any of the fower men of the same parishe, shall one daye | in the yere; that is to weeto in and upon the feaste daye of All Saynctes comonlye called Alhallowe daye, psently after Evenynge Prayer, call all y^e | Parishioners together w^{th}in the saide Churche of Hevytree, and theire to geve them Accompt what wee have receaved of the Churchwardens for that yere. | As likewise what we receive for the howses and grownde of Saynct Loye, that the Parishioners may be prevye and witynge what the totall some is that | remayneth to the said Parishioners' use for that yere.

Item that wee the fower men of the Parishe above named and they that at any tyme hereafter shalbe wth the consent of bothe the wardens or one of them shall upon | good cause remove and place to theire will and pleasure in every seige in the Churche accordinge as shall by theym thought Good. |

Item that if the fower men now beynge, or any other hereafter to be appointed to the office of Sidemen shall not well and truly to the uttermoste of theyre | powres keepe fulfill and observe all and singular the Articles above mencyoned. Or if they for the tyme beynge or any one of theym, or any succeedinge | then shall not faithfully deale in Churche causes for the best mayntenaunce of the said Church and other necessaryes concernynge the comon utilitye of | the Parishe, when and as often as occasion shall serve, in what they or any of theym may, that the churche wardens for the tyme beynge wth fower of the | Elders and best lyvers of the Parishe shall dissappoynt hym or any of theym the saide Sidemen so offendynge, and shall forthwith nomynate electe and constitute other fower as they shall think more meete for that office, And he or they so deprived and voyded of theire office, shall yelde upp suche | cheste, kaye or kayes monye goods leases deedes and convoyaunces appertayninge to the Churche fourthwith and upon the nomynacon of any one or | others as yf hee or they had not byn men chosen or elected to suche office. Anythinge to the contrary Notwithstandynge.

Item that if any some of mony beynge in the chest may be att any tyme conveniently spared, Then yf any Inhabitant of the Parishe beynge to his power | a well wisher towarde the benefite of the Churche upon good and reasonable cause shall neede to borrowe some parte thereof for a season, That such a one | shall not be denyed, So as hee leave a gaydge or other sufficient Assurance for repayment thereof.

Item itt is finallye concluded That whereas the landes and Tenementes comonly called Saynct Loyes have usually heretofore byn taken of | the Lordes of the same by the fower men of this parish to the use of the mayntenaunce of the Churche, and other necessaries concernynge the comon utilitye | of the same Parishe. By the assent and consent of the Parishioners aforesaid, That yf at any time hereafter any of the saide fower men or any of the | Parishioners or any other person or persons w^{cn} hereafter shall be elected of the fower men of this Paryshe, or become one of the Parishioners, shall by | hym selfe or by any other pson or psons whatsoever to his, or to his owne pryvate use or uses and comodityes, and contrary to use and order before mencyoned, take any | parte of the lande, tenements or hereditaments called Saynct Loyes. That then they or eyther of them offendynge the contents of this Article | shall for everye offence forfeit unto the fower men of this paryshe for the tyme beynge the some of fortye Poundes of good and lawfull mony | of England. To be levyed of them and of every of them to the use and mayntenaunce of the saide Churche.

That these Articles and orders may contynue of force, and be kepte for ever in the foresaid chest for a ppetuall memorye. We the aforesaid fower men have not only hereunto sett oure handes and seales, | But for the more confirmation hereof have caused the inhabitants of the same pishe to doe the lyke. And | for the strengthenynge and farther establishinge of this oure good proceedings and Orders, we have desired the worshipfull | Mr. Stephen Townesende Doctor of Divinitye and Deane of the Cathedral Churche of S. Peter in Exeter, owre Ordynarie to Ratifie confirme and allowe thease o' mutuall consents and agreements.

x John Isake	x Rychard Rowe	x Coory, John [?]
x John Ligh of Wonford	x George Glanfyld	x Thomas Leigh
	x James Taylor	x Edward Pookay
x Rychard Ducke	x Rychard Taylor	x William Tucker
x John Ligh of Myre	x John Lang	x Willm.Monstephen[?]
x [Undecipherable]	x [Undecipherable]	x Willm. Bruton
x John Pym	x Thomas Brodmor	x William Powl [?]
x William Liegh	x Robt. Chubb	
x Roger Mynyfye	x Nycholas Hearn [?]	G.R.

38. THE WHITCHURCH FEE.—In Domesday, a certain number of properties in Devon, which I will designate "The Whitchurch Fee," belonged to one Ruald Adobat. Early in Henry II.'s reign (if not before) the Whitchurch Fee was held by the Giffards of the newly created Earl of Devon. The fact that each possession of Ruald had then passed to the Giffards, as tenants of the Earl of Devon, suggests that this Whitchurch Fee had been appropriated, with other land, by the king to make up the number of manors necessary to support the new earldom. I think the earldom of Warwick was created in similar circumstances. If this is correct it would appear very probable that the Giffards were enfeoffed by the Earl of Devon, Redvers, "*in free marriage*," as that was a very common form of becoming the tenant of land in those days. I am most anxious to know how, and where, I should look for verification of this theory? H.F.G.

39. RALEGH FAMILY.—In his account of *British Cyprus*, published in 1879, Hepworth Dixon reports:—

"The mosque of Santa Sofia in Famagosta, Island of Cyprus, was formerly a Christian Church. The interior contains tombs of knights; the slabs still rich in names and shields. Some of these stones bear English names; one slab is carved with the arms of Raleigh, and is probably the gravestone of a crusading ancestor of the famous knight." (p. 287).

It is to be regretted that the author did not describe these arms so as to be able to show they really belonged to the

Ralegh family, of whom no record has yet come to light that any member died in that island. Can any of your correspondents explain it ?   T.N.B.

NOTICES OF BOOKS.

40. In one respect, at all events, Ottery St. Mary certainly is one of the most favoured places in Devon, for, with the exception of the Cathedral, we know no church in the County which has received such full and able treatment from competent hands. In the earlier volumes of the Transactions of the Exeter Diocesan Architectural Society, are valuable papers by members of the family with which the town is so identified, containing a full history of the Church and its restoration, besides other papers by other writers. Then Dr. Cornish in 1869 published his "Short Notes on the Church and Parish," and now we have the two pamphlets by the Rev. F. B. Dickinson mentioned below.* The first on the history of the Church is admirable. It is a model for any parish priest who will undertake the writing of a history of his own church, and although there are not many churches of such importance, or with such a history as that of St. Mary of Ottery, there are very few that would not furnish material of interest and value, not only to those living in the parish and neighbourhood, but to many outside. The second pamphlet is equally good. The importance of the Ottery Registers in connection with this large parish cannot be over estimated. Commencing in 1601 they are contained in no fewer than twenty-eight volumes, and besides the ordinary entries of baptisms, marriages, and burials, there are occasionally curious and interesting notes. Mr. Dickinson has dealt with these Registers in a most pleasant manner. Here, too, our author sets his fellow clergymen an example. If those having charge of such documents would take a little trouble to decypher them, they would be surprised at the amount of information and amusement they would obtain.

                        J.B.R.

---

* A Lecture on the History of the Church of St. Mary of Ottery, by the Rev. F. B. Dickinson, M.A., 1/- ; H. D. Badcock, Ottery St. Mary, A Lecture on "Our Parish Registers," by the Rev. F. B. Dickinson. M.A. Privately printed, 1899.

1. Week Down Cross.
2. Shorter Cross, Week Down.
3. Hele Cross.
4. North Bovey Cross.

41. SOME NOTES ON THE MORE RECENT HISTORY OF A FEW ANCIENT CROSSES WHICH ARE TO BE FOUND IN THE NEIGHBOURHOOD OF NORTH BOVEY.—Much has been written on and but little is known of the origin of those ancient Crosses which adorn the district of Dartmoor.

Erect and prostrate, entire and mutilated, self-contained and with arms, with shafts and without them, they are still to be met with in various places under different conditions, although many have been destroyed and others have been moved.

Conspicuous on the summit of a lofty Tor, noticeable on the sloping side of some lonely moor, buried in brushwood, marking boundaries of Church properties or Sanctuaries, at the intersection of cross roads, built into wayside walls, adorning market places, records of battle, murder, and sudden deaths, many of them are well known to the author of this article.

As a general rule, where they bear no inscription nothing is known with certainty of the motives which caused their erection, or of the date of their foundation, but some of them are said to be of pre-Christian origin, erected before A.D. 600. These are generally self-contained, and it is possible that they were originally nothing more than pagan sepulchral stones, and that the crosses inscribed upon them are of later date than their erection, and were cut by Christian hands. The plainer crosses with arms are of somewhat later construction, but if the late Mr. R. J. King is to be trusted, most of them are older than A.D. 936. One of them is marked upon a map which Mr. J. Brooking Rowe considers to be five hundred years old, and to which less competent critics assign a still earlier date. The cross itself thus signified may, of course, be very much older than the map. These monuments are generally of very respectable antiquity.

There is a tradition that a Cross which formerly stood at "Watching Place," in the parish of North Bovey, was erected to mark the ground on which the Moorland Christian British awaited the onslaught of their Saxon invaders, and on which a battle was fought. It was known as "Beetor Cross," and was taken down by a landowner to be converted into a gate-post about a quarter of a century ago. It was of plain construction, rudely cut from a granite block. The shaft stands up four feet from the surface of the ground, and the arms, slightly damaged, are sixteen inches across.

In Churchyards and out of them, some Crosses stand above the graves of individual men, as was formerly the case near Fox Tor Mire, where Childe of Plymstock is said to have died, in the reign of Edward III, in the year 1350, or about that time. Some Crosses were erected to denote places appointed for public proclamations, and prayers and preachings, and others may well mark the spots where travellers have in moments of great danger been providentially preserved. No matter for what object they were created they were likely to be respected, and it is probable that this consideration has often determined their formation when otherwise plain stones would have equally well fulfilled their purpose. There is, indeed, a tradition current in the County that much ill-fortune befell a man who was guilty of the desecration of a Cross, and his sad fate should be a warning to others (and they are many) who are still thus evilly disposed.

These monuments were erected during the ages of faith. Some were, possibly, the objects of superstitious reverence during the ages of credulity, they were maltreated during the ages of fanaticism, they were neglected during the period of materialism, and they are being restored in an age of intelligence.

They have experienced many vicissitudes of fortune. To the author of this paper they speak eloquently of a past period which is dear to him, and he often thinks when he sees a weather-beaten Cross, stained with the growth of lichens, spreading its short arms in some lonely situation to the sunshine and the breeze, how the prayers of the faithful have gone up from it to heaven, and to him the place which it occupies is holy ground.

In the words of one who has gone to his rest, but was once well known to the writer :—

> "In many a green and solemn place,
> Girt with the wild hills round,
> The shadow of the holy cross
> Yet sleepeth on the ground."

It is a pity that people, however little they may share such sentiments as these, should be permitted to disfigure, if not to profane, these Christian monuments by cutting letters such as D. S. (for Duke of Somerset) on Hameldon Cross; or W. B. (for Warren Bounds) on Bennett's Cross; or broad arrows, to mark Ordnance surveys, on the surfaces of other venerable monuments of Christianity. Can nothing be done to prevent a repetition of these callous enormities?

But it is time to revert to those modern histories which it is the object of this paper to record.

In the village of North Bovey there is an ancient Cross to which a more recent history is traditionally attached.

At an unknown period, probably during the Great Rebellion in the seventeenth century, it was thrown into the Bovey Brook, and in 1829, at the instigation of a Mr. Jones, then Curate-in-charge of the parish, some of the farmers of the place took down a team of horses and drew it into the village, where they set it up in order to demonstrate their delight at the passing of the Catholic Emancipation Act, which Mr. Jones, who was a great Radical and a very clever man, assured them would greatly conduce to their prosperity.

On Week Down, midway between Chagford and North Bovey, from time immemorial, and in close proximity, two Crosses have reared their venerable heads. The taller one stood on the Down, a conspicuous object for miles around; the other, which was locally known as "Shorter Cross," occupied a position in the lane which leads to Middlecote farmhouse below. These Crosses were not more than one hundred yards distant from each other. About twenty years ago the writer of this article was told that the enterprising occupant of Middlecote had taken "Shorter Cross" down, and, using it for a cover-stone over a well, had buried it deeply and securely underground. Loudly and long the writer remonstrated—apparently in vain, but not, perhaps, altogether fruitlessly—for through the instrumentality and at the expense of Major Yolland, R.E., who owns land in the neighbourhood of Week Down, this remarkable self-contained Cross has been quite recently disinterred, and is again filling the site which for so many long centuries it occupied and adorned.

Opposite to the front of Hele farmhouse is another and very beautiful Cross, but it is probably not of equal antiquity to those upon Week Down, and concerning it no vicissitudes of fortune are recorded.

Once again, a low Cross of Greek pattern stands at the top of Horse Pitt hill, midway between North Bovey and Moreton Hampstead. Some one has defaced it in the barbarous fashion which is—alas!—too common, in order to make it serve as a rude signpost to direct the traveller on his way.

From what has been written and here recorded, the reader will learn that the moorland parish of North Bovey contains four ancient Crosses, one of which urgently needs to be saved from degradation and restored—as has been " Shorter Cross," which is in Chagford Parish—to its former position.

A little further away, in connection with Manaton, Widecombe, and Lydford parishes, are similar tales to be recorded, but enough has been written for the present, and the author of this paper will conclude with the remark that the Crosses in North Bovey stand East and West, and the dimensions of some of those that have been described* are as follows:—

Cross on Week Down. Height, 7 feet 11 inches; greatest breadth of shaft, 17 inches; arms 19 inches.

"Shorter Cross," below Week Down. Height of pillar, 5 feet 8 inches; breadth, $17\frac{1}{2}$ inches; Cross inscribed, 21 by 14 inches.

"Beetor Cross," North Bovey, in gateway. Height 4 feet; breadth of arms, 1 foot 4 inches. W. H. THORNTON.

42. BURLEIGH DOLTS.—Can any of your readers explain the meaning of this word *dolt* as applied to the remains of an old British camp near the village of Marlborough? It is true the fortress is on a hill, and it may be only a corruption of *dùn*. A portion of the inner vallum only remains in a primitive state, and even here the meat earth has been removed from the ramparts, but when the surrounding fields are not in tillage the outlines of a very large camp can be traced, The names of these fields are very significant; they are Castle Park, Down, Beacon (the highest point directly above what was evidently the main entrance to the camp, in full view of Stanborough Camp and Bolt Head, near which was another camp), and Squirrel. What was apparently the main entrance to the camp looks out in a direction N.E. towards the camp at Stanborough, some nine miles distant. E.A.S.E.

---

*Our thanks are due to Miss Derby, a friend of the Author, for photograph of Hele Cross, and also to Dr. Stephens. of Moreton Hampstead, for photographs of the others, which form the illustrations to this paper.—ED.

43. STANZAS ON THE DEATH OF THE NOTED SLACK, BUTCHER AND STAGE BOXER.—He was a native of Braunton, and died there A.D. 1761, at which time the following lines appeared:—

"To thy departed Shade, the Muse, O SLACK!
 'Midst friends would blend a tributary sigh
Not that I'd *challenge* Fate—or call thee back—
 No—once at rest, I wish thee so to lie.

Oft has thy nervous arm, ere yet unbrac'd,
 With terrors fraught dealt round distructive knocks;
The Stage and slaughter-house alike it grac'd
 And there a Bully drop't, and here an Ox!

No laurel-wreath thy claim, nor martial song,
 For battles fought by thee in Albion's cause;
Yet, as due trophies, let thy tomb be hung
 With dislocated thumbs and broken jaws!

Mourn not, Brauntonians, his extinguish'd lamp;
 He meets the common fate assigned to all:—
And conqu'ring heroes of a nobler stamp,
 When Death the buttock tips, alike must fall!

Dread then, ye Bruisers, this alarming foe!
 By SLACK's defeat some warning take at least:—
Mighty must be the arm, that at a blow
 Could level *him* who levell'd *man* and *beast!*

These verses are by Christopher Jones, "an uneducated journeyman Wool-comber, of Exeter," as he describes himself. They are contained in his "MISCELLANEOUS POETIC ATTEMPTS," "printed for the Author by R. Trewman, nearly opposite S: Martin's Lane in the Fore Street, Exeter, 1782."

HARRY HEMS.

44. RINGING BELLS DURING A THUNDERSTORM (par. 10, page 18).—In the summer of 1863 I was staying at Engelburg, where exists the famous monastery, when a violent thunderstorm raged for the greater part of the day. The large bell of the monastery was continuously rung. The curious feature of the storm was that the claps of thunder resembled dull pistol-shots going off all round. Perhaps some scientific correspondent will be able to inform us whether the waves of air set in motion by bell ringing may not have some effect in causing the electrical discharges to take place at a distance from the spot wherein the waves originate.

O.J.R.

45. ABBOTSKERSWELL, KINGSKERSWELL (par. 27, page 47).—The origin of Place-names is a most interesting subject when properly investigated, in lieu of accepting *ad captandum* derivations, of which examples may be found in Polwhele's *Devonshire*. Omitting their first syllables, the name *Kerswell* in each of the above-named places evidently consists of two separate words.

Although in England the prefix is almost invariably *Kars*, or *Kers*, in the Domesday record it is always *Cars*. In the late Mr. R. N. Worth's paper on " The Identification of the Domesday Manors of Devon" (*Trans. Dev. Assoc.* xxv, 318), four places commencing with the latter form of prefix are so identified, the two noted above being of the number. He also mentions three other places in the County having *Kers* as their first syllable, that of *Kersbrook* in the parish of East Budleigh being a fourth example. There can be little doubt the original names commenced with *Cars*, excepting in any purely modern instances.

As the second term is undoubtedly an Anglo-Saxon one, we must accept the other to be so, otherwise the complete word would be of the hybrid class. From this point of view neither *Car* or *Caer* (not being Anglo-Saxon) are admissible; and, in the opinion of P.Q.K., neither are applicable to the Devon *Kerswells*. It is, however, not easy to suggest a possible derivation, Bosworth's *Anglo-Saxon Dict.* affords no clue. Possibly, it comes from the same root as *Carse*, so frequently employed as a prefix to the names of places in Scotland at the present day. If the term had been confined to a single place there would be a greater probability of its being a family one, but the numerous instances of its use appears to indicate it was derived from some local circumstance.

Where the place is unrecorded in Domesday, the modern term may be a corruption, as in the case of *Carshalton*, in Surrey, which is simply a perverted phonetic spelling of the original designation, *Cross-Aulton*.

The names of many manors enumerated in Domesday terminate in *well*, *will*, *ville*, or some variant representing either (1) a fountain, well, pond, or watering-place; or (2) the manor or lordship of the original settler; and, irrespective of its magnitude, the first proprietor of a vill or manor would, as a rule, call it after his own name.

A curious exception to each of these renderings occurs in the Place-name of *Whatstandwell*, near Matlock in Derbyshire; and termed by Rhodes in his *Peak Scenery* (1828), 344, *Hot Standwell*. Both of these are corruptions, and what appears to be the correct explanation is thus stated by J. C. Cox in his *Tourist Guide to Derbyshire* (1878), 26 :—" From a Charter of the year 1391, relative to the building of a bridge over the Derwent, we find that one Walter Stonewell had a mansion here, which he held of the Abbot of Darley."

The following examples may serve to show how necessary it is to trace the origin of Place-names as far back as possible, and not to assume for granted that similar names must, of necessity, have a similar origin.

Tideswell, a parish in the Peak of Derbyshire, is (or was) celebrated for its ebbing and flowing well; and this seems— as far as the existence of a well is concerned—to be corroborated in the Domesday volume, where it appears as *Tiddesuuelle*.

Tidwell, a sub-manor in the original royal one of East Budleigh, receives no mention in Domesday. Writing in the early part of the 17th century, Risdon alludes to it—evidently in explanation of the Place-name—as containing "a Pond or Pool maintained by Springs, which continually welm and boil up, not unlike that wonderful Well in Derbyshire which ebbeth and floweth by just Tydes, and hath given name to Tideswell, a market Town of no mean Account." (*Survey of Devonshire* (1714), I, 83-4). That Dr. Oliver accepted this paragraph as giving the origin of the name of the Devonshire sub-manor is shown in the following foot-note he appended to the copy of a Charter of Jordan de Toddewill, whose surname it served to explain :—" Now Tidwell, *i.e.*, Tidewell" (*Monasticon*, 252). Several other variants of this surname are noted in the same work, among them being *Toddwill, Todeville, Tudevill*; and Pole also records *Todwell* and *Tudwell*.

From these remarks, we may reasonably conclude that *Tidwell* is simply a corruption of *Tod-vill, i.e.*, the vill or manor or lordship of Tod; and this probably correct explanation appears to have been overlooked by the celebrated Exeter Antiquary.

T.N.B.

46. ABBOTSKERSWELL, KINGSKERSWELL (par. 27, page 47). —Why suggest a fancy derivation from Welsh *Caer* and

German *weil* (the latter, by the way, being only the Latin *villa* done into German), when a simple scientific derivation from two Saxon words lies close at hand? The first, *Cerse*, derived from *Kersau*, to grow, means cress or weed (like the sudd of the Upper Nile); the second, *Welle*, means a spring. Besides Abbotskerswell and Kingskerswell, a Charter of A.D. 956 mentions a Caerswylle in Ipplepen, which seems to be now Bulley Barton. Apparently that whole district was called Kerswell, or the Weed-well. The hundred certainly bore that name up to the time of the Conquest and afterwards, probably because its place of meeting was at the "Weed Well." Another hundred in the North of Devon, which held its meetings at the "Clear Well," was called Scirwell, or Sherwell, from the Saxon word *scir*, which means clear. As we still retain the Saxon *Cerse* in our "cress," so we still retain the Saxon *scir*, as when we call a thing "sheer" nonsense. The objections to connecting the first part of the name with the Welsh *Caer*, Cornish *Car*, Armorican *Ker*, is that, except a word has lost its meaning as in Pen Beacon, folk do not talk in two languages at once. Besides, the word *Kers* is quite a different word from *Ker* or *Caer*. May I add that in Domesday both Edginswell and Coffinswell appear simply as Welle without any personal prefix. O.J.R.

47. NAMED BOTTLES.—Why were names fixed on wine bottles? We should be glad to receive names, dates, and any particulars of such. The dates mostly found are in 17th, 18th, and early part of 19th centuries. Why should not old bottles be of interest and have their history? H.S.

48. DEVON GLEE CLUB (par. 16, page 29).—The following particulars of this Club have been received from Mr. W. J. Watts, of Forde House, Newton Abbot, who was a member:—

"President, Sir J. Rogers; Vice-President, Charles Brutton, Solicitor, Exeter. The members dined together three times during the winter months. Glees and madrigals were sung by the lay vicars and chorister boys. Grace before dinner, *Non nobis Domine*, was sung. I cannot say why the Club ceased to exist, but think the President's illness was the cause." J. D. PODE.

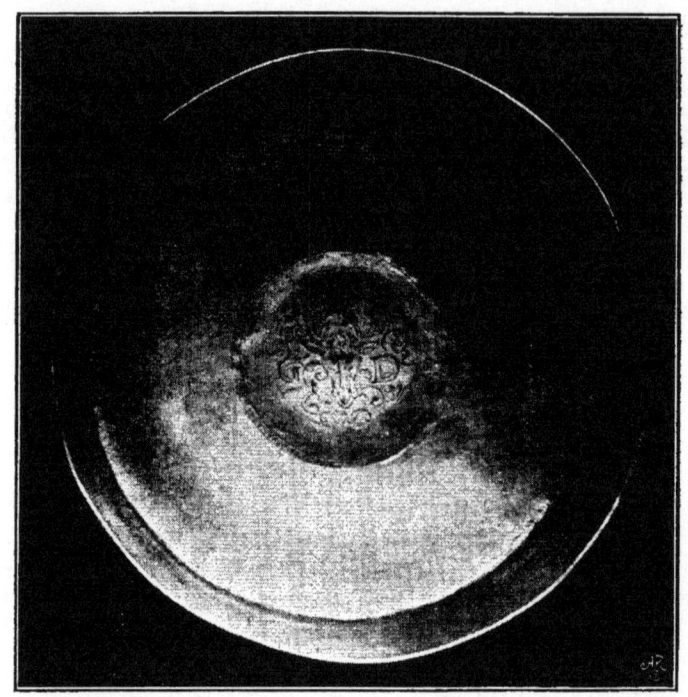

Antique Tazza in Colaton Raleigh Church.

49. SILVER TAZZA PRESERVED IN COLATON RALEIGH CHURCH.—The silver Tazza or Paten shown in the accompanying illustration, is preserved in the Church of Colaton Raleigh, and I am indebted to the Vicar, the Rev. F. Bullock, for much information respecting it. It is stated to have been presented to that Church during the incumbency of John Vickry, or Vicary, in 1749, by Dr. Charles Lyttleton, at that time Dean of Exeter: and is further reported to have belonged originally to St. Michael's Chapel, within the Deanery.

It is $4\frac{3}{4}$ inches high, and consists of two distinct portions, the Tazza and the Pedestal or Stem : the workmanship of one being wholly different from that of the other.

The Tazza, of plain hammered silver, is 6 inches in diameter, with a rim about one inch high, sloping outwards, and decorated on its outer surface with a chased pattern of scroll and interlaced work. Its base is formed of a separate piece of metal, and is united to the rim by a rolled edge. The inner aspect is slightly concave, with a centre somewhat flattened, and occupied by a circle of $2\frac{1}{4}$ inches diameter, within which is the representation of a stag's head caboshed, with the initials "G. D." one on either side of it with scroll work, all in plain chasing : no doubt intended for the arms of the Deanery. Dr. Oliver affirms the stag's head to be "ensigned with a cross pattee fitchy" (*Eccles. Antiq. of Devon*, III, 98), but, as will be noticed in the illustration, the latter is absent; and, most probably, when the Dr. was writing out his account of it, he had in his mind's eye the arms over the entrance to the Deanery, where this cross is represented. The stamp of a hall-mark can be discerned on the outer face of the rim, but is too faint to be deciphered.

The Stem on which the Tazza rests appears to be more massive than the latter required, and is of thicker metal and ruder in workmanship. It is $3\frac{1}{2}$ inches high, and terminates below in an expanded base of $4\frac{3}{8}$ inches diameter; and above, in a knop-like ornament close to the under surface of the Tazza.

It is built up, as it were, of five distinct parts, all of hammered silver, and (except the outer ring of the base) their respective edges are soldered to shape. These consist of the shaft, the round moulding immediately below it, the first expanded piece, and finally the outer ring; the jointing in all being very marked.

The construction of the upper member is peculiar: the bold round moulding, similar to the knop of a medieval chalice, is soldered to the under side of the Tazza, while below it terminates in a free round edge. A cursory examination shows this enlarged part to be quite independent of the main shaft, the latter being continued inside it, up to the Tazza to which it is soldered, separately to the other. With the exception of the base, which bears a stamped pattern, the entire decoration of the Stem is of bold repoussé work, with tooling, that of the shaft being continued beneath the capping, and presenting a striking contrast to the plain chasing of the former. The result of this examination proves the shaft to have been originally taller than the present one by, at least, the depth (one inch) of the expanded portion, which at first formed the terminal of the shaft, but was cut off, reversed, and then slided over the latter in the manner depicted in the illustration.

There are several points in the Tazza from which we may infer the comparative date of its manufacture. The initials " G. D." on its inner surface, when taken in connection with the circumstance of the arms being those of the Exeter Deanery, show them to be intended for Gregory Dodds, who was Dean from 1560 to 1570. Now between the first of these dates and 1580, there are many records extant of pre-Reformation Chalices being exchanged for Communion Cups during the early Elizabethan period. Thus, in the accounts of St. Martin's Church, Leicester, the following appears among the entries of the year 1567:—" Sold by Mr Willm Manbye, by thassent of ye pishe one Chales . . . and also bought by the sayd Mr Willm Manbye one Communion cup wth a kever." (*Chronicles*, T. North (1866), 169). During those years a large number of such Cups was made by John Jones, a silversmith, living in St. Petrock's Parish, Exeter, and one highly decorated was presented by him to the Church of that parish (where it is yet preserved), in which he had served the office of Warden for two years. Others manufactured by him are to be found in the Churches of East Budleigh and Clayhanger in this county, and there is one in the South Kensington Museum. In addition to his known plate-mark, all possess a peculiar style of chased decoration, that on the Tazza being of the same character. We may, therefore, assign its manufacture to the

Exeter silversmith, J. Jones, circ. 1570, and the circumstance of its being sent from Exeter points in the same direction.

We cannot so easily attribute a date to the Stem, there being no plate-mark or other fact to guide us. Apart from its massive appearance, the manner in which its height was reduced proves it to have been primarily intended to support a larger or heavier article than the present Tazza. Moreover, the general character of the workmanship, and the style of its decoration, demonstrate it to have been the work of some other maker. Although there is nothing on which to base an opinion, yet it appears to me to be much older than the Tazza, and this seems to be indicated when we pause to consider the kind of article it was originally intended to uphold. Bearing in mind that only a few years had elapsed between the time when the Cathedral was despoiled of its plate, and that of the appointment of Gregory Dodds as Dean, it is by no means improbable it belonged to some article used in the services of the Cathedral prior to the Reformation, *e.g.*, the support of a Pyx, as in the example of one exhibited at Ironmongers' Hall, in 1861 (*Catalogue*, 524); or of an Incense-Boat or Ship, as it was often termed from its shape, used to hold incense. Thus in the Wardens' Accounts of St. Helens, Abingdon, is this entry under the year 1555:—" For a shippe for frankincense . . . . . 0s. 20d." (*Archaeologia*, I, 12). A similar kind of Stem was employed in articles of domestic use during the mediaeval period, such as Drinking Cups, Hanaps, Nefs, &c., shown in plate 2 in *Miscellanea Graphica* (1856); and in several plates in a *Catalogue of Antique Silver Plate*, formerly in the possession of Lord Londesborough (1860); and especially of an "Encensoir," for distributing perfumes (pl. 6). But for the reasons already mentioned it is more likely to have belonged to some piece of ecclesiastical service plate. It is fairly certain that the curved base of the Tazza proves it to have been designed to be supported by a Stem of some kind; and it is not unreasonable to believe the possession of the latter may have been the cause of the former having been designed for it.

Assuming it to have been intended for ecclesiastical purposes, was it a Paten, as designated by Dr. Oliver? A Paten during the early part of Elizabeth's reign was of small size, and when reversed acted as a cover to the Chalice, or, to call it by its later name, Communion Cup. Now the diameter of the mouth of the Cup in East Budleigh Church is 3⅞ inches, and the cover fits it exactly. Many similar examples of this period are figured in Nightingale's *Church Plate of Wilts* (1891); and an excellent illustration of an "Elizabethan Communion Cup and Paten," dated 1571, belonging to Hillmorton Church, Warwickshire, is given in Bloxam's *Ecclesiastical Vestments, &c.* (1882), 190.

Although it may have been occasionally used as a Paten, it could not—judging from what has just been stated—have been originally designed for one ; more probably it was intended to hold the unconsecrated bread. Perhaps, on the whole, it is better to term it simply a Tazza, *i.e.,* "a saucer-shaped bowl or vase."

The living being in the patronage of the Dean of Exeter, may, perhaps, assist in explaining the reason of the gift ; and as Dr. Lyttleton was appointed Dean in the same year as J. Vicary was instituted to the living (1748), possibly the presentation was made by him. Moreover, the Dean had a vested interest in the parish. Pole notes, "the Deane and Chapter of Exon hath a manner in this place" (*Devon,* 163), and the Dean's house and garden (still in existence) are alluded to in *Bp. Grandisson's Register,* in the year 1347, as being exempt from the payment of tithes ;—" manse Domini Decani cum suis gardinis nunc existentibus exceptis " (edit. H. Randolph, 1021).

The Tazza was exhibited at a meeting of the Society of Antiquaries, on March 16th, 1899, and a short description of it is printed in their *Proceedings,* xvii, 2nd S., 369-70.

T. N. BRUSHFIELD.

50. FORMATION OF THE ROYAL NORTH DEVON HUSSARS, 1803.—A few years ago I had the opportunity of copying the following from the original document :—

"February 7th, 1803.

"We whose names are hereunto subscribed Inroll ourselves in defence of our King our Country and glorious Constitution as Volunteer Cavalry under the command of Lord Rolle and other officers.

"We will march to any Part of the Western District on actual Invasion or Insurrection if required by our **own** Officers.

"We will as the Law directs assist the Civil Magistrate within our own district to suppress Riots or Tumults.

"We will if there should be a Wreck on any part of the Coast within our own district use our utmost exertions to preserve the lives and protect the Property."

Here follow 104 signatures, including that of Lord Rolle.

GEORGE M. DOE.

51. "TOWN LIVING" AS THE NAME OF A TENEMENT.—Can any of your readers tell me what is the origin of the name "Town Living" as the name of a tenement in a Devonshire parish? There are many such in nearly every parish with which I am acquainted. In most cases they seem to be small holdings in, or adjacent to, the chief town, village, or hamlet in the parish, and if that were universally the case, the explanation would be obvious. But probably most of your readers will know many exceptions to this rule; for instance, in this parish there is a "Lethbridge's Town Living," so named in the Tithe-map, that is a small farm situated near the Monkokehampton border of the parish, and a considerable distance from the village or "town" of Exbourne.

ROPER LETHBRIDGE.

52. THE WHITCHURCH FEE (par. 38, page 63).— THE HONOUR OF PLYMTON AND THE WHITCHURCH FEE.—The list of "Fees of the Honour of Plymthon of the Earl of Devon" given by Testa de Nevil, p. 181, shews that the Earl about the year 1240 held the overlordship of the following Domesday estates:—1, The Earl's lands of North Tawton, Witheridge, Tiverton, Beaford, Topsham, Bradston, and the crown-lordships of Plymton, Ermyngton, and Blackawton; 2, All the estates of Ruald " the dubbed Knight," here called " the Whitchurch Fee," excepting Poughill; 3, All the estates of William de Pollei; 4, All the estates of Robert de Albemarle; 5, The lands of Robert Bastard and Harvei de Helion's wife; 6, The lands of the Frankling Knights, viz.: Osbern de Salceid, Ralph Pagan, and Girard; 7, The lands of four of the King's military thanes, viz.: Godbold, Fulcher, Nicolas, and Haimeric de Arcis; 8, The lands of the King's civil thanes not

held by serjeanty; 9, The land's of the English thane Ode Edric's son; 10, Four of Baldwin the Sheriff's estates, viz.: Whiteway, Little Torington, Wooladon, and Hele Poure; 11, Three of Judhel's, viz.: Egbuckland, Compton Giffard, and Hooe; and 12, One of Odo Fitz-Gamelin's, viz.: Plymtree. According to the amounts of the collectors of the King's aids in Testa de Nevil, pp. 187 b, 195 a, the honour included 89 Fees, and in Devon was second only to that of Okhamton with 92½ Fees.

The Earldom of Devon was created in the person of Baldwin de Redvers, some time after the year 1123 and before 1155, in which year Baldwin died; for as Mr. Round has shewn (*Feudal England*, pp. 486, 473) in 1123 Baldwin attests a Charter of Henry I., signing simply as Baldwin de Redvers. The great territorial lordship constituting the honour of Plymton appears, however, to date from a much later time. There is no trace of its existence in the Black Book of the Exchequer, in 1166 A.D. At some time or other between 1166 and 1243—consequently, after the death of Baldwin de Redvers—all the estates enumerated above, which in Domesday times were held direct of the King, must have been granted to Baldwin's successor in the Earldom, not as property but to be held as superior lord, this grant constituting the honour of Plymton.

Now the Giffards (from the statement of H.F.G.) appear to have held "the Whitchurch Fee" before the grant of the honour to the Earl, which should dispose of the suggestion that they may have obtained it in *frank marriage* from the Earl. Besides, as Baldwin de Redvers had only two daughters—one Matilda, stated to have married Ralph Avenell, the other Hedwisia—and only one granddaughter—Mary, through whom the Earldom eventually came to the Courtnay family—the only way in which a Giffard could have acquired estates in *frank marriage* from Baldwin, had Baldwin been possessed of the honour early enough, would have been by marrying Hedwisia. As to this there is no information.

It seems more probable that the Giffards obtained "the Whitchurch Fee" by grant from the crown when Ruald "the dubbed Knight" entered religion at St. Nicholas' Priory (*Oliver Mon.*, p. 119). Thereby his estates would escheat to the Crown—saving Poughill, which he gave to St.

Nicholas—and the Crown would grant them to whom it pleased.

Note also that the Hundred Rolls of 4 and 5 Edward I, have this entry:—" Osbern Giffard has a warren at Hechebocland, Cumton, and Havetnolle, by charter from King Henry." As Egbuckland, Compton, and Hooe, are the only three of Judhel's estates belonging to the Honour of Plymton, it looks as though Giffard brought them to the Honour of Plymton, not *vice versa*. O. J. REICHEL.

53. A FORMER EXETER CUSTOM.—In his account of the Scilly Isles, published in 1750, R. Heath gives the following description of a custom formerly in vogue in Exeter, and which it is believed continued in practice until the commencement of the present century:—

" Of Kin to this Custom in Scilly of throwing stones, the Boys at Exeter, in Devon, have an annual one (not so hard) of throwing water; that is, of damning (*sic*) up the Channel in the Streets, at going the Bounds of the several Parishes in the City, and of plashing the Water upon People passing by. This I was convinced of in May, 1744, going that Way to Scilly. Neighbours, as well as Strangers, are forced to compound Hostilities, by giving the Boys of each Parish Money to pass without Ducking; each Parish asserting its own Prerogative in this respect." (p. 128). T.N.B.

54. JOWER NETHERTON.—In the Exchequer Plea Rolls, Trinity Term, 22 Elizabeth, is entered the complaint, made on 23 March by Robert Paddon, clerk, against Oliver Whyddon, clerk, Rector of the church of Comb-in-teignhead, for forcibly entering and ejecting him from 4 acres of land, 4 acres of meadow, and 4 acres of pasture, situate in Jower Netherton, in the parish of Comb-in-teignhead, called by the name of two closes, the one called Cleyve Park *alias* Bywyll, and the other Lytle Genlete, demised to the said Robert by his father, John Paddon.

The name of Jower Netherton does not appear in the *Index locorum* to Chancery Proceedings, Ric. II. to Eliz., or in those of Inq. P.M. and Escheats temp. Edw. III, Hen. V, Hen. VI, Edw. IV, Ric. III, and according to Kelly's Devonshire Directory, although the hamlet of Netherton in

Combin Teignhead is mentioned, the preceding name of Jower is omitted. This name is unquestionably a family name, and one really belonging to Suffolk, in which county it occurs as early as 1339, on the third of August in which year a pardon was granted, at the request of Ralph de Ufford, to Hugh Jour, of Burgh, for the death of John Sweyn. The family continued at Burgh, at any rate, for over a hundred years after, and under the form of Jowrie, Jury sometimes, but generally Jower. The latter spelling occurs in the Lay Subsidy Rolls in 16 Hen. VIII, and in Chancery Proceedings in 1630, and their wills are to be found at Ipswich.

In 1390, John Jour, of Stisted, in Essex, appears in connection with land and tenements in Southwark and Newington, in the *Pedes Finium* for Surrey. This doubtless led to the settlement of a line of the family in the latter county, for in 1474 the name of John Joure occurs as the largest copyholder in a Court Roll of the Manor of Tongham in the parish of Seal, and about 1500 they held a messuage and thirty acres of the Manor of Peperharrow from the Brocas family, and fifty years later William Jour took proceedings in Chancery against an attempt to evict him by the husband of the heiress of Brocas.

The line continued at Tongham (with a branch at Normandy in Ashe, and another at Easeborne in Sussex) until the end of the last century, but the descent of this family in Suffolk and Surrey has no interest for Devon people, and is only mentioned here to show that although much is known relating to this family, yet nothing is known of their connection with this county, and it would be most interesting if some light could be thrown upon the point, for it must have been more than a passing connection, one would think, to cause the additional name to be used. The entry on the Exchequer Plea Roll is very clear, and is hardly likely to be an error for "Lower." ARTHUR J. JEWERS.

55. THE COMMONS OF DEVON.—Can any reader of *D.N.&Q.* suggest the reason why, of all the freeholders of Devon, the inhabitants of the boroughs of Barnstaple and Totnes are excluded from rights of common in "the Devonshire Commons," and from right of pasturing their cattle at a first rate of agistment in "the Forest proper of Dartmoor"? O.J.R.

Thomas, First Lord Clifford of Chudleigh.

56. THOMAS, FIRST LORD CLIFFORD OF CHUDLEIGH.—
The portrait of the Lord Treasurer Clifford, which we give
with this number, is from a print of a painting by Sir Peter
Lely, at Ugbrooke, and may be of interest to those of our
readers who may attend the Meeting of the Devonshire
Association, to be held at Totnes in August next, under the
presidency of the ninth Lord Clifford of Chudleigh, whose
ancestor, the subject of this sketch, was elected Member of
Parliament for that ancient borough.

In April, 1660, Thomas Clifford was chosen with Thomas
Chafe as representative of the Borough of Totnes to the
Parliament or Convention which recalled Charles II. to the
throne of England, and again in 1661 he was re-elected with
Sir Edward Seymour, of Berry Castle, afterwards Speaker of
the House of Commons, and continued to represent Totnes
until he was raised to the Peerage as Baron Clifford of
Chudleigh in 1672.

Thomas Clifford, who was born at Ugbrooke in 1630, was
the son of Hugh Clifford and his wife Mary, eldest daughter
of Sir George Chudleigh, Bart., of Ashton, and through her
the Cliffords are now the representatives of the Chudleighs of
Ashton, an account of whose family was given in last year's
Transactions of the Devonshire Association by Mr. Maxwell
Adams*

After leaving Exeter College, Oxford, he entered the
Middle Temple, and further improved himself by foreign
travel. On entering Parliament he was a decided oppositionist,
and possibly to that he owed his election to the Borough of
Totnes, as the Puritan party was very strong there, but
gradually he became a strenuous supporter of the Court and
thus attracted the notice of the King, and had conferred on
him the honour of knighthood, probably on account of the
prominent part he took as a diplomatist in carrying to a
successful issue treaties of alliance at the Courts of Sweden
and Denmark.

In 1668 the King appointed him Treasurer of the Household and declared him a Lord Commissioner of the Treasury,
and during Lord Arlington's absence in Holland he was
directed to execute the duties of Principal Secretary of State.

---

* Vol. XXXI, page 185.

At that time the leading men of the Cabinet were Clifford, Ashley, Buckingham, Arlington, and Lauderdale, known as the Cabal, a word which their initials happened to compose.

In 1672 the King raised him to the Peerage, and through the influence of the Duke of York, the King's brother, he was advanced to the most profitable office in the kingdom, viz., that of Lord Treasurer, the King " thinking nobody fitter for it."

In 1673 the Test Act was passed, and Lord Clifford having become a Roman Catholic, was unable to accept the test, and resigning all his appointments, retired to Ugbrooke, where he died the 17th of October the same year, and was buried in the vault of the private chapel there.

A full account of his life may be found in Prince's "Worthies of Devon," p. 221, ed. 1810, and in a paper entitled "Lord Treasurer Clifford," in the Devonshire Association, by Mr. E. Windeatt, Vol. XVI, p. 559.   J.S.A.

57. EDWARD CALVERT, ARTIST.—It would seem to be not generally known that Calvert was a Devonshire man. There is no mention of him in Pycroft's "Art in Devonshire," and I make haste to confess that I was in ignorance of the fact until recently, when I had the opportunity to study his work in the Print Room of the British Museum, side by side with the "Memoir" written by his third son.

Edward Calvert's early manhood was spent at Plymouth, where he made valuable and lasting friendships, and I like to indulge the hope that these notes may be the means of gleaning some information as to the whereabouts of the sketches he undoubtedly made in Devon and Cornwall. These early sketches do not seem to be in the possession of his family, and it is quite possible that some of them may still be preserved in the portfolios of connoisseurs and collectors, who have either inherited or acquired them. It would be exceedingly interesting to ascertain whether this is so, and I for one should be very grateful for an opportunity of seeing them.

The main reason, however, for inviting attention to the life and work of Calvert is that he was an artist of singular charm and rare individuality, too little known in his own day, and certainly not too well known now.

Until the appearance of the "Memoir," the main sources of information concerning Calvert were contained in the article in the Dictionary of National Biography, in a sympathetic note by the Editor in the *Hobby Horse* of July, 1891, and in sundry obituary notices and Press criticisms. The first volume of the " Catalogue of Drawings by British Artists," recently issued by order of the Trustees of the British Museum—a catalogue which, when completed as promised, in five or six volumes, should be of inestimable value to art students and others—contains a short biographical notice of the artist which may conveniently be quoted here:—

" Calvert, Edward (*b.* 1799, *d.* 1883).
Painter, engraver and lithographer; born in Devonshire; entered the Navy, but soon resigned his commission in order to give himself to painting; came to London where he chiefly worked and fell strongly under the influence of Blake, whose style he partly followed in some beautiful engravings on wood, copper and stone; a set of these is in the Department; exhibited little, but produced a number of classical compositions in oils; visited Greece in 1844, and made many sketches there."

But, in view of the interest attaching to the early years of his life as an artist in Devonshire, this brief record may be amplified from his son's " Memoir," which is the only adequate tribute to the man and his work. It may be mentioned in passing that there is a handbook on Calvert, by W. B. Yeats, announced as forthcoming in the useful " Artists' Library " published by the Unicorn Press, which one hopes will do much to increase the number of the admirers of what Mr. Sidney Colvin aptly describes as his " exquisite pastoral dreams and harmonies."

The " Memoir " was published by Sampson Low and Marston in 1893, in the form of a handsome illustrated 4to, limited to 350 numbered copies. The dedication is as follows:—

" To George Richmond, Esq., R.A.,
The last of that little band of Idealists who knew and reverenced William Blake,
This book is respectfully dedicated by the third son of his old friend Edward Calvert."

It is, I think, probable that even this limited issue was not exhausted, and if such be the case it may help to explain why his work is so little known outside a comparatively small circle of enthusiasts.

Calvert was born at Appledore, North Devon, in 1799, his father, Rowland Calvert, captain of the Bideford Yeomanry, and subsequently of the Devon Guides, dying when the lad was only twelve years of age. Not long before his death, however, Captain Calvert removed from Starcross, where he had been stationed, to Lostwithiel, in which neighbourhood Edward Calvert's boyhood was spent with his devoted mother. By her he was placed at the Bodmin Grammar School, with his brother, and here in his playtime he wandered in the meadows and by the hedgerows and streams, letting, as he said in after life, the enjoyment of nature enter into his soul.

At the age of fifteen he entered the Navy, and served as a midshipman successively on board H.M.S. "Chesapeake," "Weymouth," "Trident," "Queen," and "Albion." It was on the last named that he experienced exciting and perilous service, "the 'Albion' being one of those most actively engaged in the heroic bombardment of Algiers, under Lord Exmouth. At this time he had not completed his seventeenth year. Though himself only slightly wounded, his boon and happy companion, Midshipman Jardine, was shot down by a cannon-ball at his side." Soon after this he appears to have decided to leave the Navy and devote himself entirely to art, and at the age of twenty-one he exercised his prerogative and left the service.

This decisive step taken, he took lodgings at Plymouth and set seriously to work, studying everything of an artistic nature which was available in private collections, and at the local Athenæum. Here he made the acquaintance of Ambrose Bowden Johns, the landscape painter of whom, as Devonians, we are all so proud. This was the beginning of a friendship which only ended with the death of the latter. Johns, always helpful to young artists of real ability, was greatly interested in Calvert's work, and gave him many useful lessons; he also introduced him to Thomas Ball, an artist resident at Plymouth, who had studied in the Parisian and Italian Schools, "was a great enthusiast in Classic Art, and as punctilious in the principles of drawing as was Fuseli himself. Calvert became an intimate pupil of Ball, and under his tuition drew boldly from the antique, and increased his admiration for the old masters."

Even in these early days of his artist life young Calvert had a decided preference for classic and pastoral landscape, and a warm admiration for the work of Claude and Poussin. His taste in art, however, was always catholic, and he fully appreciated the work of his contemporaries David Cox, Fielding, Barrett, Varley, and Girtin.

For the work of Johns, his friend and teacher, his enthusiasm was unbounded, " his open heart yearned to these gems of rich and embowered landscape, beautifully self-contained and harmonious." There is a charming letter from Calvert to Johns, written many years after these Plymouth days, which is worth quoting. Calvert says:—

" I have been thinking about you, and preaching about you and your trees—the noble pine trees and the breezy skies that gladdened me so much. Northhill, with its dear inmates, is one of the sweetest memories of my life. Nor can any other ever fill your place in my soul. You first introduced me to the art I so fondly love, and are ever associated with its difficulties, its joys and its glories."

Another important and lasting friendship Calvert made at this period was with Mr. Joseph Hine, then the proprietor of an important school at Plymouth. Hine was a Cumberland man, and an early companion and ever-valued friend of William Wordsworth. He was, the Memoir says, "a noble fellow, of great mental calibre, full of anecdote and originality." At Hine's school Calvert gave class-lessons in drawing.

About this time Calvert first met Miss Mary Bennell, who came from London on a visit to Plymouth with her family. The acquaintance soon ripened into love, and, after a short courtship, the young couple were married. It is enough to say here that the union was in every sense an ideal one.

London was now decided on as the proper field for study, and leaving Plymouth, the Calverts took up their abode at first in Arundel Street, and, armed with letters of introduction from Johns and Ball to Fuseli, the keeper of the Academy, he entered the Academy Schools, where we are told that his studies in anatomy were very thorough.

So ends Calvert's connection with Devonshire, for the remainder of his long life was spent in London.

In 1825 Calvert exhibited for the first time at the Royal Academy, the subject being "A Nymph," and the picture was greatly admired. He followed this up with "A Shepherdess" in 1827, but after 1836, when he sent "Eve" to the gallery, he ceased to exhibit.

On settling in London, the young artist was again happy in the choice of his friends. He was introduced to William Blake, the poet-artist, and became one of that little band of Idealists who gathered around him in his last years with reverent affection.

This little band of brothers in Art included such men as George Richmond, John Varley, Samuel Palmer, and John Linnell, the elder, truly a notable group, whose influence has done much to keep alive the best traditions of English Art.

Blake's influence on Calvert was at first very pronounced, and it was at this time that most of his engravings were executed. They are now exceedingly rare, but there is a set of them in the Print Room of the British Museum. One of the most powerful and impressive is "The Ploughman," sometimes called "The last furrow of life."

To attempt to describe these little engravings would require a longer article than this, but it is safe to say that for poetic feeling and imaginative power they have seldom been equalled.

So interesting is Calvert's connection with Devonshire that I have left myself little space to speak of his life's work as a painter; dreaming his pictures (as Corot was wont to say), working out his own colour schemes and golden harmonies, and refraining from exhibition after 1835, his art was almost unknown outside the circle of his friends.

To the fine taste and enthusiasm of Mr. Sidney Colvin we owe the beautiful and representative collection of his chalk and pencil studies and sketches in oils now in the Print Room of the British Museum. To Mr. Colvin, too, the art-loving public was indebted for the exhibition of these works in 1891. This little exhibition at the Museum was followed by a larger collection of his oil paintings in the Old Masters Winter Exhibition at the Royal Academy of 1893, and came as a revelation to lovers of idyllic and pastoral landscape. Critics vied one with another in appreciation of "his exquisite classical grace, his feeling for atmosphere, poetic suggestion and delicate harmonies of colour."

The Director of the Luxembourg Gallery in Paris was so much struck by the beauty of Calvert's pastoral compositions that he acquired one, from the family of the deceased artist, for the National Collection. It is greatly to be desired that a really fine example of his work—such, for instance, as the exquisitely beautiful " Shepherds moving their flocks," reproduced in the Memoir—may before long find a place in our own National Gallery.

The number of his finished pictures is, however, small. Fastidious to a fault, he often destroyed his work, never sacrificing his high ideal, but struggling with the Angel of Colour even to the last.

One would like to linger over his tour in Greece, his Notes on Art, and his " Suggestions in view of a Musical Theory of Colour," but space forbids, and, in conclusion, one may say of Edward Calvert, as he himself said in generous tribute to a brother artist:

" All honour to the sincerity, and the courage, and the beauty which have passed to the other shore. He served Art well, both as a thinker and a worker."

JOHN H. RADFORD.

58. CAN any of your readers tell me (1) If the " Plimmouth Memories" cited by the old Dr. Yonge (who embalmed Sir Cloudesley Shovel) in his MSS. Diary as its sequel, *circa* 1712, is still extant?

[The two manuscript volumes of James Yonge were presented by his descendant, James Yonge, M.D., to the Plymouth Institution in 1831, and they are now at the Athenæum. One is the autobiography of the writer, the other a collection of notes relating to the Municipal History of Plymouth, entitled "Plimmouth Memoirs." This latter has been printed in the Transactions of the Society, Vol. V., 1876, p. 509. EDS.]

(2) What is the meaning of the "*signum voc' Merill*" which in Elizabeth's time was carved on all wreckage washed on the beach of Chapter Manors? JOHN Y. A. MORSHEAD.

59. ABBEY OF ST. SAVIOUR.—I recently received a copy of a MS., and I hope the translation I give below may be of interest. By the kindness of Mr. Rider Haggard, the owner, the original was sent to me, and I found it to be one of the best written and preserved manuscripts I have met with.

I should be glad to have the opinion of Devon or other antiquaries as to the Abbey of St. Saviour mentioned. Could it be Tor Abbey, which Oliver tells us is called in old charters the church of St. Saviour, or Holy Trinity, indifferently?

"To all the sons and daughters of Holy Mother Church, both present and future, be it known that Oliver de Tracey gave and granted for ever in alms to the Abbey of St. Saviour and the monks there serving God, ten shillings sterling annually, out of the tolls of Barnstaple fair, which he fixes to be paid to them at the Nativity of St. Mary until he charges these said shillings on the rent of land. This donation he granted for the soul of his Lord, King Stephen, and for the souls of his father and mother and of all his ancestors, and for his own salvation and that of his friends. These being witnesses, Robert and William Chaplain, Thomas Beaumont, his wife Adeliza, Philip and Isabel Beaumont, Gervase de Carrepüs, Godfrey de Plassey. The said Gervase has granted to the said abbey six pence annually." THOS. WAINWRIGHT.

North Devon Athenæum, Barnstaple.

50. A TOUR ACROSS DARTMOOR INTO NORTH DEVON, by REV. JOHN SWETE, 1789.—By the permission of Mr. G. Buller Swete, we are able to print from some Manuscript volumes in his possession, the substance of an account written by his grandfather, the Rev. John Swete, of Oxton House, of a tour into North Devon taken in 1789, and illustrated by water-colour sketches. It does not appear that this MS. has ever been published, and as it describes what the writer actually saw of places and remains on and around Haldon and parts of Dartmoor, it may be found interesting to antiquaries of these days.

The Rev. John Swete has never been sufficiently recognized owing, most probably, to his having assisted others, such as Polwhele and Chapple, rather than publishing his own work. He was the elder son of Mr. Nicholas Tripe, who practised as a surgeon at Ashburton, and built and resided in the house now the *Golden Lion Hotel*. He was born at Ashburton in 1752, matriculated at University College, Oxford, in 1770; took his B.A. 1774, and M.A. 1777. In 1781 he took the name of Swete by Act of Parliament, and the same year was made a Prebendary of Exeter Cathedral.

Peasants Gathering Moss.

Sandy Park, or Dockerman's Bridge, on the Teign.
From Watercolour Sketches by Swete in 1789.

He inherited the Swete property of Train, in the parish of Modbury, and Morleigh Court in the parish of Morleigh; also, from his father, Oxton in the parish of Kenton, as representative of the ancient family of Martyn, formerly of Dartington. Mr. Swete was a cultured and accomplished gentleman, with a love for literature and antiquarian lore. He wrote several pleasing poems, and contributed sonnets to Polwhele's collection of poems by gentlemen of Devon and Cornwall, published in 1792. He read some learned Essays before the Literary Society at Exeter, the MSS. of which are still in the possession of the family. He appears to have personally visited, measured, described, and sketched many objects of interest in the County on which he gave his opinions. In 1780 he assisted his father in exploring the great Barrow on Haldon, which was described by Polwhele in 1792, apparently from Swete's information. Polwhele's account of the Remains near the Drewsteignton Cromlech, which have since disappeared, is identical with the measurements and descriptions given by Swete in 1789. It is, therefore, probable that in the Swete MS. we not only have earlier descriptions, but the originals from which Polwhele, and others following him, drew their facts.*　　　　　　　　　　　　　　　　Eds.

A TOUR TO THE NORTH OF DEVON.—Having long projected a little excursion to the North of the County, on Friday the fourth of September 1789, I mounted my horse in company with two neighbouring gentlemen, the principal object of the day being to dine with a friend at Moreton.

Quitting the grounds of Oxton we rode up Holloway lane and having mastered the ascent of a mile we gained the level heights of Haldown; turning short to the right we inspected a large Barrow known by the country round by the name of the great Stone-heap; which although originally it was of a conical form (as are all the tumuli of these parts) yet being now intersected by an opening made in the year 1780 afforded a very conspicuous object to the subjacent country.†

---

* See Trans. Devon Association, Vol. XIV., p. 52, as to the relations between Swete and Polwhele. The phraseology and spelling of the Author have been followed in these extracts.

† It appears that Dr. Tripe of Ashburton, father of Rev. John Swete, and then owner of Oxton, opened this Barrow, but the author was present at the time.—EDS.

The form of this Barrow was nearly circular being rather more than 200 feet in circumference and about 15 in height. By the aid of 14 men a passage into it was effected almost due East about 8 feet wide; at about the same space from the margin was discovered a dry wall about 2 feet high which was separated from without by very large stones in the form of piers or butresses. On arriving near the center were seen a great many large stones (all of them flint) placed over one another in a convex form; and in the middle thereof a large stone nearly round, 2 feet in diameter, 6 inches thick, covering a cell on the ground about 2 feet square, formed by 4 large stones placed on their edges; in this was an Urn, and what was rather a remarkable circumstance, inverted; containing the ashes and burnt bones of probably a youth, as they were small and with but little muscular imprission. When the Urn was removed these appeared as white as snow—tho' soon after they were exposed to the air they lost that whiteness—from the size of the tumulus and this circumstance we may gather that they were the remains of a person of dignity whose surviving friends in honour of his memory had taken care to have them well-burnt and blanched by the intensity of the fire. . . . . The Urn is 13 inches high, 10 inches diameter at the top, 5 at the bottom, near half an inch thick and holds about 10 quarts, it is made of unbaked earth smoked and discoloured by its exposure to the fire, and consequently without inscription or embellishments. . . . . From local circumstances and from the contents of tumuli, a gleam of light is not unfrequently thrown on the matter. With respect to these on Haldown we might be induced to ascribe them to the Danes and that perhaps without much temerity when we consider the numerous encampments in the vicinity which are generally attributed to that nation. From the line in which the Burrows on Haldown are ranged it should seem that some road past that way, and indeed they have a direct tendency to the station now visible in the park of Lord Clifford.

Passing the ridge of the down we rode over the old race ground to the extreme Northern point of Haldown, terminated by Pen-hill finely planted by Sir Robert Palk, on the apex of which he hath lately erected a vast tower which from its elevated situation is discerned at an immense distance. On the skirts of the down are seen the remains of an encampment, which from the abruptness of the Eastern descent must have been of considerable strength.

From whence dropping down the Western side we came to Ashton, where are the ruins of a Mansion house lately belonging to the Chudleighs. The last of that family, Sir George Chudleigh, quitted it and built a magnificent fabric on the plan of Buckingham House now vastly improved and in the possession of Sir Robert Palk.*

The Park here (Ashton) a few years since was embellished by some of the finest trees in the county, which have been cut down by the present owner Sir John Chichester. Two miles onward brought us to Canon-teing, so-called from its site on the river of that name, and from its having been a Religious house belonging to Canons Regular of the Order of St. Augustin, which since its dissolution hath been converted into a Mansion belonging to Helyar Esqr tho' from its architecture it appears to have been built anew out of the old materials. The woods descending from an elevated down above the House are extensive, in the centre of which a vast rock projecting its broad whiten'd front relieves the sylvan gloom. In the chasm of the West side a cascade rushes precipitately down forming a beautiful and enlivening object amid the deep recess, some ancient ashes in front of it contribute to enhance the beauty of the scenery. Leaving Canon-teing house we ascended a steep hill for about a mile, then past over several small downs on the last of which before we entered the Moreton turnpike road was seen close on the path, that huge Moorstone rock called Black-stone distinguishable at an immense distance. On the South side it appears to be 40 feet high and nearly perpendicular, but on the North it declines precipitately, on the summit it is crowned by another Mass which, considerably less than the rock itself, seems as it were artificially placed on it. A Quarter of a mile further North are another collection of vast Moorstone Masses, called from the contrast of colour White-stone.

Ere we rose from the vale to the town of Moreton, on the North we beheld an excellent Parsonage house, lowly seated

---

*Sir George Chudleigh built Haldon House in 1735, and it was purchased in 1769 by Mr. Robert Palk, who was created a Baronet in 1782. The castle on Pen-hill was erected in memory of General Stringer Lawrence, whose statue as large as life, on a black marble pedestal, ornaments the entrance.—EDS.

at the base of the hill on which the Church forms a conspicuous object. Here making good cheer with our hospitable Friend Mr. Fynes we past the remainder of the day.

On the following morning we made an excursion to the curiosities of the neighbourhood. The first object that drew our attention was Cranbrook Castle. This entrenchment, Saxon or Dane, is on a high eminence, the view on the West glances over a country chequer'd by the towns of Chagford, Gidleigh and Throwleigh, terminated by the rounded summit of Causan down, reputed to be the highest point of land in Devon. The Western mound of this encampment is the highest, reaching not quite to the top of the hill, and the foss is here deepest. It seems nearly circular and its diameter from S. to N. is about 240 yards.

Descending a very steep rugged hill we soon after reached Whiddon House, an old edifice blocked up toward the Park which hath the wildest, most romantic appearance. Oaks detached and in natural clumps, scatter'd over the plain and the hill, intermixed with variegated masses of rounded rocks and washed toward the North by the waters of the Teing.

The river not being at this season fordable, we winded round to Sandy park or Dockerman's bridge, which in a field a little below afforded a charming appearance, its foundations rose on rude detached masses of granite, arches overhung and chequered with old ivy, thro' which the waters fell and foamed. The side screen of the right, rich in wood which also in the most striking manner form'd the composition of the background (*vide* illustration). Crossing the bridge we turned off the road to the right and passing down a common, arrived opposite Whiddon park at the usual place of fording. Here as the path was contracted we dismounted and left our horses, pursuing the track by the margin of the river and thro' a cluster of grotesque rocks which thro' a succession of ages, have tumbled from the craggy hills on the left, in a quarter of a mile we reached the " Moving Rock." This we found to be a stupendous block of Moorstone, detached and resting at its base on a rising narrow point of another mass deep grounded in the channel of the river, an equipoise was thus wonderfully form'd, which tho' by accounts given in the neighbourhood was not so sensible as it had been in former times, was yet to be put in motion by pressing with some force against it.

Drewsteignton Cromlech.

Reprinted from "Rowe's Perambulation of Dartmoor."

How this equipoise was occasion'd, whether by the irresistible violence of waters at the deluge; or by the intervention of floods which in process of time undermined the circumjacent strata borne them away while this Colossean Monument withstood all the attacks and braved their fury is left altogether to conjecture. . . . The dimensions of this moving stone are enormous, at the West end it is 10 feet high and from its West to East points may be in length about 18 feet. The hills rise majestically high on the North, on the right is Whiddon park with its clumpy woods, finely contrasting the craggy declivities on the left.

From hence returning half a mile we left Drewsteignton to the East and after two miles we came in sight of the famous Cromlech which is certainly one of the most perfect in the world. It stands in a field belonging to a farm, called perhaps from this curiosity Shel-stone. The covering stone or Quoit hath three supporters, it rests on the pointed tops of the Southern and Western ones, but that on the North side upholds it on its inclined surface, somewhat below the top, its exterior side rising several inches higher than the inner part on which the superinpendent stone is laid. This latter supporter is 7 feet high, indeed they are all of them of such an altitude that I had not the least difficulty of passing under the covering stone erect and with my hat on. This latter stone I made a measurement of and found the dimensions to be, from N. to S. edge 14 feet and half, it was also of similar length from E. to W. The edges or angles seemed to present themselves (as far as I could make an observation from the sun) exactly to the cardinal points; across it was in width 10 feet, the form of the stone was oblate, not gibbous, but rounding from the under face, rising toward the North about 13 inches higher than the other parts, yet so plane on its surface, that I could stand and move about on it without danger. . . . The use and intention of the Cromlech or crocked stone was primarily to distinguish and do honour to the dead, and also to enclose the venerable Reliquiæ, by placing the supporters and covering stone, so as to be security to them on every side, they were *tumuli honorabiliores*.

In an adjoining field toward the West I remarked several conical Pillars about four feet high. On the Southern side there are three standing in a direct line from East to West,

the distance from the most Western one to the middle one was
212 paces, from the middle to the one on the East 106, just
one half of the former, by which it should seem that an intermediate one at least had been removed. In a parallel line to
the North are two other remaining erect, the one from the
other distant about 52 paces, nearly one fourth of the greatest
space on the opposite line. The area between is 93 paces in
the midway of which at the Eastern extremity stands the
Cromlech, and if conjecture may be permitted I should not
scruple to assert that this originally grand Vista or Druid way
beginning on the environs of the Cromlech as soon as rising
from the valley it became visible was intended to inspire those
who were approaching the Monument from Dartmoor with
greater awe and reverence.* . . .

Somewhat on the South of this *via sacra*, descending the hill
we arrived at a circle, form'd by a vallum which on the outer
part declines and is about 4 feet high tho' the greater part of
the stones which were erected on the top of the mound are
gone and those that remain are deep sunk in the ground yet
there are as yet sufficient, clearly to make out the whole round
of the circle, the diameter of which (for it is exactly circular)
is 31 paces: Contiguous to this (indeed one vallum in the
point of approximation serving for both) is another circle
of nearly the same proportions. (The author gives a
sketch of the two circles.). More down the hill we were
struck with the wildness of the scenery where the Rocks were
seen divuls'd into gloomy chasms or terminating abruptly in a
precipitate perpendicular manner. One rock in particular
about 16 feet high detach'd from other masses and plane on
the superfices, the Quoit or impost of which superimpending
the stratum below projects three or four feet over, appear'd to
be wonderfully well suited for an Orator to address a Multi-
tude. Adjoining this spot was another detach'd body most
singular in its appearance for which it seemed to be more
indebted to Art than to Nature—having two ledges or strata

---

* These stones were similarly described by Polwhele in *Historical Views of Devonshire*, 1793, who appears to have adopted Rev. J. Swete's measurements. In 1838, Rev. W. Grey, of Exeter, mapped some remains of circles in a field West of the Cromlech, of which no traces have been found although searched for by the late Mr. G. W. Ormerod. For full account and plan *vide* Transactions Devonshire Association, Vol. V, 1872, page 73.—EDS.

approaching toward each other, yet not touching being separated by a perpendicular hollow of about a foot wide through which might be discern'd other rocks lying behind—over these in the manner of a Crom-leh a transverse enormous impost superimpends, decorated in most luxurient manner with old fantastic ivy and tinted with a moss peculiar to the Moorstone, a sketch of which is given where women are introduced collecting this moss, which is called Cupthong Orchil, or, botanically, *Lichenoides saxatile*, which after rains is scraped off from the Moorstone (for in dry weather it is brittle) and sold to the Dyers, by them it is dry'd, and being steep'd in urine, or in a solution of tin by aquafortis is converted into a most vivid scarlet dye. Nothing can well exceed the scenery of this place. Rocks the most grotesque and dissimilar imaginable, vast Hollows deepening into gloomy recesses, over which the dark green ivy trailed its parasitical branches, and from every interstice started the Mountain Ash beautifully decorating the scene with its orange-tinted berries. Returning to where we dismounted, we called to dinner; and instantly on a knoll of greensward overshadowed by some friendly oaks was display'd a cold refreshment, drawn from the wallet of the servant of our provident Host, which we devour'd with most ravenous ardour, and having cheer'd our spirits with some humming October, congratulated one another on having dined with more satisfaction and *goût* than the luxurious Apicius ever did tho' gormandizing on Mullet and his Lucrine Oysters. The little eminence chosen for our repast, over-hung what a year or two since was called Bradford Pool, a vast hollow excavated thro' a succession of ages by miners, the tin works however had been given over for a considerable period owing to a vast quantity of water which had overwhelm'd the bottom. It had been drained lately by some enterprising persons by means of adits drove under the hill on which the Cromlech stands. The scenery from where we sat, was uncommonly wild tho' by no means deficient in pleasing traits, the sloping banks ornamented with trees, various brushwood, and the rude shap'd hollow afforded a very agreeable picture.*

---

* Bradford, or Bradmere, Pool is now again a mountain tarn; it covers an area of about three acres, being about 180 yards long by 40 wide. A most romantic spot.—EDS.

Here with regret taking leave of my companions who returned to their respective homes, I proceeded on my tour and passing over a tolerably cultivated country, contrasted on the S.W., by the bleak aspect of Causan Hill I rode through the little town of South Zeal, to be noticed only in that it possesses a piece of antiquity resembling a town hall in the centre of the street, which from its tower at the Western end composed of four pillars, inclosing a bell would give room to suppose that in days of yore, it had seen better cheer. Here I crossed the river Taw leaving S. Tawton and its lime kilns like ramparts encompassing the town about half a mile to the right and rode thro' Sticklepark (*sic*) a mean village washed by a stream which in a most violent hurry, ran to join its waters with the Taw, not long after I entered Okehampton.

(To be continued.)

NOTICES OF BOOKS.

61. This is a very well written little book, concerning Men and Manners in the good old town of Ottery St. Mary* The reader loses much which the listener must have enjoyed in hearing the lecture, but he has the facts concisely and pleasantly put and in a permanent form.

62. This is the first part of a new Genealogical Magazine of which there are already several published in the United States.† We welcome it and wish it a successful career and a useful one. As the Editor says, although in a new country the pursuit of wealth leaves but little time or desire until that is accomplished, the wish to know something of our ancestors, and to learn from whom and what manner of man one is descended is a natural and laudable ambition. There are articles on the Holmes, the Hughes, the Pearl, the Pope, and the Peet families, with pedigrees carefully compiled.

---

* The History of the Town of Ottery St. Mary. A Lecture delivered Sept., 1897, by Lord Coleridge, Q.C. Privately printed.

† "The California Register," Vol. I., No. 1, April, 1900, San Francisco, published by the California Genealogical Society.

Sir J. Millais' Studio at Budleigh Salterton.

63. THE BOYHOOD OF RALEGH.—The recent addition to the Tate Gallery of the late Sir J. G. Millais' painting of "The Boyhood of Ralegh" has directed the attention of the public to one of the most valuable works of that artist; and there are several reasons for its being of especial interest to Devonians. It was painted at Budleigh Salterton during a visit of the artist in 1869-70; the scenery of the background belongs to that place; it contains the portrait of a sailor who resided there at that time; it depicts an incident, and a very probable one, in the life-history of one of the greatest of the worthies of the county — Sir Walter Ralegh; and it is believed to be the sole work of the painter relating to Devonshire.

It was purchased by Mr. James Reiss in 1870, who paid either £800 or £900 for it, and, I am informed, would never allow it to be engraved. At his decease, it was bought by Mrs. Tate for the sum of £5,460, and was presented by her to the Tate Gallery. It is said: "This particular work was one that Sir Henry Tate was very anxious to obtain, so that he might make the series of pictures by Millais as complete as possible; and, as no opportunity of securing it occurred during his life-time, his widow has now devotedly carried out his wish;" and the nation now possesses, to quote a remark in the *Athenæum*, "one of the most sympathetic and poetical of the great artist's works."

In 1869, Millais resided for a short time in a quaint looking structure in Budleigh Salterton, known as Octagon House (shown in the accompanying illustration), situated at the commencement of the Parade, opposite the last house on the other side of the roadway, to the left of which there was an uninterrupted view of the sea. The lower room on the ground floor was his studio, and in it he painted his Ralegh picture.

The canvas, 46 by 55½ inches, depicts the figures of two boys and a sailor of the Elizabethan period. The latter, on the right, has his back to the spectator, and is seated on a balk of old ship timber, a rusty anchor lying close to it. He wears a slouch hat, wide red baggy breeches, and a coarse shirt; and has bare arms and legs, which, with his face, are much sunburnt. His right arm is extended seawards, and he appears to be relating to the two boys whom he faces, some of his wondrous experiences during his voyages to foreign countries. The two boys are sitting on the ground; one on the left has his hands clasped round his knees, and although his face is directed towards the speaker, his thoughts are evidently far distant ; the other, in the centre, rests his chin on his hands, and gazes at the sailor in a quiet listening attitude. A low stone wall extends across the background, and beyond it is the open sea, with a headland just peeping on the left ; the foreground consists of sand and pebbles, and a tuft of thrift occupies the right hand corner. A toy ship and some articles of foreign origin lie scattered about.

In *Notes on Some of the Principal Pictures* of the artist, exhibited at the Grosvenor Gallery in 1886, and edited by Ruskin, is the following account of this painting, transcribed from *The English School of Painting*, p. 31, and there termed " The Youth of Raleigh ":—

" The scene is laid on the sea-shore. Young Raleigh and his brother listen with eager attention to the wonderful accounts of a sailor who has touched at every port. He tells them of the regions of the sun, and of the lands of enchantment in the East; he shews them some embroidered Indian work, and parrots' feathers, and they, in their childish imagination, wander in this world of fancy, traverse the Eldorado, enter the palace of the Aztec kings and the Inca temples ornamented with massive golden suns. They come upon secluded spots containing hidden treasures, where Indian captives seek concealment, and where spring the fountains of eternal youth. Raleigh little foresees the block and the scaffold awaiting him in the future. His one dream at present is to sail for the glorious land, Westward Ho.'"

There is a short account of the picture in the *Life of Millais*, by his son, J. G. Millais, 1899, and in it is recorded that the figures of the two boys were portraits of the writer's brothers, Everett and George (both now deceased) ; but for the sailor, who is entrancing them with romantic tales of the Spanish main, a professional was employed. The background was painted at Lady Rolle's place, on the Devonshire coast " (II., 11, 474). A few remarks on this statement are necessary. The younger boy, George, died of consumption at Cambridge, in August, 1878, æt. 19, so that he would be about eleven years old when the picture was painted. Everett was fourteen years old at that time, having been born in 1856; their portraits appear in the same volume (II., 92, 228).

The third figure is the portrait of an old sailor, a resident of Budleigh Salterton; he had been many voyages, was afterwards in the coast-guard, and in 1870 acted as ferryman across the river Otter at the end of the parade. He was a dark-visaged man named Vincent, a native of Jersey, and a well-known resident of the place. He frequently alluded with much pride to the circumstance of having had his portrait painted. My information was derived from the late Miss Gibbons, as well as from my friend, Dr. R. Walker, who saw the picture in progress on many occasions, was acquainted with Vincent, and knew he acted as a model to Millais. It is probable that the professional model noted by the painter's son (who informs me he was a Spaniard), was only employed when the painting was being completed in the artist's London studio, preparatory to its exhibition in the Royal Academy.

It is scarcely correct to say that the "background was painted at Lady Rolle's place." Budleigh Salterton is included in the Rolle estates, and after the death of Lord Rolle, in the early part of the century, they were inherited by the Hon. Mark Rolle, who still retains them.

The stone wall shown in the background of the picture still remains, and is almost immediately opposite the lower right hand window of the painter's local studio. It acts as the boundary to the road, as well as to the termination of the brook on its passage to the sea.

During the progress of the work, Sir John had some pebbles brought from the adjacent beach, and some thrift from the cliff, and placed them in front of the wall; these are depicted on the canvas. In a sketch of the figures contained in the *Art Annual* of 1885 (and reproduced in the *Life of Millais*, II., 17), that of the sailor is represented to be seated on a chair, but in the finished work this was altered, and a piece of timber substituted. The left hand corner contains the artist's monogram, with the date, 1870, the year of its first exhibition in the Royal Academy.

Being desirous of learning the authority for the scene he

depicted, I wrote to Sir John, who courteously sent me the following reply:—

"7 *Jany.*, '93,
Perth.

Dear Sir,
   The subject was suggested by Froude's "English Worthies." Raleigh's brother died young, he says, if I remember rightly.
           Y^{rs} very truly,
                J. E. MILLAIS."

The only passage in Froude's writings that may have suggested the subject, is contained in this extract from his "England's Forgotten Worthies":—

"At Greenway, near Dartmouth, Humfrey and Adrian Gilbert, with their half-brother, Walter Raleigh, here, when little boys, played at sailors in the reaches of Long Stream; in the summer evenings doubtless rowing down with the tide to the port, and wondering at the quaint figure-heads and carved prows of the ships which thronged it; or climbing on board, and listening, with hearts beating, to the mariners' tales of the new earth beyond the sunset." (*Short Studies*, I. [1868], 318). This article was first published in the *Westminster Review*, 1852.

The second boy was more probably intended for one of the Gilberts, and not for Sir Walter's elder brother, Carew, who was known to be living as late as 1623 (we must bear in mind that Sir John's letter was written 23 years after he had executed the painting). However, the interest centres in the figure of Sir Walter, whose attitude in the picture serves to remind one of Kingsley's lines respecting him, as "looking down" from one of the Dartmoor heights "upon the far blue southern sea, wondering when he shall sail thereon, to fight the Spaniard, and discover, like Columbus, some fairy-land of gold and gems." (*Works*, XVI. [1880], 87-8; first published in the *North British Review*, 1839).

There could not have been a more appropriate place for depicting Ralegh in his youth than Budleigh-Salterton, situated in the parish where he was born, and only a little over two miles, as the crow flies, from his birthplace. His father was in some way connected with the shipping interest, and both here and at Exmouth, young Ralegh probably listened to many tales of foreign climes and of the wonders to be seen there.

It is a matter of great congratulation that the artist's great painting has found a permanent abiding-place in the Tate Gallery. The present account of it (many of the particulars were kindly furnished by the author of his father's *Life*) may fittingly close with the following lines, comparatively unknown, which fully embody the spirit of the painting.

"*On Sir John Millais' Picture :—*
THE BOYHOOD OF RALEIGH AND GILBERT.

Seaward he points across the sunlit bay—
    That western sailor with his rings of gold,
    Whose gorgeous spoils, whose scars and gestures bold
Make real the wonder that his words convey.
And breathless on the jetty near him stay
    Two boys ; one fired to win some treasure-hold,
    One seeming, poet-like, in his heart to fold
Visions of sunset making western day.
But Gilbert perished in the Atlantic storm,
    And others took his land ; Raleigh in vain
    Searched Orinoque for El Dorado's form.
    Wealth fled and vision faded : yet again
    Their sunset is our western sunrise warm,
    Ours are the marvels of the Spanish main.

(*The Greyfriar*, II. [1892], 98).   L. H."

T. N. BRUSHFIELD.

64. THE GRAND JURY AND THEIR PORT WINE.—On March 27th, 1800, an advertisement by the Grand Jury, signed "Reymundo Putt, High Sheriff," announced that whereas Mr. Land, of the New London Inn, and other Exeter innkeepers, had charged them and other gentlemen of the County 4s. a bottle for port wine, and considering that the accustomed charge of 3s. 6d. a bottle was a most liberal allowance, they resolved to support any house that would sell good sound port at the old rate. On April 3rd, John Land advertised that he continues to sell *good sound port wine* at 3s. 6d. a bottle, but adding the expense of keeping for several years in order to render it of superior excellence, obliged him to charge 4s. for *old* bottled port wine, and he hoped the nobility, etc., will consider that advance to be barely equal to the interest of money and the loss by keeping a heavy stock so long to improve its flavour.   P.F.S.A.

65. JOHN WILCOCKS.—From the Calendar of State Papers, Domestic Series, 1634-1635, it appears that John Wilcocks, apparently of Plymouth, and others, had license for the sale in divers towns in Devon and Cornwall, of tobacco which they were importing from St. Christopher's. They petitioned to be allowed to land their tobacco at Plymouth instead of London. Can some one give me further information regarding him? May he have been the John Wilcockes concerning whom there are some twenty-six references to be found in the Dutch records of New Netherlands, now in the office of the Secretary of State at Albany? The earliest reference is under date October 16th, 1642, and the latest under July 17th, 1648. He appears during this time to have made his residence at Fort Amsterdam, and he traded with the Indians at Rhode Island. He sold his post in the Narragansett country to Roger Williams. He traded also with the Swedes on the Delaware. There is reason for thinking he traded also at Accomac, Virginia. He sold a ship named "Abigail" to Jan Evans, of New Haven, merchant. He seems to have been unlettered, somewhat convivial and hot-headed, but a man of energy, a large trader, and of many good qualities. In an affidavit dated August 7th, 1647, he is said to be thirty-three years old. There was an Edward Wilcox at Aquidneck, Rhode Island, in 1638. May he have been the Edward Wilcockes mentioned in Visitation of Leicestershire, Harleian Soc., Vol. XIII, as thirty-two years of age in 1619? And if so, may this Edward have been the father of John mentioned above, of Daniel, of Little Compton, 1634, and of Stephen of Portsmouth, 1655? The names in the Visitation of Leicester County are Rodolphus, William, Robert, Thomas, Galfredus, Edward, and Richard. The Aquidneck Edward disappears here after 1638. Among his grandsons are two Edwards, two Thomases, and a William. In the next generation are two Edwards, four Thomases, two Roberts, and three Williams.

Scranton, Pennsylvania, U.S.A.   WM. A. WILCOX.

66. CHURCH PLATE.—Can any of your readers give me the name of a maker of Church Plate whose mark was LP. (presumably his initials), Assay Office, Exeter, date 1789? I shall be glad of any particulars of him, and of examples of his work.   J.H.W.

67. DOLBEARE OF DOLBEARE.—In the "Visitation of Devon" there is a short pedigree given of this family. The first mentioned is Ralph de Dolbeare, 16 Edw. I.; his son, Richard de Dolbeare, 3 Edw. III.; his son, John Dolbeare, the elder, 17 Rich. II., *m.* Joan, dau. and h. of John Purcombe—their son, John Dolbeare, the younger, 11 Henry IV., was father of two daughters: Margaret Dolbeare, wife of John Hockmore, who *d.* 10 Aug., 1507, and Isabel Dolbeare, who *m.* William Burgoin. The Dolbeare family appears to have resided for many generations in the neighbourhood of Ashburton, Buckfastleigh, etc. Elizabeth, dau. of Richard Prideaux, of Ashburton (*d.* 1596) *m.* Richard Dolbeare, of Ashburton ("Visitation of Devon," 624). The Rev. Thomas Dolbeare was vicar of Buckfastleigh *circa* 1618. In Parliament held before Sir Philip Champernowne for the Warden .... of Exeter, 25th Sep., 1534, amongst the jurats was John Dolbeare (Anct. Stanny. of Ashburton, Devon Assn., Vol. 8, p. 320). Any further light thrown on the pedigree of this ancient Ashburton family would be of much interest. Also any reference as to the origin of the name and what arms the family bore.
G.W.R.

68. ARMS OF COTTELL (Exeter Town Hall).—A few years ago I noticed that almost the last (if not the last) coat of arms on the left hand side and at the top of this Hall was *Or. a bend gules.* As this is the coat of Cottell of Devon, I shall be glad to know whether it refers to Thomas Cottell, of North Tawton (whose house at Barton Bathe still stands), who was Escheator or Sub-Escheator for the County of Devon, 1560-1587, or thereabout.
W. H. COTTELL.

69. COCKTREE.—Cocktree (now a farmhouse), a property adjoining North Wyke, in the parish of South Tawton, was acquired by Wm. Wyke, of North Wyke, on his marriage, c. 1400, with Katherine, dau. and heir of John Burnel, whose family had been settled for some generations at Great or "Mychel" Cocktree. In endeavouring to discover the origin of the name and its application to this place, I have made the following notes:—

In 1218, one Jordan de Coketrewe acknowledges the right of Robert, son of Richard de Bremelrigge, to one ferling of land in Bremelrigge (which is in the neighbouring parish of Crediton.—E.L.W.)*

At Croke Burnel, Robert Burnel had his dwelling, temp. Hen. III.†

33d Hen. III. Robert Burnel and John Burnel, de terre in Caketrewe.‡

Examinacis feodorum Devoniae, 1303, Hundredorum de Suth Tawton .... Rogerus Burnel tenet in Coketrewe.§

De loco de la Trewe ... et aliis ... concessis ... Thome Cok ... senescall gascon.‖

In 14th Hen. VI., a Richard Cocktree is witness to a grant by Roger Weeke of land in Stone in decima de Croke Burnel.¶

The H.E.D. gives M.E. tree, tre; A.S., *treo, treow* .. etc.; all from Teuton type. Trewa, a tree. In the Inq. P.M. of Thos. Giffard of Halsbury (4th Ed. VI.), occur the place-names of Hollytrew in pŏch de Puworthy, and Trew (perhaps near E. Clifford?), and in the Inq. P.M. of Henrico de Bellocampo (24th Hen. VI., No. 43), I noticed the name Trewe St. Jacob's (query whether Jacobstowe, near Winkleigh, as it occurs between Winkleigh and S. Tawton in the list). Close by the present house of "Little Cocktree" stands the ruin of a large oak, which, considering the slow growth of such trees in this Dartmoor region, may well—in accordance with the local tradition of its being many hundreds of years old—have flourished in the days of Katherine Burnel.

ETHEL LEGA-WEEKES.

70. RAPID TRAVELLING.—In June, 1800, the *Mercury* coach was started to run from the New London Inn, Exeter, every morning at quarter to four, arriving at the Swan with Two Necks, London, the following day at noon. Fares: outside, £3 10s. 0d.; inside, £1 18s. 0d; luggage, 2½d. per lb. The London Mail, *via* Salisbury, left Exeter every morning at quarter to five, and arrived at the same Inn in London at six the next morning. Fares: £4 4s. 0d. and £2 3s. 0d.; luggage 3d. per lb.   P.F.S.A.

---

* Worthy's Devon Wills.   † Polwhele.   ‡ Le Neve' Index, Vol. 12a, p. 36.
§ Feudal Aids.   ‖ Rot. Gas. 25th, Ed. III, No. 9.   ¶ Risdon.

The Steen, A.D. 1790.

Cottage by the Churchyard, North Bovey.

71. NORTH BOVEY SUPERSTITIONS.—It is the fashion with some folks to give expression to commonplace truisms, and to say, for example, that "the schoolmaster is abroad." He might possibly be better employed at home, but being abroad he is supposed, amongst other achievements, to have banished superstition from the land. The people who think so are as much abroad as the schoolmaster can be, at least in this locality.

A few years ago I buried a remarkable woman. She lived with her old husband until he was ninety-one years of age, and she followed him to the grave when she was about eighty-eight. They were both born in the very early years of the expiring century.

Those were hard times for poor people, and yet husband and wife grew up to be robust as well as long-lived, but they had very little education. There were no schools for people of their class at North Bovey in those days, and they were put out to service at seven or eight years of age. They married young and had a numerous family. When I made their acquaintance they were between sixty and seventy years of age. The old man was peaceable and respectful in his manner towards me; the old woman was of a different character. While he was gardening and making bee butts, she was not infrequently plaguing me. I hardly knew how to deal with her, but she amused me greatly, and on one or two occasions she persuaded me to do things for which I was afterwards sorry. Although she was very poor and scarcely able to write, she managed to denounce me to the Charity Commissioners and to gull and deceive them, in company with one of Her Majesty's judges, as completely as she took me in. I was not her only victim. There was another old witch in those days, let us say ten years ago, who resided in the parish, and, upon the well-known principle that two of a trade can never agree, they were not friendly and told me tales of each other. But Deborah was far the cleverer of the two. It may have been a strange fancy, but she frequently made me think of Lady Hester Stanhope, and I believe now that if this old woman, who kept a husband and reared ten children on ten shillings a week, had possessed the other's opportunities she might have done what she pleased with the Bashi Bazooks. " You wicked old woman," I would say, half laughing, "what made you, who have no paper and no ink; you who cannot write and have no money for postage stamps—what made you write all these sheets of false stories to the Charity Commissioners to get me into trouble with them?" Then the old woman of eighty years would fix her one eye—a very bright shrewd eye—on me, and say that she had had a *revelation*.

"I don't understand your brogue," she said, "but I heard my man's uncle's box-lid slamming at midnight—that was Uncle Jasper who was lost at sea in a man-of-war in 1830—and the box was locked, and I knew he would not go slamming for nothing, so I got out of bed and looked at the stars, and there I saw all about it. I know what the stars say right enough." "The stars must be mighty liars, Deborah, if they told you that a Mr. Langdon left a large fortune to the poor of North Bovey, who always had the interest until I was appointed to the living, and that I am so indolent that I have never taken up the money, and the poor people now have to do without it. The Charity Commissioners know nothing of Mr. Langdon, Deborah, neither do I." "Yes, fye, you do, and the Earl of Devon has taken away scores and scores of acres of land that belong to the poor of the parish, and there is also a charge of twenty bushels of wheat upon Sanduck Farm, and I have eaten the corn when I was a child often enough, and now he has taken *that*." "I tell you what I will do, Deborah. I will ride out and ask farmer John to Shapely. He has lived in the parish for one hundred years, and ought to know if anybody knows of these matters. Where is the land situated, Deborah, that rightly belongs to the poor?" "Right a-top of the hill as you pass on to Moreton Hampstead; but don't 'ee go to farmer John. You go and ask Ann, up to village, and her'll make one of her toads tell 'ee, for all her's no better than a bastely witch. If you're not what I told the volks up to London you was, you'll take a little trouble, too, and get me those £700 that uncle Jasper had for prize-money in the great war time from the people at Doctor's Commons. Now, do 'ee, there's a dear." "Tell me about Ann's toads first, Deborah. How long has she had them?" "Her keeps them in the steen under the dresser, and the other day when my grand-daughter went to the house her dared her to put a finger to the lid. There's 'Croppy,' and 'Rumbo,' and the great wicked one 'Krant,' and a dozen besides. Her works with 'em in the churchyard at midnight when it is very dark. Her can tell you all you wants to know about the land, and a bit besides, I promise you." "Ann is a spiteful old woman, Deborah, and if she can do harm with her toads, I wonder that her neighbours fare as well as they do." "Oh," said my informant, "her can't hurt *everybody*. When her wants to do an injury her first takes the Bible and puts the door-key in the leaves, and then ties the book tightly together, then with the handle of the key her sets the Bible on edge, and if it does not move her knows it is useless to go on, but if the book turns round her takes out her toads and begins. Ann is as bad as ever was one, and her ought to be burned."

I did not go to old Ann, but I went to farmer John, who could go back with the help of his father for 170 years of parish history, and I found that he had never heard either of common lands abstracted or Sanduck wheat levied, and I spoke to the good Lord Devon, who promised immediate restoration if old Deborah would produce a little better evidence than the slamming of an old box-lid.   W.H.T.

72. JOWER NETHERTON (par. 54, p. 79).—Jower Netherton is clearly a mistake for Lower Netherton, *i.e.*, if the entry has been read correctly, as a glance at the old Ordnance Map will shew. Had there been any family of Jower giving its name to Netherton, the name would have read Netherton Jower, not Jower Netherton. Withecombe Clavil, Buckland Brewer, Combe Raleigh, Combe Royal, are all evidence of the Devonshire use in this respect. But there is no trace of any such family in Devonshire annals.

Next to Domesday, in which Netherton appears as Esseministre, held by William Capra (p. 683 in reprint), the earliest reference to Netherton is in Testa de Nevil, No. 816, p. 183a, where under the Honour of Braneys (William Capra's Honour) is this entry: "John le Barun and Walter per Tut hold in Netherton 1 fee." Burton's extract from the Tax Roll of 31 Edward I. has under Exminster Hundred this entry, No. 78: "Nitherton is [part] of the fee which Eustace Le Barron holds and Isabella de Brent holds the other half of the fee." We see, therefore, that in 1303 Netherton was divided, one half being held by Eustace le Barron, or Le

Barun, who held the adjoining Buckland, called after him Buckland Baron, the other half being held by Isabella de Brent, In 1346, according to *Feudal Aids*, p. 388, "William Baron holds ½ fee in Nitherton of the Honour of Braneys which Eustace le Baron formerly held," and "Peter Clyfford holds ½ fee in the aforesaid Netherton [with a different spelling, however], of the Honour of Braneys, which Isabella de Brenta formerly held." In 1428, A° 6 Hen. VI., *Feudal Aids*, p. 482, "Nicolaus Carrowe and Joanne his wife, and Matilda, sometime the wife of John Fokeray, William Fokeray, William Werthe, and William Medborne hold ½ fee in Nitherton, which they hold separately among themselves, and no one of them holds an entire fourth share, the same having been of old held by William Baron." Also "Nicolaus Carrewe and Joanne his wife, and Matilda, sometime the wife of John Fokeray, William Fokeray, William Werthe, Richard Clifford, and William Medborne hold ½ fee in Nitherton, which they hold, etc. [as above] the same having been of old held by Peter" [Clifford.] These estates have been since known as Higher and Lower Netherton. Excepting the last quoted passage, there is no evidence even of their having been known respectively as Nitherton Baron and Nitherton Brent.

OSWALD J. REICHEL.

73. "YEND," "VOACH."—In some parts of Devonshire it used to be said, they *yend* a stone instead of throwing it, and *voach* on your corns instead of treading on them. What is the etymology of these words? A. J. DAVY.

74. DEVONSHIRE SOCIETIES.—Can any reader give details as to the date of foundation, length of life, publications, leading officers, and any other information respecting :—

(a) The Devon and Exeter Graphic Society.
(b) The Exeter Naturalists' Club.
(c) The Teign Naturalists' Field Club.
(d) The Literary Society of the Devon and Cornwall Railway Company.
(e) The Torquay Natural History Society.
(f) The Plymouth Institution.
(g) The Barnstaple Literary and Scientific Institution?

T. CANN HUGHES.

75. CHRISTOPHER JONES (par. 43, p. 69).—An interesting brief autobiography of this Devonshire poet in the *Town and Country Magazine* for 1775, pp. 325-6, is introduced in a somewhat curious manner. There are, in the first place, some "Stanzas addressed to Christopher Jones, a Journeyman Woolcomber, with a large Family, at Crediton in Devonshire, Author of several elegant little Poems." The set of seven four-line verses is signed " J. Jones," but whether he was related to the poet is not mentioned. This is followed by an "Ode to Benevolence. By Christopher Jones," commencing :—

"Let Fame her thousand temples raise,
Her ardent sons to charm," etc.

This is succeeded by a long foot-note containing the autobiographical fragment :—

" Extract from a letter sent by the author of the above to John Jones, of Kidderminster :—' Born in obscurity, I lived in rural innocence about eleven years; my father having a numerous family, took me at that age from a very good country school to assist him by my labour, and it happened, unfortunately, to be the last advantage I ever reaped in that manner. At fourteen it pleased heaven to deprive me of a father, when I was taken by the friends of my mother, who was also dead, and put apprentice to a woolcomber. A genteel premium was given, and a considerable sum, the gift of my grandfather, was lodged in my master's hands, on his own bond, for the purpose of putting me into business, the interest of which served to purchase books, etc., as I always delighted in reading ; but, alas, I never enjoyed a penny of the principal, my master dying, honestly poor, about the expiration of my term. Our trade, ever unhappily fluctuating, has occasioned me many a painful pilgrimage. From the great decline in our branch, I have been more than twelve months of the last three years in want of labour ; to amuse these painful intervals I have made some trifling attempts in poetry, but truly sensible of my inability, my diffidence frequently gains the precedence of my desires. A trifle of mine, written at a time when I was forced to repast on an ideal dinner, occasioned my being noticed by Dr. Downman, a benevolent physician in Exeter ; he has frequently assisted me in my distress, and has lately given me many books, such as Johnson's Dictionary, Lowth's

Grammar, "The Seasons," "Night Thoughts," some volumes of Swift's prose works, etc., etc. Indeed, without assistance, and that of a few other benevolent friends, life would ere now have been quite a burthen to me, as I have a wife and two small children. The difficulties in which I am involved frequently destroy that serenity of mind I should otherwise enjoy, and which is absolutely necessary to be felt by those who would pay their address to the muses, etc.'"

In the same year as the above (1775) was issued by him, anonymously, a poem entitled "Sowton; a Village Conference," noteworthy for being the earliest work supposed to have been printed and published at Crediton. There is a short account of him, with a transcript of one of his poems, "The Lamb Forgot," in *West Country Poets*, pp. 278-9.

The concluding history of this local poet is thus narrated in the *Gent's Magazine* for August, 1792:—

"At Keynsham, near Bristol, C. Jones, well known through that extensive county by the name of the Crediton Poet. His death, after a lingering and tedious sickness, was attended with all that penury and distress which too frequently accompany true poetic genius. While resident in Devonshire he published a little volume of poems, by subscription, which was honoured with the names of very many literary characters, and obtained the approbation and patronage of the late Dr. Johnson."

T. N. BRUSHFIELD.

76. TOWN LIVING (par. 51, p. 77).—The term "Town Living" seems to be equivalent to what is elsewhere called a "Barton Farm" or a "Town Barton," and is applied to a messuage which has sufficient land attached to it to make it worth while to have a "towned" or fork-fenced rickyard, as opposed to the small tenement of a villager or copyholder. The word "living" is the English rendering of the Saxon "cotlif," which again is the Saxon rendering of the hide of Domesday and the manse of the Charters. A manse or hide is the homestead of a single free family with the necessary amount of arable land, pasture and wood for its support, the quantity varying from 64 acres in some districts where the land is good to 160 in others, but normally taken as 120 acres, and in this county as not more than 90 or 100. The term

"living" in this sense has become well-nigh obsolete, except when applied to an ecclesiastical benefice. One of the laws of the Franks incorporated in Egbert's Excerptions posterior to A.D. 830 (No. 23) runs: "Let one entire living (*mansa, cotlif*, or *hida*) be given to every Church without other service." The custom has accordingly survived to our own day to speak of a beneficed clergyman's homestead and appurtenances as his living.

The term "Barton" is derived from Bere—that which the land beareth—whence the word barley, and "town" a fork-fenced enclosure from "tynan" to fork-fence. Some homesteads had only " mows," or simple enclosures made by a hedge or water running round them to protect their bere or produce. These were called Huishes or Hayes. Those which were more strongly protected as when buildings enclosed them were termed Bartons. A "towned" homestead if let to farm would be known as a "barton farm"; if occupied by its owner, as a "barton or town living"; if spoken of regardless of tenure, as a "town barton." Of this a good example is supplied by the two Tetteburnes held in Domesday under Baldwin the Sheriff. One of them held by Rainer, which was strongly enclosed, is now known as "Town barton." The other, which was only slightly enclosed by an owner or occupier of the name of Cole, is now known as Colehay or Colley.

OSWALD J. REICHEL.

77. REYNELL, STEEDE, EASTERBROOKE, SAINTHILL.— Can anyone give me anything touching the ancestry and connections of the following members of the Reynell and allied families :—

1. Richard Reynell, Esq., Recorder of Bradninch in 1620, *vide* Bradninch, Visit. Devon 1620. (Colby).

2. Richard Reynall, whose son Abell was buried 1 Mar., 1644, at St. Petrock's, Exon. *Vide* Par. Reg.

3. Richard and Patience Reynalls, whose dau. Mary was bap. Sep. 22nd, 1644, at St. Petrock's, Exon. *Vide* Par. Reg.

4. Richard Renell, whose son William Renell was bap. May 27th, 1653, at St. Petrock's, Exon. *Vide* Par. Reg.

William Reynall, who md. Mary Easterbrooke, of "Tapsham," at St. Petrock, Exon, Aug. 12th, 1664. *Vide* Par. Reg

6. Ezekiel Steede and Elizabeth Reynolds, of Exeter, spinster, mar. lic., Oct. 23rd, 1666. (Bishop's Act Book).

7. "William Rynolds and Elizabeth Steed ware maried" Sep. 20th, 1687, at St. Petrock, Exon. *Vide* Par. Reg. [William Renell, of Topsham, Admor. P.R. Exon, granted 24 Apr., 1702, to Hannah Steed, sister of relict Elizabeth Renell. Richard Renell joined in the bond.]

8. Richard Rennell, of Exeter, who with son William Rennell, Jos. Marshall, John Hoppyng, Richd. Hele, "Doctor in Phisick," and John Ridler, goldsmith, worked a glass factory at Countess Ware, near Topsham, 1691-4, on land which was the "joynture" of Elizabeth, wife of William Rennell. *Vide* Rennell *v.* Marshall (Chan. Proc. B. & A. bef. 1714. Bridges 2, 113).

9. Richard Renell, of Topsham, gent., who in 1701 owned a "glass house" at Countess Ware. *Vide* Chan. Proc.

10. Richard Reynell, admor. with John Snell (during minority of son) of estate of Elizabeth Sainthill, relict of Samuel Sainthill, of Exeter, mcht. P.R. Exon, 14 Feb. 1675. (Sainthill ped. Vivian's Visit. Devon).

11. "Henery Renell" md. Elizabeth Sainthill, Feb. 3rd, 1664. (Register St. Thos. Aple, Exon).

12. Henry Reynolds and Dorothy Sainthill, of Totnes, wid., mar. lic. Jan. 31st, 1664. (Bishop's Act Book).

Is it possible that the two last items refer to the same event? Referring to No. 6, Ezekiel Steed, of Exeter, in his will (pvd. P.C.C. Mar. 1699) names his daughter Elizabeth Rennell and her children William and Hannah. His wife, Frances Steed, extrix. She (his second wife) was daughter of George Kekewich, Governor of St. Mawes' Castle (*vide* Kekewich ped., Vivian's Visit. Cornwall. I want marriage of Ezekiel Steed with his first wife, Elizabeth Reynolds, and her parentage, and the ancestry of William Renell, of Topsham (No. 7 above), who wedded her daughter, Elizabeth Steed, at St. Petrock's, Exon, 1687. Most Exeter Registers and those of Topsham give no clue. Tradition says the Renells were dissenters at Topsham. W. REYNELL UPHAM.

78. RICHARD RENELL, OF TOPSHAM, GENT., who owned a glass house at Ware, near Topsham, in 1701 (Chan. Proc. P.R.O., B. & A. bef. 1714. Collins 3, 552, 246).

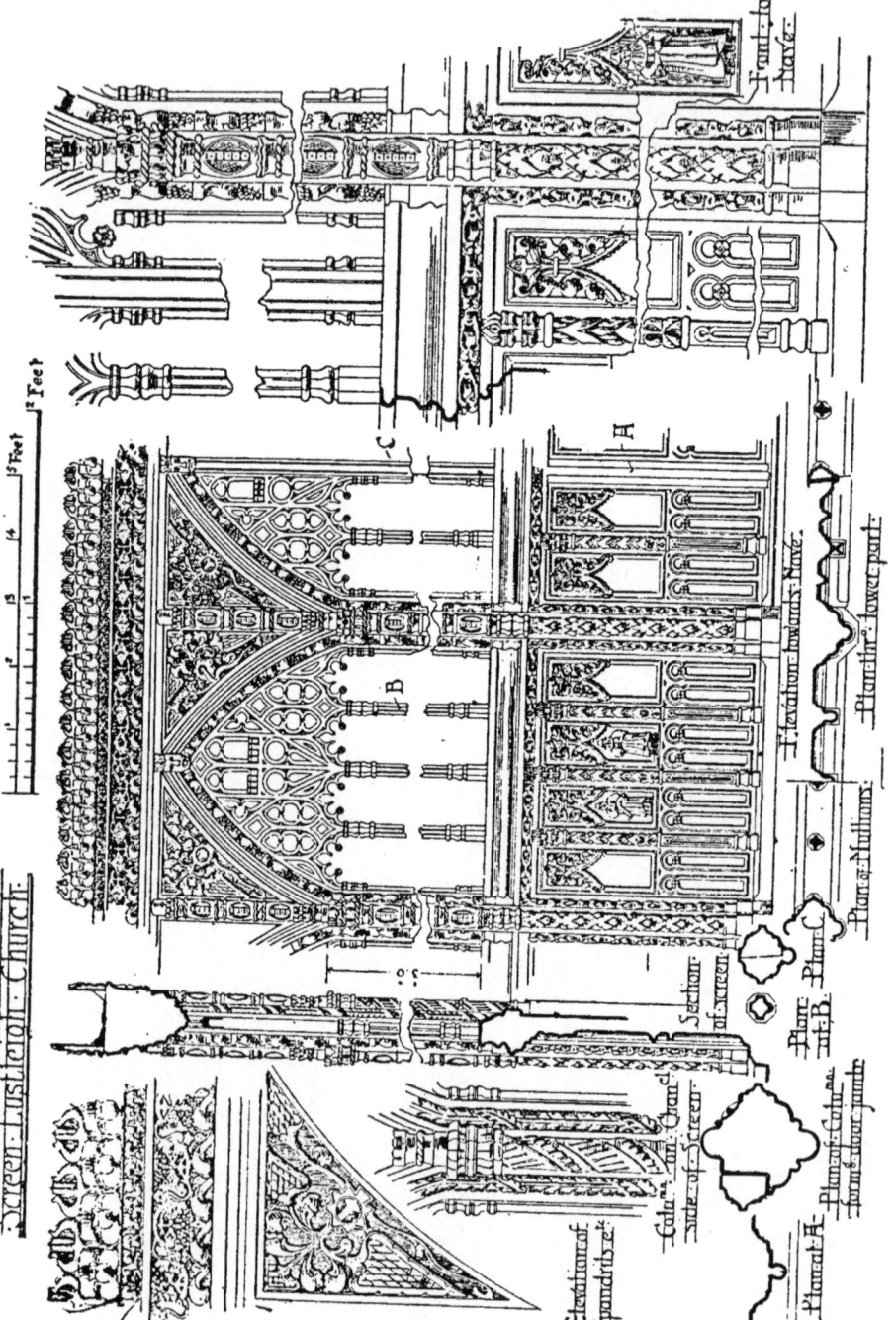

Carved Oak Screen in Lustleigh Church.

Thomas Raynell and wife Agnes, who had son Thomas bap. at Topsham, Aug. 11th, 1698.

William Reynell who took oath for executing the office of bailiff at Exeter, 30th January 1687 (Jenkins' Exeter, 2nd Edit., p. 8).

1687. John Snell, mayor, John Gandy, Richd. Burell, Richd. Periam, Thomas Salter, removed by King's mandate, and Sir T. Gifford, kt., mayor, John Curson, Anthony Vicary, William Atkins, William Reynell, appointed in their places (*vide* Jenkins). Why? W. REYNELL UPHAM.

79. THE SCREEN OF S. JOHN THE BAPTIST'S CHURCH, LUSTLEIGH.—The screen of S. John's Church, Lustleigh, is the most interesting I know of the many beautiful screens of which the county of Devon has reason to be proud; and it bears evidence of individuality and tradition combined in its design wholly wanting in the general run of Devonshire screens, which from their great similarity of major and minor detail can hardly fail to be the result of long tradition handed down through either a monastic or lay school of carving. Whether this screen was designed entirely *de novo*, or whether a later clothing, so to speak, has been put on an early skeleton, it is difficult to judge; but, personally, I should say it was the work of an artist familiar with the results of tradition, but having thrown them over, and working on his own lines of thought and under the influence of the new ideas of design at that time spreading through the country. As in many other places this is merely a *choir* screen and no longer a *rood* loft; the door of the staircase to it is in the north wall. Of post-reformation times, the beautiful vaulting we usually see branching over on either side, supporting the platform, has been ruthlessly swept away, and a modification of the rich cornice which always completes the vaulting has been retained only. The most curious thing about this screen is the clinging in some ways to the old traditional form as regards structure, whilst abandoning it in many ways so far as ornamentation is concerned. The designer, although strongly under the influence of Renaissance feeling, yet cannot make up his mind to adopt thoroughly what would be the most natural form for him to use, namely the colonnade and cornice, but retains the main outline of the

old work with pathetic insistency, or want of courage, it is difficult to know which, whilst he at the same time lands himself in a difficulty by taking up the columns between the arches to carry practically nothing at all. The tracery also is a curious evidence of inconsistency; either it is an actual reproduction of what was there before, or the designer must have been wholly unable to conceive tracery with classic feeling about it, and he has consequently filled up his arches with the standard Devon pattern we see everywhere, to the great detriment of his screen from an artistic point of view. Coming to the question of ornament, the designer has evidently felt himself able to break almost free from tradition, which has hitherto held him more or less, and the result is very interesting. The first thing to be noticed is that apparently being unable longer to use colour for the decoration of his work, in deference, I presume, to the feeling against it existing at that time, his only resource is a lavish use of carved ornament, and here he certainly has not stinted himself; cornice, spandrils, columns, strings, panels, no matter where, we find the same redundancy. Still, it is used with artistic knowledge and care. He has not broken entirely free from old example, as the cornice follows local forms very closely, and the ornament on either side of the columns and round the arches on the choir side also retains the Gothic feeling; but, as a whole, he has adopted Renaissance forms for his decoration. There is a curiously archaic look about the ornament in the spandrils, which may, I think, be accounted for by the fact that the inspiration for it is no longer sought entirely from natural forms, but is largely conventional; and the designer has not been sufficiently familiar with this style of decoration to treat it in the wholly free and much more successful manner which was adopted later; at the same time it is carefully managed and retains well the appearance of diaper or surface decoration. The ornamental columns, although they shew a singular mixture of Gothic and Renaissance treatment, are, as a whole, very happy and rich in their effect, harmonising well with the highly ornate strings supporting them, though these latter are quite emancipated from Gothic influence. The cornice is very closely modelled on the generally existing forms, but it, too, bears the impress of Renaissance modification, more especially in the beautiful open cresting and the lower curved ornament; as a whole, however, it adheres very closely to old traditional lines, with vine foliage and fruit, though these are handled a little unusually. It is when we come to the lower solid portion of the screen that the new influence shews itself most strongly, and the departure from the generally accepted form is most complete. Here we get a thoroughly Renaissance feeling in general treatment and in the sections of the various mouldings, whilst the decoration has thrown off all reference to Nature and is wholly conventional in form, and a great improvement on the halting between two opinions expressed in the spandrils above. A most singular instance of the conservative tendency of the artist's mind is, I think, afforded by the panels. Living in more or less Puritan times, he hesitated to use colour, and would also be prevented from giving the representations of the rather hypothetical saints hitherto common; at the same time he was evidently unwilling to give up everything of the kind, and has therefore provided us with *carved* figures wearing, I should say, contemporaneous costume, but whether representing clerical or lay dignitaries I am unable to decide, though I should imagine the former. Altogether, I think this screen, in a small church, in an out of the way part of Devon, shews, in a very instructive way, the gradual and hesitating manner in which important architectural changes were introduced in times long since passed away. A. L. TATE.

[In reference to this screen, Mr. Baring-Gould writes:—"I strongly suspect that the screen is a post-reformation structure. The details are *very* late, too late for pre-reformation work, and there are significant omissions. The rood-loft is no longer there; the place of the saints is taken by clerics in surplices, hoods and stoles, and Elizabethan caps. A good deal of ecclesiastical carving was done at this period, mainly bench ends with sea monsters on them in place of the instruments of the passion. At Morwenstow the earlier pew ends with the sacred emblems were actually removed and laid as supports for the new flooring."—EDS.]

80. WALTER (OR WALTERS) FAMILY OF DEVON.—Any notes respecting this family will be appreciated. There is a pedigree in Vivian's "Visitation of Devon," but he does not attempt to bring it up to date. There was a Richard Walter who married Anne, daughter of John Yonge, Esq., and widow of Christopher Crymes, Esq.; she died 1693. Query, whether any issue. G.W.R.

81.   EXETER JEU D'ESPRIT, 1838.
Dedicated without permission to the Liberals of Exeter.

    Oh ! what a model is our Mayor
    Of thriftiness and frugal care !
    On Saturday sells gin to all,
        Preaches Sunday,
        And on Monday
    Sits in judgment at the Hall—
    Inflicts the fine for fight and fray
    Caused by the gin of Saturday ;
    And when his duties all are o'er,
    Struts home the street to count the score.
        Gin, justice, and a little prayer,
        Oh ! what a model is our Mayor.

    In our Whig Mayor, say have we not
    A foe to each gin drinking sot ?
    Then be consistent, worthy Mayor,
        And let thy text
        On Sunday next
    Be " Of gin, tho' watered well, beware ! "
    Preach loud, your Worship, 'gainst the sin
    Of drinking draughts of ardent gin ;
    And when 'tis o'er, invite thy flock
    To turn with thee and taste thy stock.
        Gin, justice, and a little prayer,
        Oh ! what a model is our Mayor.

    The Councillors—thy Curate Gill,
    Shall dot the chalks and count the till,
    Assist thee in the Hall by day ;
        Or hold the glass
        To lad or lass,
    With a dash to each of caraway.
    Or with thee will on Sunday teach,
    And jointly with his worship preach ;
    Keep order 'mid the maids and men,
    And when all's o'er will croak—Amen !
        Gin, justice, and a little prayer,
        Oh ! what a model is our Mayor.
            WILLIAM JOHN PLAYTER WILKINSON.

82. DRAKE MONUMENT IN WERRINGTON CHURCHYARD.—Looking through some old letters, I came across the following enquiry from the late Rev. Edward King, Vicar of Werrington :—" Do you know to what family an old monumental slab belongs. It is outside the present church, under the

east window. A man, lady, and four boys, all kneeling; costume Elizabethan, I should say. It came from the old church, I believe, but has no inscription or armorial bearings."

I replied that I should think it probable it was to Sir Francis Drake, who sold the Werrington property to Sir William Morice, to which Mr. King replied:—" Pray accept my best thanks for your letter with its information. I should have thought the monumental stone here about 1590-1600 by the costume, but it must be to Sir Francis Drake, the first Bart., who had by his second wife exactly four sons and no daughters. He was created Bart. 1622 and died 1637. The lady has the high collar and the boys the ruffs of Queen Elizabeth's time. She might have died some years before him, and he may have erected the slab to her."

Is this monument still in existence, and could it not be saved by being put under cover " inside " the church?

G. T. WINDYER MORRIS.

83. CARY OF FOLLATON.—Whitehall, 5 May, 1900. The Queen has been pleased to grant unto Agnes Mary Cary (calling herself Agnes Mary Stanley Cary) of Manson Place in the County of London, wife of Stanley Edward George Cary, of Follaton, in the Parish of Totnes, in the County of Devon, Esqr., and only surviving daughter and co-heir of Arthur William Jerningham, late of Catherine Place, in the City of Bath and County of Somerset, Admiral of Her Majesty's Fleet, by Sophia Mary, his wife, late of Catherine Place aforesaid, daughter of Richard O'Ferrall Caddell, late of Harbourstown in the County of Meath, Esqr., both deceased, Her Royal license and authority that, in compliance with the directions contained in the last will and testament of her mother, the said Sophia Mary Jerningham, she may take and henceforth use the surname of Caddell, in addition to and after that of Cary, and bear the arms of Caddell quarterly with those of her paternal family, the said arms being first duly exemplified according to the laws of arms, and recorded in the College of Arms: otherwise Her Majesty's said license and permission to be void and of none effect.

And also to command that the said Royal concession and declaration be registered in Her Majesty's College of Arms.

J.B.R.

84. VASTBY (BARON DE).—An Essay | on the Causes of the | Revolution and Civil Wars | of | Hayti, | Being | a Sequel to The Political Remarks | Upon Certain | French Publications And Journals | concerning | Hayti. | By | The Baron de Vastey, | Chancellor of the King, Member of the Privy Council, Field | Marshal of the Army of Hayti, Knight of the | Royal and Military Order of St. Henry, | etc., etc., etc., etc. | Translated From The French, By | W. H. M. B. | Exeter | Printed at the Western Luminary Office, For The | Translator, For Private Circulation. | 1823. 8vo., 2*ll.* + x *pp.* + 250 *pp.* + cxviii. *pp. Fine Copy, uncut and unopened edges. Orig. bds.* Exeter, 1823

On page IX the translator states that only 100 copies were printed for private distribution to a few of the more zealous friends of the African cause, not for sale. Rich. II. 153, N. 46 : " The French original was publ. at Sans-Souci (Haiti), 1819 ; Leclerc, 1417, gives a biogr." "Le Baron de Vastey, né au Quartier de la Marmelade, île d'Haiti, abandonne les drapeaux de la République française, en 1795, pour embrasser ceux de l'Espagne, alors en guerre avec la métropole. Il fut tué au Cap le 8 Oct. 1820, propre jour où son maître le roi Christophe était réduit à se brûler la cervelle pour se dérober à la vengeance populaire."

The above description of a work printed at Exeter is from a recent catalogue of a second-hand bookseller. Is anything known of the translator ? A copy of it is in the British Museum library. W. P. COURTNEY.

85. RELICS OF THE CIVIL WAR. — Since coming to Membury in October, 1897, some interesting relics of the Civil Wars have come into my possession, though one has since been deposited, at my suggestion, in the Exeter Museum by its former owner, Mr. G. Summers, of Rock Mills, Membury. These relics consisted of three cannon balls, weighing respectively nine, four and three pounds, and a bullet weighing one-and-a-half ounces, and it is the first of these that is now in the Museum. The three-pounder was given me by an old man living in a cottage close to the churchyard, who told me that, together with the bullet, it was found in the wall of the old cottage pulled down to make room for the present one. It is known that fighting between the opposing parties of King and Parliament took place here in 1645 on two occasions, and it is remarkable that in the register under date October 12th, 1645, is recorded the burial of a soldier that was " killed

by the Church." Could it have been my cannon ball or bullet that did the deed? On February 4th, 1645, Sir Shilston Calmady was buried, having been killed in the gateway of what is now Ford Farm. When the church was restored in 1893, a Norman pillar was discovered built into the wall by the tower at the end of the arches between the nave and south aisle. If any of your readers have met with mention of a church at Membury in Norman times, I should be glad to know it. It is stated by Oliver that what is now called the Yarty Aisle was originally Our Lady's Aisle, and that what is now called the Brinscombe Aisle was called St. Catherine's Aisle. But the oldest inhabitant has never heard either of them called by those names. What is Oliver's authority? He further states that the church was ordered to be re-seated on May 15th, 1588. Again I should like to know his authority?

F. E. W. LANGDON.

86. MOLFORD FAMILY, OF DEVON.—Can any brother genealogist supply me with the date and place of birth of John and William Molford, or Mulford, born about 1620 (said to have been officers in the Civil War), who emigrated to Massachusetts and founded the notable family of Molford? I have a copy of the pedigree from the Visitation of 1620, but this, while it does not go far enough to include the above Mulfords, indicates Cadbury and South Molton as the parishes where such baptisms should be recorded. We have three printed pedigrees of Mulford in America, all incomplete, and I am aiding in the preparation of a comprehensive one.

New York, U.S.A. STUART C. WADE.

87. THE COMMONS OF DEVON (par. 55, p. 80).—Your correspondent, "O.J.R.," under the heading "The Commons of Devon," asks if any reader can suggest the reason why the inhabitants of Barnstaple and Totnes are excluded from the rights of common on the Devonshire Commons. I read a paper on "The Venville Rights on Dartmoor" at the meeting of the Devonshire Association at Plympton, in 1887, when the same question was asked. My reply then was, and I am still of the same opinion, that, as by Charter of the 18th May, 1204, King John disafforested all Devonshire up to the metes and bounds of Dartmoor and Exmoor (see Percival

Birkett, p. 12, in the volume published by the Dartmoor Preservation Association) and all ancient rights of common were then granted to the aforesaid men of Devon and their heirs within the regards of those moors as they were accustomed to have, the whole of Devon had been before afforested, that is, subject to the forest laws; but it was most probable that Barnstaple and Totnes, being at that time very important towns, perhaps supplying shipping for the Crown, were exempted from afforestation of Devon, and consequently were not included in the disafforestation when the grant of the customs "within the regards of those moors" was specially made. W.F.C.

88. ON THE FONT IN DUNSFORD CHURCH there are eight shields, one of which is charged with three harps. What family bears these arms? No tinctures are given. The other seven shields represent the arms of Fulford impaling Moreton, Fitzurse, Courtenay, Fortescue, Bozom, Richard I. (as Earl of Poictou), and St. George. M.A.

[The shield on the Dunsford font must be that of Harpesfeld, Co. Herts, *argent, three harps sable, stringed or.* What connection the family may have had with Dunsford we do not know, but Nicholas Harpesfeld was Rector of Ash-reigny (Reigne-ash, Aysh-reyne), having been instituted on the presentation of Joanna, Vicountess Lisle, and Thomas Specket, gent., 21 Feb.. 1497-8. There is a good account of Sir Nicholas Harpesfeld and his family by Mr. F. G. Baigent, *Jour. Arch. Assoc.*, Vol. XIX, p. 191. See also *Herald and Genealogist*, Vol. V, p. 127. EDS.]

89. "THAT'S EXTRA."—Many years ago it was frequently said in Devonshire, "That's extra," as the old woman said when she saw "Kirton" (Crediton). What was there in Crediton to give rise to such an expression? A. J. DAVY.

90. DEVON GLEE CLUB.
5 Feb., 1830, "at this meeting it was Moved and Seconded:
 'That there be a Ladies' night . . . . the Funds of the Club to be in no manner drawn on to meet the expenses thereof, but that the same be defrayed by such Members as may be willing to contribute thereto, and that a Committee be appointed for conducting the same, and for forming such resolutions as they shall deem expedient.'

Okehampton Castle, 1789.
From a Watercolour Drawing by Swete.

" But it was Resolved :
  ' That the same be referred to and taken into consideration at the next General Meeting to be held on the 5th of March, and that the Members be requested to attend at Half past Four o'clock precisely on that day.'   By Order,
CHARLES BRUTTON,
Treasurer."
G.L.B.

91. TOUR IN NORTH DEVON BY REV. JOHN SWETE (*continued from page* 96).—After leaving Stickle park not long after I entered OKEHAMPTON—a borough town, not very respectable in its buildings and chiefly remarkable for its Castle, which about half a mile to the S.W. is seated on a proud eminence, beneath which runs the West Oke from whence the town deduces its name. Few places have more of the picturesque in them than this—the ruins of a magnificent castellated Pile, crowned by a keep, high towering over the other buildings, in feudal times rendered almost impregnable by Nature, and effectually made so by the assistance of Art, which on the West, hath cut off all possible access to the Castle from the hill beyond, by an effort of indefatigable labor, effecting a gulph or chasm of considerable width and fearful depth, while on every other quarter the hill slopes away from the exterior walls so steep and rapid that a near approach of an enemy must have been hazardous in the extreme. In the Keep the walls at the doorway are seven feet in thickness, immediately on the right of the entrance is a circular staircase which ran to the top of the building originally consisting of two stories, this room the dimensions of which are a cube of 21 feet, communicates with another 28 by 18. The plane on which the keep is erected is about 60 feet by 33. From the base of this partly artificial mound, the ridge falls gently, contracting as it goes, till it is compressed into a point, where are still the remains of a Gatehouse. Within the walls is an area, which inclusive of the building would have compris'd an acre and a half—here are still to be traced the remains of eight rooms besides the gateway and two in the keep, the hall which is 45 feet long and the Chapel are easily distinguishable. This place was the

Barony of Baldwin de Brioniis, given him by the Conqueror with the title of Vicomis of Devon. The Park separated from the Castle by the West Oke, is of great extent being 9 miles in circumference. It rises gently from the rivers and is beautified with thick woods of almost every kind of trees that this country can call indigenous.

Sleeping here, the next morning being Sunday I walked to the Parish Church, which seems to pay no compliment to the people of the Town, by leaving them at half a mile distance. Here when the service was concluded one of the inconveniences which this year must frequently have resulted from the distance of the Church to the town, presented itself to the congregation, in the shape of a thunder-storm. After a detension of an hour, I accompanied Mr. Clack to a pleasant farm of his about two miles distant, seated a little to the left of the road to Tavistock. In the evening we mounted our horses and had hardly proceeded a quarter of a mile behind the house, when all at once open'd upon the eye such a scene, as no description of mine can give any but the faintest idea of. The beauty, the grandeur of the scenery exceeding everything I had before seen! An intermixture of woods, of water, of hills, rarely to be paralell'd; above the others East Tor (Yes Tor) which I should not hesitate to affirm surpasses its neighbour, the hill of Causan in height. These hills, tho' barely clad, are admirable sheep tracks and are ever verdant, the bases of them charmingly skirted by the West Oke, into which from the midst of the hills, where the grounds somewhat expand, a rivulet called Hollow lake (lake being here synonimous to rill) empts itself. Here the Park begins, here the woods are seen in the most rich and picturesque stile, creeping as it were up the hill, diminishing in size and quantity gradually as they ascend, overhanging the wild river on either bank and at times bending down their branches close to its surface, seemingly with an intent to stop its hastening waters, which mantle as they fall over the obstructing rocks, forming a succession of cascades of diverse appearance and varying beauty, not one of them having a trail like the rest. Various sorts of trees contribute to improve the scenery, some by their tints, others by their fantastic shapes; old oaks and ash, thorns, quickbeam and hazle. From some of the oaks are found suspended an extraordinary and very curious moss, consisting of strings of considerable length which appear of the texture and strength of common thread, on which are strung beads of various sizes, generally of an oblong figure, thicker and more rounded in the middle. These when the moss is dry, are as beads, easily to be moved from one part of the string to another and carry with them more of the appearance of Art than Nature.

Above the Park by the river have been lately discovered masses of a metalline mixture, in weight and form similar to the scoriæ from a smith's forge, very ponderous, seemingly all iron and evidently formed by fusion, which as there are no vestages of an eruption from the earth, the least traces of a volcano, nor the appearance of any metal having in old times being smelted here, would seem (and it is the opinion of the place) to have thus coalesced by a recent stroke of Lightening and what adds to this conjecture is, that they have been newly discovered tho' the spot was well known and had been year after year frequented by the fishermen of the neighbourhood.

Not long the next morning had the sun risen, when I hastend thro' the village that I might once again feast my eyes with the scenry I had yester-eve been delighted with, and took a sketch of the prospect before me, all my cares, every sollicitude were forgotten.

From such harmony I turned away reluctant, and my watch told me I might be delaying the family breakfast. This over I took my leave of hospitable Kerslake and crossing the turnpike road in front of the house I rode over extensive commons for several miles and entered the road leading to Hatherleigh. This is a very neat town on a red soil. Somewhat further on toward the West I saw Inwardleigh Church, the tower of which was in a most ruinous state, having been reduced to two thirds its height, about a year or so since by lightening. At some distance from Hatherleigh I rode by a seat of Luxmore, Esqr. placed on an eminence without reaping any advantage from its situation, the front being toward a plain unmeaning field. The taste of the Architects of Houses in these parts, from this and other instances, seems to militate strongly against the *natural taste* of the present enlightened times, the one wish to exclude from the view everything that is worth notice, the other to comprehend the minutest trait of unembellish'd or wild Nature.

Passing over the Trowridge by Hele Bridge, of four arches rising nobly over the widened waters, and having gained the ascent of a steep wooded hill, I stopped my horse and turning round was gratified with a fine view of the country I had past over, the spire of Hatherleigh gracing the mid-ground of the picture which terminated in the noble horizontal line of East Tor (plainly at this distance a convincing test) super eminent to Causen and the other inferior hills.

I soon reach Heanton, a seat of Lord Orford, a vast pile, built at different periods, having a date of 1639 engraved in a tablet of Moorstone, which is certain from the architecture not the oldest, but ascertaining the time in which the portal over which it is placed was erected. As the body and wings form the letter **E**, in front, and as we know in the days of Elizabeth, this compliment was paid her Majesty, of building in the form of the Initial Letter of her name, so we may refer the original building to that date. The principal rooms of the house are a large hall, a dining room, and a drawing room in either wing, and a vast number of bed chambers, furnished with antique beds of net work flowers and other embroidery. One bed was in a recess, and another, probably the one of State was separated from the other part of the room by a railing, breast high, with a door on each end, giving the whole the appearance not only of snugness but of grandeur; it had been hung with silk, and decorated with paintings, but the one was faded and rent, the others that were not daubings had long been removed to form a part of the Houghton collection. In the small room over the entrance, was a trap door, which by a step ladder, led to a lower room about 8 feet square, where Col. Rolle secreted himself after having struck Sir Robert Walpole, dreading his vengeance. The hall is ornamented, not with cuirasses, helmets, coats of mail, the arms or spoils of heroes of yore, but with the atchievents of modern times, antlers of forest deer, some of enormous size projecting terrific, from the heads carved in wood, ranged round the walls to the number of 22, and in the quadrangular court behind were near 50 others, of lesser size but their antlers and heads both real. On the Southern side of the house is a most noble terrace of considerable width and in length 130 paces, which with the bowling green and the walks around are kept in most excellent order and are the finest of the kind I have seen. On the parapet walls, the mullions of the windows which are moorstone, and the flat pavements, I observed that a white moss had so incroach'd that it was rather difficult to discover of what substance they were. All that is seen from the terrace of any note are the adjoining oak trees, which are in general of great height and admirable bulk, particularly a clump of five or six nearest to the house, one of which was 16 feet in circumference. With regard to improvements, as the present Lord Orford hath never resided at or even visited this mansion, the old ideas of formality still exist, they have taken full posession of the environs—but they might easily and with no great expense be removed—there is so much depth in the woods, so much variety in the ground, and so much space on every side that the whole scene is capable of any embellishment, particularly by the addition of a piece of water in front, for the reception of which Nature hath done everything that could be desired. I cannot quit this antient family seat of the Rolles and Earls of Orford, without noticing an admirable rule or precept, painted in an escutcheon over the chimney in the eating room, which originated in the ceremonious etiquette of the Gentlemen of the Stag Hunt, in the late Earl's time, about seating themselves at table. "He that sits down first gives least trouble." How numerous these assemblies were, and what the hospitable cheer, is the story in the mouth of every old man in the vicinity, I shall however add what I myself saw, and what to me was greater conviction. A large oblong tub, called the Punch-bowl, which during these *fetes de la chasse* tho' holding two hogsheads, was constantly filled with punch.

Having been here hospitably entertained by Mr. Mallet the Steward, the next morning I proceeded on through a pleasant track of country toward Torrington, having past a villa commanding an extensive view, and arriving within a mile of the Town, I turned in on the left to Cross, the charmingly situated seat of H. Stevens Esq., placed on an eminence the grounds declining rapidly from the front, it of course comprehends all the subjacent country and the opposite hill, on which the town of Torrington full in view, exhibits a conspicuous and romantic object, the houses on the south verging toward a precipice, and suspended as it were over the river Towridge, meandring round the bottom in a wavy channel with its waters kissing the very margin of the meadows " without o'erflowing full."

Accompanied by Mr. Stevens I went in quest of the Ruins of Frithelstoke Priory, passing over the bridge at the S.W. end of Torrington rose a steep hill to a down, precipitous toward the river but having a delightful prospect on the North, of " Beam " a seat of Dennis Rolle Esq., a most lovely and sequester'd spot. Having again crossed the Torridge by another bridge we came to the Ruins of the Priory, which tho' not grand or extensive, have a good deal of the picturesque in them and posess a peculiarity in the rounding of the western windows of the Chapel rarely, if at all to be met with. The remains consist chiefly of the side and end walls of what is now one room, the area of which in length is 30 paces and in width about 9. There are two very antient walnut trees, overhanging the Southern Walls and with the ivy contributing greatly to enhance its beauty.

In our return we made a circuit through the town of Torrington, which hath been notable for a Barony from the Norman Conquest. The Northern street by which we entered, tho' not elegant, was yet neat and ornamented with several very decent looking houses, this brought us to the center of the town by the church side, the tower of which is rendered a conspicuous object at a distance posessing an handsome spire cased with lead. In this part of the town was also a respectable town hall, opening into a small square or market place. Hence we past on to the Eastern Cliffs on the verge of which once stood a castle, time however hath now brought its honours to the ground, and its only remains are a mere heterogeneous mass of earth and stones, saving that the Chapel yet exists, tho' converted to the use of a School-house. An area of an acre and half adjacent hath been used as a bowling green, till (being in the posession of Mr. Rolle) it was suppress'd by him a year or two since, on account of the reputed dissipation of the gentlemen of the town, who were accustomed it seems, now and then to game, and to execrate their ill-fortune ' by words,' which were not deemed proper for gentlemen of character and decency to make use of. The consequence is, that its turf is destroyed, its fences broke down, and a pleasure house dismantled, which commanded a most extensive prospect towards the S. the W. and the East.

(To be continued.)

NOTICES OF BOOKS.

92. Mr. STUART CHARLES WADE* proposes in this book to give, not only an account of the origin of the name, and of the hero Wada, the son of King Vilkinus and the Mermaiden, and his descendants, and particulars and pedigrees of famous Englishmen of the name of Wade, but also genealogies of the families of Wade of Massachusetts and New Jersey and other pedigrees. The Wades of the United States, a large and widespread family, seem to be the descendants of Nathaniel, Nicholas, and Jonathan Wade, yeomen from Norfolk, who settled around Boston in 1630. This is the first part, and the continuance of the work, which it is proposed to complete in ten parts, apparently depends upon its sale. The price per part is not mentioned. There are given portraits of members of the Wade family, and heraldic and other engravings. The author has a query in this part of *D.N.&Q.*, No. 86, p. 119.

93. Better late than never. It does, however, seem strange to issue an account of the proceedings of a Society for a period ending March 1882, in 1900.† But the result is a very interesting little volume, and it would have been a great pity not to have completed the Transactions of the Club, and so lose the record of much valuable work. But for the industry and perseverance of the Editor, Mr. Harper Gaythorpe, F.S.A. Scot., many facts now safely preserved would have gone out of memory. The illustrations are, upon the whole, good; but the two plates supposed to be humorous could have been done without.

---

* "The Wade Genealogy," compiled by Stuart Charles Wade, 8vo, Part I. New York, 1900.

† Furness Lore, being the Transactions of the Barrow Naturalists' Field Club for the 4th, 5th, and 6th years ending 24th March, 1882, together with historical and descriptive notes of the monuments, ancient heraldic and painted and stained glass, pre-reformation and 18th century bells in Aldingham and Keswick Churches, and other interesting information relating to the topography and archæology of the Furness District. Compiled and edited by Harper Gaythorpe, F.S.A. Scot., Kendall : printed by T. Wilson, Highgate, demy 8vo, 1900.

94. Mr. James Dallas and Mr. Henry G. Porter have rendered yeomen's service to County archæologists by transcribing and printing "The Note Book of Tristram Risdon, 1608-1628. London, E. Stock, 1897." Those who have hitherto been obliged to content themselves with "Dugdale's Baronage" for the earlier genealogies, and remember having glanced at Hornby's Book, published in 1738, criticising Dugdale (Museum Press Mark 607 g. 5), must have often felt misgivings as to Dugdale's earlier pedigrees. Our editors tell us that "attention is called to the change in the early part of the Courtenay pedigree brought to light by researches into the records of King John's time, which corrects all the Courtenay pedigrees to be found in the usual works of reference." They add that "the collection of Brevia [given by Risdon] contains an enormous mass of most important genealogical matter taken from original deeds which doubtless at one time or other passed through Risdon's hands . . . the entries have been so far compared with the Fine Rolls and other Records as to prove conclusively their great accuracy and value." For this we are most grateful to the editors.

In their own notes, however, many of which are extremely valuable and shew much independent research, it does not appear to be brought out with sufficient clearness that the barony of Hurberton (p. 73) was one portion of Judhel's barony of Totnes, the other portion being usually described as the barony of Totton (p. 60). "Testa Nevil," p. 176b, and 198a, gives a list of the "tenants of Reginald de Valletort of the Honour of Hurberton," and on p. 183b. a list of the tenants of William de Cantilupe of the Honour of Totton." It will be seen that the estates of both of these Honours were in Domesday held by Judhel. The Editors' note on p. 64, "William de Falesia is written in the top margin of the page, but has no bearing upon the text. Eds.," is surely uncalled for, seeing that the Domesday estates of William de Faleise are exactly those which constitute the Honour of Dartington. A note on p. 70 speaks of "Walscinus de Duac*us* in the Exon Domesday," and another on p. 71 of "Mil*es* de Cogan." These are, however, only gnats in the ointment.

O.J.R.

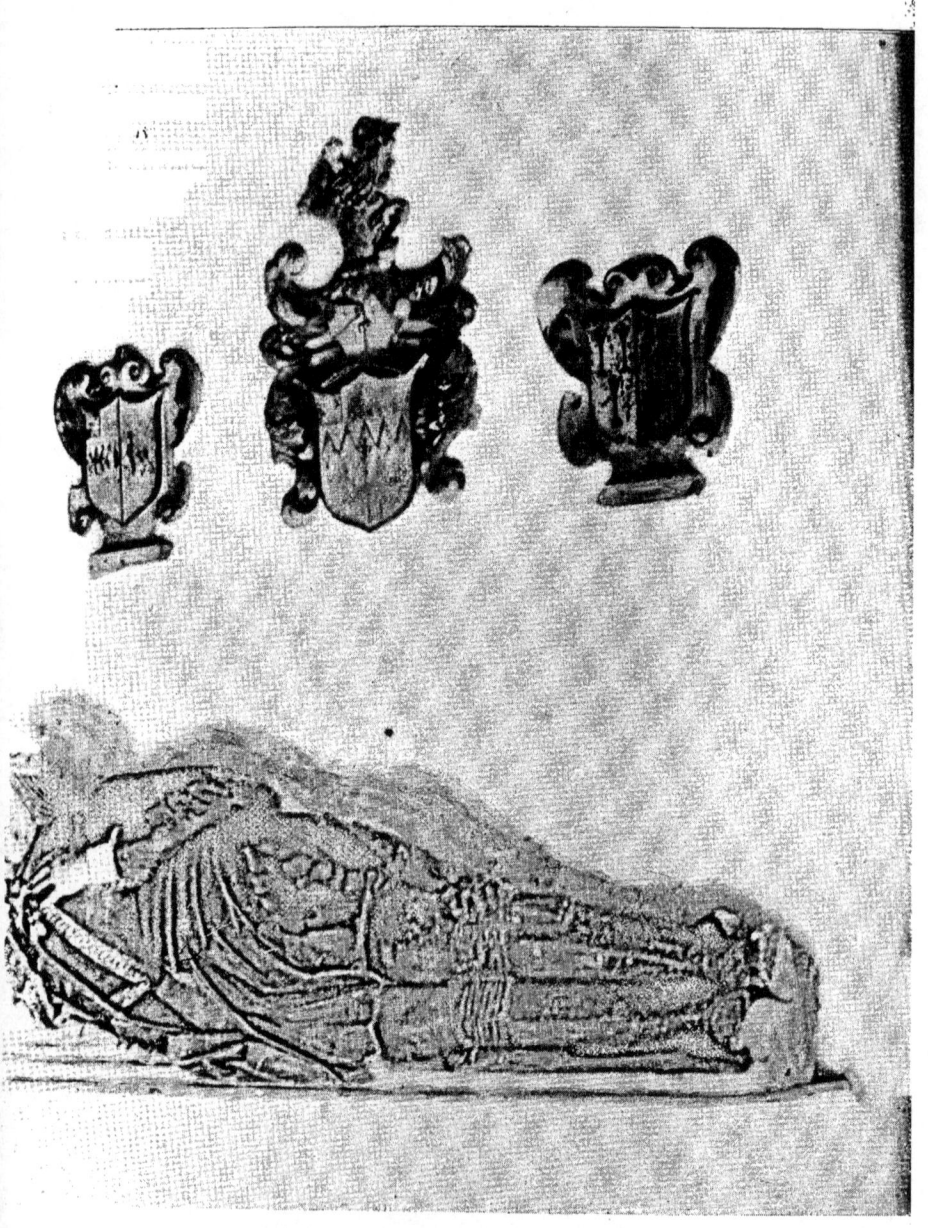

onument of Thomas Chafe in the Church of St. Giles-in-the-Heath,
Great Torrington

95. THE MONUMENT OF THOMAS CHAFE IN THE CHURCH OF ST. GILES-IN-THE-HEATH, NEAR GREAT TORRINGTON.— The interest which Thomas Chafe inspires arises from his connection with Tristram Risdon. He seems to have been a clever and somewhat eccentric man, who did not get along well with everyone. His mother, as appears from her will, did not approve of his proceedings, and she blames her son-in-law, Risdon, for leading him into extravagant habits. He was, however, evidently, an affectionate warm-hearted man. Some account of Chafe is given by the late Charles Worthy (Transactions Devon. Assoc., Vôl. xix., 1887, p. 530). He took his degree at Exeter College, Oxford, and was called to the bar, but apparently soon took up his residence at Doddescott, in the parish of St. Giles, where he died in 1648. His monument was erected in pursuance of the following direction in his will. "Further I require my executor to inter my body as near as he can by my sister Risedon," this was Pascha Chafe, the wife of Tristram Risdon, " and I do ordain appoint and require £30, rather more than less, to be bestowed in a monument of my effigies by my Executor, of whose love herein I am not diffident, who have reaped so many gratuities formerly from me, and now in present burthening his conscience for effecting it, as he shall answer Coram Deo. I desire him to inscript in my monument some memory of his good aunt Rysedon and of the family deceased there interred, also of my wife and her two children, no great onus to an ingenious generous and gratefull mind."

In compliance with these directions, Thomas Chafe, the nephew, caused to be erected in St. Giles' Church a monument, with effigies and armorial bearings. "Rather more than less" must have been bestowed upon this. It was placed in the chancel, but during a restoration of the church in 1863, it was shamefully treated. It was taken down altogether, and those portions, which the architect thought fit to preserve, were placed against the south wall of the tower of the church. In its original state the monument was a high tomb, probably like the Fulford tomb in Dunsford Church (par. 3, p. 5), on which was the effigy. Over the effigy was a canopy supported in front by two Ionic columns, on either side were two small female figures, and in front of the tomb was an incised medallion portrait of a man in a black gown, with a book in his hands. It was of stone and marble. There were six shields of arms and the whole was ornamented with foliage and scrolls, and painted and gilded. It was very handsome, and the most interesting thing in the church, and yet it was cast out and mutilated as I have mentioned. At the back was a tablet with the following inscription :—

In
Piam
Thomæ Chafe
Generosi memoriam

ex per antiqua Chaforum de chafecombe familia in comitatu
Somerset

oriunde eq' Collegio Exoñ in academia Oxoñ artium magister.
probitate virtute ac ingenio insignis qui in apostolica fide viri
constanter versatus in beati justorum resurrectionis spe
animum spiravit 25° die Novemb' Anno Salutæ 1648
aetatis suo climacterico magno.

e XUVI as sVas eXvit Me DICV's.

Uxorem reliquit Margerium.
filiam Philippi Burgoyne clarissima Burgoynorum
prosapia orti matronem religiosissimam bororumq' operam
plenissimam

qua et obdormivit in Domino Anno
A Chrō nato 16   ætatis suæ
Abstulit a nobis miseri [*qy. miseræ*] qvem tem' [*qy. terræ*]
ademptum

Abstulit e vivis mortis iniqua manis
Nec cecidit svlis namq' et prudentia virtus
Candor amoʳ pietas interiere simul
Teste vel invidia vita est lethoq' beatus
Vivus erat Domini mortuus in Domino.

What did the restorers please to leave us? The effigy, three of the shields, and the tablet with the inscription. These were ruthlessly torn from their surroundings, and stuck up against the wall, far from their original position.

The figure of Thomas Chafe is in the costume of the period. He wears a coif, doublet, and short cloak, with, perhaps, a cuirass under, plain hose, the stockings gartered below the knees with large rosettes, which the shoes also have:—"*with two Provencal roses on my razed shoes.*" (Hamlet. Act iii, scene 2).

The six shields contained the following:—

1. *Az. 5 'fusils conjoined in 'fess argent, a canton of the last,* with mantling; and crest, *a demi lion rampant or. holding between its legs a 'fusil az.* Chafe. This remains.

2. As the last. It is gone.

3. *Az. a talbot passant ar. armed and langued gules.* Burgoyne. Gone.

4. As 1, Chafe, impaling 3, Burgoyne. This remains.

5. As 1, Chafe, impaling *Az. 3 escallops or. a crescent for difference.* Malet. Gone.

6. *Ar. 3 bird bolts erect sable.* Risdon, impaling 1, Chafe. This remains.

We may return to Thomas Chafe and his family on some other occasion. J.B.R.

96. MULFORD (par 86, p. 119).—Monuments in South Molton Church. One over the chancel doorway is very handsome, and has a rather pathetic interest, being in memory of the last member of a family long associated with South Molton, whose residence was at Garliford in the adjoining parish of Bishops-nympton. Inscription, translated—"Beneath repose the mortal remains of John Molford, gentleman, a youth of seventeen years of age, whose ashes by the most evident display of Divine love (for those whom the gods love die young) mingle with those of his Father, Grandfather, and Great Grandfather, too early having joined them, since by his death the only hope of the noble race of the Molfords perished. He died the 21st of June in the year of the Christian Era, 1692." The British Museum has a quarto tract, entitled, "A Sermon preach'd at the Funeral of John Molford, Esq., of Nymet Episcopi, in the Diocese of Exeter, who dyed (aged 18 years) the 21st day of June, through the sad occasion of a fall from a horse, and was buried at South Molton the 27 day of the same month. By Thomas Easton, A.M., Vicar of Nymet Episcopi." There is a large house in South Street, South Molton, known as Mulford House, now, 3rd Oct., 1900, occupied by a medical man. It formerly belonged to the Rev. J. Bawden. The Bishop Nympton register can probably supply further information. HELEN SAUNDERS.

97. SIDBURY, DEVON. — In Antony Wood's Life and Times, occurs the following:—"25 July, 1664, about 11 o'clock at night one Richard Kastlecke (*i.e.*, Kerslake) of Exeter Coll: bible clerk, was killed over against Wilcokses the barber by the Star, by —— Turner, commoner of Wadham, son of Sir Will: Turner, civ(ilian). He held up his hand at the next assizes and downe upon his knees for his life. By means of his father Sir William Turner, Dr., his life was saved. Kastleck was bible clerk. Richard Karslak, pauper scholaris, came to Exeter Coll. 6 Apr. 1661." He was son of Richard Karslake, of Sidbury, Devon, and was twenty-one years of age at the time of his death. The name Carslake is found in Sidbury at the present day. William and John, the sons of William Turner, D.C.L., matriculated at Wadham, Coll., 21st Feb., 166½. The evidence does not show which of these two was the homicide. *Vide Life and Times of Antony Wood. Oxford Hist. Soc., Vol. ii., p. 18.*

John Trivet was Devon Fellow of Exeter Coll., Oxon, in autumn, 1362. A family of Trivet lived in Sidbury.

John Parkhouse, also Devon Fellow of Exeter Coll., 1500-1519; Principal of Hart Hall, 1506-10; Canon of Exeter; Vicar of Sidbury, 1536; *ob.* 1541. Vide Boase's "Registrum Collegii Exoniensis," p. 49.

In September, 1799, the Earl of Clare was created Baron Fitzgibbon of Sidbury, Devon, in the peerage of Great Britain. Did he own property in this parish ? A. R. BAYLEY.

98. PORTRAIT OF SIR HUMPHREY GILBERT. — Cockram's Tourist's Guide to Torquay and its neighbourhood, published some sixty years ago, says " His (Sir Humphrey Gilbert's) portrait was to be seen at Compton (Castle in Devonshire) in the time of Prince, who says: ' This noble knight's lively effigies is yet remaining in his grand-nephew's house at Compton, Humphrey Gilbert, Esq., which I have there seen, in this figure, the one hand holdeth a general's truncheon and the other is laid on the globe of the world, Virginia is written over ; on his breast lies the golden anchor with the pearl at peak,' " etc.* Does anyone know of the present location of this portrait ? It is generally considered that Compton Castle was built by the Gilbert family. A. J. DAVY.

---

* Prince's Worthies, p. 419, ed. 1810.

99. DESERTERS.— The Hon. Mrs. Marker sends us a copy of an entry written on the fly-leaf of the register of the parish of Gittisham. There are other entries of merely local importance.

"An Hue & Cry granted by Mr John Newcomb, Mayor of Exon, dated ffebruary 25, A.D. 1703, to search for & apprehend Cornelius Carnell, a Scotch Irishman, squatt & thick, about 5 feet & 7 inches high, wearing his owne haire very black, and a red coate lin^d wth green and a black coate under it, his speech very much ye Irish tone.

John Richards a tall young fellow about 5 feet & 10 inches high wearing his owne haire, being browne & a red coate lin^d with green.

Austin Rice, a German borne, about 5 feet & 9 inches high wearing a red coate lin^d wth green & under it colourd cloaths & speaks broken English, w^h 3 lately deserted ye company & service of Colonell Evans. Whoever apprehends y^m & brings y^m to Mr Tho. Robinson at ye New Inn in Exon shall have 2 guinias for each."

100. THE COMMONS OF DEVON (par. 55, p. 80, and par. 87, p. 119).—W. F. C. is no doubt right in saying that previously to the disafforestation by King John, on 18th May, 1204, the whole county of Devon was a royal forest, subject to the Forest Laws (see Pipe Rolls, pp. 493, 498, in Trans. Devon Assoc., vol. xxix.) He is also probably right in saying that Barnstaple and Totnes being important mercantile towns were not included in the forest, and therefore did not share in the common rights definitely bestowed on the holders of the disafforested lands by the Charter. Then comes the difficulty. How came the inhabitants of Lidford and Exeter to have common rights? They must also have been without the forest, seeing that Lidford was a town equal in importance to Barnstaple or Totnes, and that Exeter, according to Domesday (*Devon Assoc. edition*, p. 3) was by far the most important city and did service as much as Barnstaple, Totnes and Lidford together.

O.J.R.

101. WHITE ALE.—The following lines were published anonymously in *The Torquay Directory*, 1877. Probably all that the public will ever know of the constituents of the mystic com-

pound known as "White Ale" will be found in a paper read by Mr. P. Q. Karkeek before the Devonshire Association at the meeting at Kingsbridge in 1877. The verses were supposed to have been found under the table after Mr. Karkeek had read his paper, and were written by the Bishop of Marlborough, the present Dean of Exeter, the President for the year. (See Transactions, Vol ix., p. 188).

"Three spirits condemned to eternal distress,
Compounded, 'tis said, this most horrible mess."

I. A dipsomaniacal monthly nurse,
With toothless gibber, and grumbling curse.

II. A fraudulent brewer, delirium's prey,
Who was drunk upon small beer every day.

III. And a chemist, whose principal trade was in drugs,
Which find their dark way to the publican's jugs.

Monthly Nurse's Ghost *(loquitur)*—
"Refuse caudle, stolen gin,
Stale cold gruel—pour them in;
Stolen from the room of Death,
Tainted with the patient's breath—
Pour them in, and pour them out,
Grin and groan, and stir about."

Ghost of fraudulent Brewer *(loquitur)*—
"Musty seeds of Paradise,
Mouldy malt and verdigris,
Drippings from the leaky vat,
Smallest small beer add to that,
Bilge from Charon's ferry boat,
Drink for Cocytean throat;
Pour them in and pour them out,
Grin and groan and stir about.'

Chemist's Ghost *(loquitur)*—
"Sweepings from my still and shop,
Draughts that long without a stopper have stood in dust and sun,
Mix them all, the work is done,—
Stir with cunning hand and wrist,
Draught to cheat the analyst,
Till we make a vile potation,
In thy name, Adulteration."

Omnes— "Pour them out and pour them in,
Drink to every mortal sin."

A. J. DAVY.

102. HOLMAN FAMILY.—Who was the father and what is the ancestry of the two brothers, both lieutenants R.N., Robert Holman, of Plymouth, living in 1827, seniority as lieutenant dating from 1810, and James Holman, F.R.S., known as the blind traveller, born 1787, died 1857? Their father and sister died between 1827 and 1832. James Holman described himself as a kinsman of my grandfather, John Bagwell Holman, of Topsham, but I cannot trace the kinship.

H. WILSON HOLMAN.

103. GLASS MANUFACTORY IN DEVON.—In Llewellynn Jewitt's "Half Hours among English Antiquities" (1877) is a list of glass houses in England and Wales, and the only one in Devon is "Topsham," and its product was "bottles." I have made many enquiries about this factory, and am told that near Topsham is a lane called Glass House Lane, but the oldest inhabitant does not know why. In par. 78, page 112, in a note on the Reynall Family it is stated that certain persons worked a glass factory at Countess Weir near Topsham in 1691-4. Seeing this, I venture to ask if the history of this glass house is known, and if there are any specimens of its products to be seen. PAUL Q. KARKEEK.

104. ARTHUR FAMILY.—Can any of your readers throw any light on the connection between the Arthurs of Essex, Somerset, Ireland, Devon and Cornwall? They all bear the same arms, viz., *Gu. a chevron arg. between three rests (clarions) or. Crest, a pelican in her piety, sa. the nest or.* Am I right in supposing Essex to have been their original home, whence they migrated westwards? A Sir Richard Arthur appears in the Somerset Visitation in Edward I. time. A Nicholas Arthur de Tyntagel was admitted Vicar of Madron, 3rd November, 1309; whilst the Irish branch was settled at Limerick, before 1340, when one of that name was mayor of that city. The Devonshire branches are said to have settled in this country from Cornwall, about the time of the Restoration (Burke's Peerage, G.C.A., Sir Arthur, Bart.), whilst others settled at Barnstaple still later. Besides the Nicholas Arthur above referred to, there was a John Arthur, of Tintagel, in Henry VIII. time, and there are several references to them in the Tintagel Registers, from 1677 to 1798. Also is it not

curious that the Arthurs should bear arms so similar to those borne by their near neighbours at Tintagel, the Grenvilles, of Stow? Does this point to an early connection? If so, may it not be in connection with Hamon Dapifer, the younger brother of Robert Fitzhamon and Richard de Granville, who is known to have had large possessions in the East of England, and whose name appears in the Essex Domesday Book?

QUISQUIS.

105. ANTI-CROMWELLIAN SONG.—At the beginning of this century the following song was in general use. I have only been able to get the first verse, which is as follows:—

> "I'll bore a hoale in Crumwell's noase,
> And therein putt a string,
> And laid 'en up and down the teown,
> For murdering Charles our King."

It is said to have been sung by old nurses and others of the humbler classes, and adapted to the music of the chimes. Does any reader of *D.N.&Q.* know anything of its origin or if there are more verses? It is supposed to have been a loyal song.

A. J. DAVY.

106. NORMAN TYMPANA IN DEVON.—The only example known to me of a Norman Tympanum, still preserved in any Church in Devonshire, is that over the south door of the Church of Down St. Mary. Should any other belonging to this county be known to any of your correspondents I should feel obliged for an intimation.

T.N.B.

[Dr. Brushfield read an illustrated paper on "Norman Tympana with reference to those of Derbyshire" before the British Archæological Association, which is printed in their Journal for September, 1900. Information, therefore, relating to similar examples in Devon will be most acceptable.—EDITORS.

107. HAMLET OF "BASON."—Can any of your readers inform me if there is a township or hamlet called "Bason," in the County of Devon, or if not known by that name now, whether there was such a place about the middle of the 18th Century?

H.

Screen—Church of St. Thomas of Canterbury, Bridford.

108. THE SCREEN IN THE CHURCH OF ST. THOMAS OF CANTERBURY, BRIDFORD.—We have here another very interesting screen, similar in many features and in general design to the one at Lustleigh, and originating I should say from the same source. It is in some senses even more worth studying, for being earlier, but still breaking free from the old traditions, it shews almost more signs of hesitation on the part of the designer than the latter does. In this case he has adhered more closely to Gothic forms in the mouldings, and in some of his bases, capitals, strings, etc., whilst his decoration and foliage are just as conventional as in the Lustleigh screen and very similar. This is also undoubtedly a post reformation screen (shown by the figures in the panels) earlier than Lustleigh, as we have here the full evidence of the rood vaulting having once existed though subsequently destroyed, whereas at Lustleigh, so far as we can now see, it has never been erected. This screen is said (*Murray's Handbook, Devon*) to carry the date 1508. I confess I have been unable to find it, and I should say that the evidence of the screen itself points to a later date. As I believe rood-lofts were mostly destroyed about 1566 it probably came into existence somewhere between 1545 and 1555, though I admit the pomegranate, the device of Katherine of Aragon, points to its being earlier, however, I know of no documentary evidence giving its exact date. It is said to have been the gift of the Rev. Walter Southcote, who was Rector here from 1508 to 1550,* if so, all honour to his name; it must, however, have been towards the close of his tenure of the living that he presented it, if it is his gift. An additional proof of its being an earlier screen than Lustleigh, lies I think, in the fact that it was fully coloured and gilt, a great deal remaining to the present time (the feeling against colour not, I presume, having arisen as yet), whereas at Lustleigh I can find no trace of either colour or gilding. The series of triangular panels now hanging loosely on the front, and formerly filling the spaces which existed between the main cornice and the inverted cones of the vaulting when it was complete, are the only instances I can recall of these spandrils being filled with foliage carving. As a rule they are filled with ordinary tracery corresponding in section with the moulds of the

---

*See Trans. Exeter Dioc. Architectural Soc., Series II, Vol. II, p. III.

vaulting ribs. This wealth of carving, gilt and coloured as it seems to have been, must have been very fine, and proves that the men of the earlier days of the reformation were entirely free from the narrow gloomy bigotry which ultimately led to the suppression of all beauty and refinement in art so far as churches are concerned, and that they did not hesitate to give lavishly, in the same place as they made it, some portion of the wealth which undoubtedly flowed into Devonshire at that time, as the result of the wool and other trades there carried on. The main cornice, now fixed against the screen, instead of occupying its former place on the outer face of the vaulting is far away the finest piece of the whole. At first sight it appears both from design and workmanship to be earlier than the remainder, but careful examination shews that the same pomegranate decoration, which is universal in the lower parts, is introduced here largely also. The much greater beauty and refinement of this cornice, both in design and execution, can only be attributed, either to more skilful artists having been employed upon it, or to the increased manual dexterity gained by carrying out the lower portions; the result, however, from whatever cause, is highly satisfactory. The cresting, unfortunately for us, has been entirely destroyed. The tracery is of the usual pattern, which seems to be rather stereotyped throughout the county; in this case it is a little diversified by a small scroll at the springing of the cusps, also two nicely designed crockets on the centre mullion, both quaint conceits which are artistically carried out, and are decidedly unusual. One curious feature in this screen is the doorway, or, rather, ways, for there are two of them. In each case they are filled with a door in one piece, instead of being divided in the centre and opening in two wings. I do not remember having met with another instance. The figures in the lower panel are very similar to those at Lustleigh, but show a greater variety. There appears here to be a mixture of clerical and lay, some having the appearance of jesters, being in grotesque attitudes; what these can refer to in a remote village it is difficult to surmise, unless, the date of the screen's erection being about the time of great prosperity of trade, probably many fairs were held, accompanied, no doubt, by strolling players, and these may, perhaps, have been immortalised in these rather profane times. The northern bay of the screen has been restored in later days when the Saints had regained their old position in men's minds, and four are here represented by rudely carved figures vested somewhat like the others and carrying distinctive emblems. The decoration of this lower portion, follows the lines of Lustleigh screen so closely in other respects as to call for no comment. A. L. TATE.

109. BRIDFORD AND LUSTLEIGH SCREENS (par. 79, p. 113).—The screen in Lustleigh Church is one of a pair which differ essentially in the style of their ornamentation from all the rest of the screens to be found in the district comprised between the Exe and the Dart. The other is in Bridford Church, situated in a lonesome, windy region, high up among the hills in a N.N.E. direction, about four miles from Lustleigh. These two screens should, undoubtedly, be examined in their relation to one another. Both have, or rather had, several distinctive features in common, but the Lustleigh screen has been so altered by recent treatment and by modern additions, hereafter enumerated, as to completely mislead nearly every beholder with regard to its original appearance, and which have rendered it practically worthless from an antiquarian point of view as a subject for attentive study. The Bridford screen, though also deprived of its rood-loft, still retains its other features intact, and excepting the lower panelling of the two end divisions, north and south, has remained, most fortunately, for the most part untouched and wholly unrestored to the present hour. The original colouring and lavish amount of gilding from top to bottom still exists perfect throughout, though charmingly subdued by age, and the uncommon introduction of white and blue into its chromatic decoration, renders its appearance exceptionally lovely. The base of the northern division, alluded to above, appears to be a modern restoration, and the panelling of the last section at the south end has been used to ornament the pulpit.

Both churches have nave with a north aisle only, separated by arcades of the same design, which, though also occurring elsewhere, afford a very perfect type of the granite architecture of the district, whilst the rude workmanship of the arches and columns, and their peculiar capitals, express themselves in solemn harmony with the strange grim spirit of the moorland wastes around. It may be assumed that these two churches were erected at the same period, late in the fifteenth century, and probably by the same craftsmen, the nave at Lustleigh, however, being tacked on to a thirteenth century chancel.

The two screens are of the same height, a little over 9 feet, and accommodate themselves to the width of the aisles, the northern division at Lustleigh being 9½ feet broad, at Bridford about 6 inches wider, and the screen which spans the nave measures in each case exactly 16 feet. Each compound screen consists of eight open-traceried arches supporting a continuous cornice, broken only by the intervening column. The carving of the Bridford screen is so superior to the other, that, if they were both the work of the same sculptors, it would unquestionably be the later production of the two, but judging from the design also of the adjoining parclose, doubtless of contemporary workmanship, and which is of pure Gothic character with graceful flamboyant tracery in one of its compartments, this can hardly be the case. One is therefore led to conclude that the Lustleigh screen is really a much later work, being, in fact, an imitation by inferior workmen, for it is quite obvious that the makers of the later one must have been well acquainted with the design and details of the other.

At Lustleigh the entire surface of the screen has been retooled in quite recent times, a deliberate piece of destructive vandalism still going on unchecked at several other churches in Devon, and which cannot be too strongly censured and condemned. Very small portions only, namely the traceries of the first and third arches, reckoning from the north, and the side mouldings of one or two others, effectively illustrate also that remarkable absence of veneration, which characterizes present-day treatment of old things, having been scraped and sand-papered. There is a stretch of the ancient cornice of about the width of two of the arches over the nave section, the rest of it being of new wood. The upper portion of each divisional column from the spring of the arch is also quite new work. This continuation of the columns does not exist at Bridford, and never did at Lustleigh either till the "restorers" introduced it. The triangular straight-sided spandrels, common to both screens, have been falsified at Lustleigh by being spliced with new wood on which the carved design has been continued, and they are therefore about one-third larger than they were originally, whilst two of them are manifestly quite recent productions. The outer rim now curves to the line of the arch, which has also been provided with a new outer moulding, the old wood being easily distinguished from the new by its grey tone. These spandrels were evidently always exposed to view, and appear to have folded together back to back to form the brackets for the rood-loft really to rest upon, without the usual groining masking them in front. This seems fully confirmed by the fact that, at Bridford, at each end of both sections of the screen there is a carved spandrel in excess, namely, four in all, which are now* fastened on so as to flap against the side walls,† and against the divisional granite column. How the real spandrels behind these carved wings were treated might probably be ascertained by their exposure to view. The suggestion may, I think, be safely hazarded that they were covered by a network of tracery, independently worked, following the patterns filling in the angles of the adjoining parclose, and, being easily removed, this beautiful fretwork was all destroyed when the rood-loft was abolished.

With regard to the lower band of the carved cornice of vine leaves, etc., the Bridford design follows very much the earlier examples of Devonshire screens, and is exceedingly well executed, but at Lustleigh the conventional semi-renaissance treatment entirely prevails. The Bridford screen has no open cresting, that at Lustleigh appears to be new wood from end to end, which fosters the suspicion that the whole thing is a playful flight of fancy of the modern "restorer," introduced in lieu of the upper course of ornament with its terminal bead moulding, or whatever may have finished off the design originally.

The doors of the Lustleigh screen are modern constructions, that towards the nave having incised along the table moulding, "A thankoffering from a Parishioner, 1892," but I believe that most of the alterations above alluded to were effected some years previously.

---

* October 8th, 1900.

† These two appear to have been only recently so placed at either end, and have since been taken down. They are, doubtless, still preserved either in the church or at the rectory.

The panelling of both screens is of precisely similar design, having little carved figures of men in gowns. Those at Lustleigh have all been re-carved. At Bridford they are of varied character, some apparently intended for ecclesiastics, others for laymen, the former wearing the biretta-shaped cap familiar to the reader in Holbein's well-known portrait of Cardinal Wolsey. Some of them wear also short capes painted red or green, and several hold either a scroll, or "a roll of a book,"—Fathers of the Church and Doctors of Divinity most likely. The laymen wear a nondescript kind of cap, and some of them carry what looks like a flattened leathern horn or sleeve. One of them holds up the broad end of it to his ear, as if listening to some sound within it. One of the figures swings a circlet of beads with tassel, another holds a large key dependent, and yet another, performing wildly, appears to represent a morris-dancer.

At Lustleigh the winding stairs in the wall, which gave access into the rood-loft, exist on the north side; at Bridford they are at the opposite end of the screen, and there seems to have been no rule as to their disposition. Their existence, however, is valuable evidence, as proving that the screen, the rood-loft and the rood, formed, at this period, an integral part of the design of the church, so that both were nearly coeval, whilst the exceeding richness of the screen itself was undoubtedly intended to magnify the preciousness of the crowning emblem.

The guide-books inform us that the Bridford screen has the date 1508 upon it. This date I have never been able to discover, but, previous to the renovation of the church, which took place in 1883, when the pulpit, with a large sounding-board over it, stood almost centrally against the granite column dividing the screen, there was a piece of carving up over, but now removed, having the initials "W.S." united by a scroll. Walter Southcote appears to have been rector of Bridford at that time, and he may, therefore, have placed it there. Underneath, and suspended from the scroll by a ring, was a short horizontal ribbon displaying in raised mediæval letters the devout ascription—

'Iaus deo.'

Roscoe Gibbs.

110. AN EIGHTEENTH CENTURY EXETER BOOKSELLER'S BOOK LABEL (par. 9, p. 18).—The following label of an Exeter bookseller famous in his day may be of interest to your readers:—

Sold by | EDWARD SCORE | Bookseller, in EXON ; | where, | Besides Books, Stamp-Paper, | Parchment and other Sta- | tionary Wares, | are sold | The following Medi- | cines viz. ;—*Daffy's* Elixir, *Bostock's* | Cordial, *Bateman's* Pec | toral Drops, *Anderson's Peter's* and *Hooker's* Pills *Bet* |*ton's* and *Roger's* Oil, *Squire's* | Grand Elixir, and a Sovereign | Remedy for the Cholick | Gravel and Stone. J.B.

111. SIR RICHARD WHITTINGTON AND TORRINGTON.—The late Rev. Samuel Lysons, in a little pamphlet entitled "The Model Merchant of the Middle Ages," says that next to our establishing the truth of our biographies, an additional interest is given to them where we can connect the subject of the history with ourselves, our own country, our own county, our own town, or our own village, and the pamphlet in question has afforded me with a very good illustration of the aptness of the remark, for from a note on page 73, I discovered that the subject of the paper—the famous Sir Richard Whittington was, through his wife, connected with Torrington.

The note in question states that Sir Hugh Fitzwarren or Yvon Fitzwarren was of Torrington, in Devonshire, and from the will, and by the ordinances of his alms houses, the author points out we are informed, that his wife's name was Alice Fitzwarren, daughter to Sir Ivo Fitzwarren, and Dame Maude, or Matilda, his wife. He then refers in his note to the "*Calendarium Inquisitionum Post Mortem*," Vol. III, pp. 107-141, from which I have copied the entries in *extenso* :—

Page 107. " 99 MATILDA UXOR IVONIS
FITZWARYN CH^R.
" *Toryton quattuor messuag*
" *due caruc' terr et 20 acre prati* } DEVON.
" *40 acre bosci et* 100^s *redditus.*"

Page 141. " 120 MATILDA UXOR IVONIS
FITZWARYN *(breve tantum).*
" *Toryton quattuor messuag*
" *due caruc' terr et 20 acre prati.*" } DEVON.

The question then arose in my mind as to which Torrington was referred to, for there are no less than three in North Devon, viz.:—Great Torrington, Little Torrington, and Black Torrington, but after some search I think I can claim for Great Torrington some connection with Ivo Fitzwarren, the father of Whittington's wife.

The family seat of the Fitzwarrens was undoubtedly Totley, Toteley or Totleigh, in Black Torrington, as is mentioned by Risdon (p. 254, Ed. 1811); Prince (p. 287, Ed. 1810); and Westcote (p. 318, Ed. 1845).

Strange to say in the "*Note Book of Tristram Risdon*," edited by Messrs. Jas. Dallas and H. G. Porter (1897, pp. 309, 316), we find that Fulk Fitzwarren temp. Edward III. and Richard II., who preceded Ivo Fitzwarren, held "manerium de *Whitington* in comitatu Salopie." In the same book the arms of Fitz Warren, of Toteley, are given as follows:— "*Gules, bezanty, a canton argent* (p. 21).

In the Register of Stafford (Episcopal Registers, Exon. Hingeston-Randolph, p. 103), it is recorded that Sir Ivo Fitzwaryn, Knt., was patron of the R(ectory or Chapel) of St. James, in the Castle of "Chipyngtoryton," so that though the Fitzwarrens evidently had their residence at Totley, in Black Torrington, Sir Ivo Fitzwarren was connected with Great—or Chepyng—Torrington.

In conclusion I may state that Totley is now a farm house in the Parish of Black Torrington.   GEORGE M. DOE.

112. EFFECT OF STRONG WIND ON FERMENTATION AND SPRINGS.—Can any of your readers explain *(a)* why strong wind causes cyder to begin to work again after having apparently stopped fermenting? *(b)* Why must cyder, to be bright and clear, be bottled during weather when the sky is bright? Has electricity, or a fall in the barometer, or change of temperature anything to do with either of the above phenomena? *(c)* Why do water springs diminish in volume before rain and increase their flow with wind, not necessarily accompanied by rain?   EOLUS.

113. THE DEED OF FOUNDATION OF THE CHURCH HOUSE, EXBOURNE.—The Lord of the Manor of Exbourne, as successor in title of William Chudlegh, who was Lord of the Manor in the 22nd year of King Henry VII., still receives an annual chief rent of four pence from the Rector and Churchwardens of Exbourne for the Church House of that parish. By the courtesy of the Rector of Exbourne, the Rev. D'Oyly W. Oldham, M.A., I am enabled to give a copy of the indenture by which William Chudlegh conveyed the Church House to trustees in that year, for the use of the parishioners, reserving to himself, his heirs and successors for ever the said Chief Rent of four pence. This interesting document is still preserved in excellent condition among the Parish arc ives. I will give the Latin with the abbreviations set out at length, and afterwards a translation :—

"Omnibus Christi fidelibus ad quos præsens scriptum indentatum pervenerit Willielmus Chudlegh armiger salutem in Domino sempiternam. Sciatis me præfatum Willielmum dedisse, concessisse, et hoc præsenti scripto meo indentato confirmasse Ricardo ffranke, Willielmo Howett, Johanni Downe, Johanni Clerke, Johanni Northcote, Willielmo Downe, Johanni Westlake, et Rogero Ailecote quendam parcellam terræ meæ, continentem in longitudine quadraginta et quatuor pedes, et in latitudine viginti et quatuor pedes, jacentem in Ekisborn inter le North churche stile, ex parte australi, et portam gardini ibidem vocatam Rokehay yeate, ex parte boreali, et gardinum quondam ex parte orientali, et viam regiam ibidem, ex parte occidentali. Habendum et Tenendum prædictam parcellam terræ cum suis pertinentibus prefato Ricardo ffranke, Willielmo Howett, Johanni Downe, Johanni Clerke, Johanni Northcote, Willielmo Downe, Johanni Westlake, et Rogero Ailecote, heredibus et assignis suis in perpetuum ad usum parochianorum et successorum suorum ad intentionem ad faciendum et de novo ædificandum in eâdem parcellâ terræ unam domum ecclesiasticam pro parochianis prædictis et successoribus suis quæ vocabitur a Churche Howse. Reddendum inde annualim michi præfato Willielmo Chudlegh et heredibus meis quatuor denarios sterlingos solvendos ad festum Sancti Michaelis archangeli Tenendum de capitalibus dominis feodi illius per servicium inde debitum et de jure consuetum ; salvis tamen michi præfato Willielmo Chudlegh et heredibus

meis omnibus et omnimodo serviciis et liberis consuetudinibus
libertatibus franchesiis et privilegiis quibuscunque que in
præfato Willielmo Chudlegh et heredibus meis de jure aut
aliquo alio modo imposterum evenire contigerint aut habere
poterint ratione dominii nostri de Ekisborn, exceptis tamen
pandoxacione et venditione duarum brasurarum cervisie in
eâdem parcellâ terræ, ad usum dictæ ecclesiæ de Ekisborn
prædictæ bis per annum, pro quibus duabus pandoxacione et
venditione ibidem ut præfertur prædictus Ricardus ffranke,.
Willielmus Howett, Johannes Downe, Johannes Clerke,
Johannes Northcote, Willielmus Downe, Johannes Westlake,
et Rogerus Ailecote heredes seu assigni sui nichil dent michi
præfato Willielmo Chudlegh et heredibus meis de fine pro
fractione assisi cervisiæ prædictæ. At si contingat prædictum
annuale redditum quatuor denariorum a retro fore in parte vel
in toto ad aliquod festum Sancti Michaelis per unam mensem
non solutum, quod extunc bene liceat præfato Willielmo
Chudlegh et heredibus meis in prædicta parcella terræ dis-
tringere, et districtiones sic captas asportare et retinere quo
usque dictus annualis redditus cum suis arreragiis in præfato
Willielmo Chudlegh et heredibus meis plene fuerit persolutum
et satisfactum et si contingat prædictum annuale redditum a
retro fore non solutum post aliquod festum in quo solvi debeat
per spatium unius anni si legittimo modo petatur et nulla
sufficiens districtio inde jure poterit in parcella prædicta terræ
quod extune bene liceat præfato Willielmo Chudlegh heredibus et assignis meis in prædicta parcella cum pertinentibus
reintrare et in pristino statu meo possidere hiis indenturis
maliquibus non obstante et ego vero prædictus Willielmus
Chudlegh et heredes mei prædictam parcellam terræ cum suis
pertinentibus præfato Ricardo ffranke, Willielmo Howitt,
Johanni Downe, Johanni Clerke, Johanni Northcote, Willielmo
Downe, Johanni Westlake et Rogero Ailecote, heredibus et
assignis suis ad usum prædictum contra omnes gentes warantizabimus, acquietabimus et defendemus in perpetuum. Noverit
insuper me, præfatum Willielmum Chudlegh ordinasse et in
loco meo posuisse dilectos meos in Christo Simonem Gombles
clericum et Andream Latyer meos veros et legittimos attornatos
conjuncte et diviso ad deliberandum præfato Ricardo ffranke,.
Willielmo Howett, Johanni Downe, Johanni Clerke, Johanni
Northcote, Willielmo Downe, Johanni Westlake, et Rogero

Ailecote plenam et pacificam possessionem et seisinam de et in
prædicta parcella terræ cum suis pertinentibus secundum vim
formam et effectum hujus præsentis carte mee indentate Rata
et grata habentes et habituri totum et quicquid dicti attornati
mei fecerint seu eorum alter fecerit in præmissis. In cujus rei
testimonium præsentibus indenturis tam ego præfatus Willielmus Chudlegh, quam præfati Ricardus ffranke, Willielmus
Howett, Johannes Downe, Johannes Clerke, Johannes Northcote, Willielmus Downe, Johannes Westlake, et Rogerus
Ailecote sigilla nostra alternati apposuimus Hiis testibus
Humfredo ffulford, milite, Jacobo Chudlegh armigero, Johanne
Bobisshe, Ricardo Wekys, Johanne Call, et aliis multis.
Datum vicesimo nono die Julii anno regni Regis Henrici
Septimi vicesimo secundo."

The translation of the above is as follows:—

" To all faithful in Christ to whom this present written
Indenture shall come, I, William Chudlegh Esquire send
eternal greeting in the Lord. Know ye that I the aforesaid
William Chudlegh have given, conceded, and by this present
Indenture have confirmed to Richard ffranke, William
Howett, John Downe, John Clerke, John Northcote, William
Downe, John Westlake, and Roger Ailecote, a certain parcel
of my land, containing in length 44 feet and in breadth 24
feet, lying in Ekisborn between the North Church
Stile on the south, and the gate of a garden there
called Rokehay Yeate on the north, and a certain garden
on the east, and the King's highway there on the west. To
have and to hold the aforesaid parcel of land with its appurtenances, to the aforesaid Richard ffranke, William Howett,
John Downe, John Clerke, John Northcote, William Downe,
John Westlake, and Roger Ailecote, their heirs and assigns
for ever, for the use of the Parishioners and their successors,
for the purpose of making and of building anew in the same
parcel of land one ecclesiastical house for the aforesaid
Parishioners and their successors which shall be called A
Church House. To pay thereout yearly to me the
aforesaid William Chudlegh and my heirs four pennies
sterling to be paid at the Feast of Saint Michael the Arch-
angel. To hold of the chief lords of that Fee by the service
thence due and of right accustomed, reserving nevertheless to
me the aforesaid William Chudlegh, and my heirs all and all

kinds of services and free customs, liberties, franchises, and privileges whatsoever which to me the aforesaid William Chudlegh and my heirs of right or in any other way may happen to belong or may be able to accrue by reason of our lordship of Ekisborn, except only the right of brewing of ale and of selling of two brewings of beer in the same parcel of land for the use of said Church of Ekisborn aforesaid twice yearly, for which two brewings of ale and selling there as aforesaid the said Richard ffranke, William Howett, John Downe, John Clerke, John Northcote, William Downe, John Westlake, and Roger Ailecote, their heirs or assigns shall give nothing to me the aforesaid William Chudlegh and my heirs as a fine for the breaking of the assise of beer aforesaid. But if it shall happen that the aforesaid annual rent of 4 pennies sterling shall be in arrear in part or in whole at any Feast of Saint Michael not having been paid for one month that then in that case it shall be lawful for me the aforesaid William Chudlegh and my heirs to distrain on the aforesaid parcel of land, and the distrained property so taken to carry away and retain until the aforesaid annual rent with its arrears to me the aforesaid William Chudlegh. and my heirs shall have been fully paid and satisfied. And if it should happen that the aforesaid annual rent should be in arrears and unpaid after any feast on which it ought to be paid for the space of one year if it be demanded in a lawful manner and no sufficient distraint can thence lawfully be obtained in the aforesaid parcel of land. Then it shall be lawful for me the aforesaid William Chudlegh my heirs and assigns to re-enter upon the said parcel of land with its appurtenances and to possess it in my former status notwithstanding anything to the contrary in these Indentures. And I the aforesaid William Chudlegh and my heirs the aforesaid parcel of land with its appurtenances to the aforesaid Richard ffranke, William Howett, John Downe, John Clerke, John Northcote, William Downe, John Westlake, and Roger Ailecote, their heirs and assigns to the aforesaid use will warrant, acquit and secure for ever. Be it known further that I the aforesaid William Chudlegh have ordained and in my place have placed my beloved in Christ Simon Gombles Clerk in holy orders and Andrew Latyer my true and lawful attorneys jointly and severally to deliver to the aforesaid Richard ffranke, William

Howett, John Downe, John Clerke, John Northcote, William Downe, John Westlake, and Roger Ailecote full and peaceable possession and seisin of and in the aforesaid parcel of land with its appurtenances, according to the force form and effect of this my present Deed indented. Holding and about to hold ratified and confirmed all and whatsoever my said attorneys shall have done or either of them shall have done in the premises. In testimony of which thing both I the aforesaid William Chudlegh and the aforesaid Richard ffranke, William Howett, John Downe, John Clerke, John Northcote, William Downe, John Westlake, and Roger Ailecote have respectively placed our hands and seals, the following being witnesses, Sir Humfrey ffulford Knight, James Chudlegh, esquire, John Bobisshe, Richard Wekys, John Call, and many others. Given on this twenty-ninth day of July in the twenty-second year of the reign of King Henry the Seventh [A.D. 1507.]

ROPER LETHBRIDGE.

114. BURLEIGH DOLTS (par. 42, page 68).—The query respecting this local name of the site of an ancient camp, near the village of Marlborough, of which, apparently, only a few traces of the vallum remain, also the names of the fields which now occupy the area are very interesting, and worth consideration, as they may lead to the identification of other such earthworks in cultivated land now obliterated by the plough. Bailey's Dictionary, 1745, gives "Burley" to mean big, heavy, gross, and "Doke" a ditch or furrow. Thus Burley Dokes would mean big ditches or furrows, which, I presume, fairly describes the remains as they appeared a few generations ago. The fields were probably enclosed when the camp was well known as the Castle, a common name for such earthworks, as the old maps show. A similar camp near Ashburton was first recognised by the names of two fields on the site, known as Castle Parks, in which flints are frequently found after ploughing. The road leading to the spot is called Tower Hill. "Beacon" and "Down" speak for themselves, but Squirrel is a puzzle. It is well, in tracing the names of fields, to follow the local pronunciation rather than the spelling, and some curious roots may be reached. Thus in Halliwell's *Archaic Dictionary* we find Squillery, or Squylerey, to mean a scullery, which may not apply here, but suggests an idea. P.F.S.A.

115. SIR WALTER RALEGH.—There is, in the British Museum library, a small volume entitled "Poems, Elegies, Paradoxes, and Sonnets," published in 1657, without the name of the writer, and of much interest, as it contains a poetical lament on the execution of Sir W. Ralegh. Being comparatively unknown at the present day, it is worthy of reprinting.

"AN ELEGY VPON S(IR) W(ALTER) R(ALEGH).

I will not weep, for 'twere as great a sin
To shed a tear for thee, as to have bin
An Actor in thy death. Thy life and age
Was but a various Scene on fortune's Stage,
With whom thou tugg'st and strov'st ev'n out of breath
In thy long toil ; were master'd till thy death ;
And then despight of trains and cruell wit,
Thou did'st at once subdue malice and it.
I dare not then so blast thy memory
As say I do lament or pity thee.
Were I to choose a subject to bestow
My pity on, he should be one as low
In spirit as desert. That durst not dy
But rather were content by slavery
To purchase life : or I would pity those
Thy most industrious and friendly foes ;
Who when they thought to make these scandals story
Lent thee a swifter flight to heav'n and glory.
That thought by cutting off some wither'd dayes
(Which thou could'st spare them) to eclipse thy praise ;
Yet gave it brighter foil, made thy ag'd fame
Appear more white and fair, then foul their shame :
And did promote an Execution
Which (but for them) Nature and Age hath done.
Such worthless things as these were onely born
To live on Pities almes (too mean for scorn).
Thou dy'dst an envious Wonder, whose high fate
The world must still admire, scarce imitate."

This cannot be deemed very high-class poetry, and we wonder at this the more for its being the production of Dr. Henry King, Bishop of Chichester. The son of Dr. John King, Bishop of London, born in 1559, he held several livings in London and Essex at the time of Ralegh's execution, of which, if not actually present, he must have known the full particulars, as well as the public sympathy and general belief that it was due to Spanish influence. He died in 1669. There was another issue of the original work, with a new title page, in 1664, and a new edition in 1700, entitled "Ben

Jonson's Poems, etc." According to J. G. Nichols, in Dingley's *History 'from Marble* (I., 75), "the family of King," to which the Bishop belonged, "were of Oxfordshire, and their remote ancestry, it is said, of Devonshire."

T. N. BRUSHFIELD.

116. COCKTREE (par. 69, p. 103.)—Can Miss Lega-Weekes throw light upon the claim of Cocktree to represent the Taweland held by William the Seneschal in Domesday? Taweland paid a fee farm rent to South Tawton of either an ox or thirty pence (*Dev. Ass. ed.*, p. 1135). Is 2s. 6d. paid to South Tawton now by Cocktree or by Taw Green? The reason for suggesting Cocktree is that it appears together with most of William the Seneschal's estates—Crook Burnel, Uppraed, Cadeleigh, Boleham, Mariansleigh, and Torre Mohun—among the Mohun fees which the Mohuns got through William de Brewer. It is true that Cocktree is not named in the partitioning of William de Brewer's fees by Testa Nevil, p. 200. It may, however, have been then included in the fee of Crook Burnel. Taw Green is also not named in the partitioning, nor does the name appear at all afterwards. In the *After death Inquest* of John de Mohun 7 Ed. I., No. 13, p. 66, Cocktree is written Kaktrey; in that of 14 Ed. I., No. 23, p. 90, Catrew; in that of 17 Ed. III., No. 35, p. 31, Tokeremue, apparently a mis-reading or mis-writing of Cokeretrue.

That *Trewe St. Jacobi*, which is named first among the fees (not the manors), held of Henry de Beauchamp, Duke of Warwick in 24 Hen. VI., is not Jacobstow but Trew St. Jacob, next Exeter, to which reference was made, par. 21, p. 41, is hardly open to doubt. For Trew St. Jacob, *alias* St. James' Priory, Exeter, is named in *After death Inquest* of Hugo de Courtenay, I Ric. II., No. 12, p. 2, last entry, among fees held of Plymton Castle; and it may be observed that in the *After death Inquest* of 24 Hen. VI., No. 43, p. 229, all the 'fees of Henry de Beauchamp, excepting Trewe St. Jacob, which stands first, and South Tawton, which stands last, were held of the Honour of Gloucester. Hence no inference can be drawn from the order as to the locality of these two. They seem placed first and last because they belonged to other honours than Gloucester. Besides, what evidence is there that Jacobstow was ever called Jacobstrew? Jacobstow originally formed part of Hatherleigh and appears as Branford or Broomford among fees held of the abbot of Tavistock, in Testa, No. 310, p. 178, b. The *After death Inquest* of 3 Ed. IV., No. 19, p. 321, shews "Stowe S$^{te.}$ Jacobi manerium et advocates ecclesiae," held by Joanna, wife of Robert Stracklegh.

The mutilated extract relating to a Trew bestowed upon Thomas Cole in Edward III. time, can hardly refer to Cocktree; because Cocktree was known by that distinctive name in Edward I. time, and at the date of the alleged gift was the property of John Burnel, who held it as a fee under Mohun. There is, however, a Trew in Shobrook to which it may possibly refer, and a Trew in Black-torrington, and no doubt many another Trew in the County. But is it so certain that *Trew* or *Tre* in such names as Cocktree, Heavitree, etc., is derived from Anglo-Saxon *Treo* a tree? May it not be the Cornish *Tre* which, together with *Pol* and *Pen*, is a survival from older times? OSWALD J. REICHEL.

117. REYNELL (par. 77, p. 111).—Polwhele, ii., 48, relates that Sir Robert Basset sold Shobrook to Richard Reynell, of Creedy-Wiger, Esq., who was succeeded by Peryam Reynell, his son. O.J.R.

118. COTTELL, WALTERS, MOLFORD AND DOLBEARE FAMILIES.—The following extracts, from a manuscript of ye Armes of Devon and Cornwall, 1689, in my possession, may be of some interest:—

Cottell of North Tawton (par. 68, p. 103)—*Or. a bend gu.* crest, *a leopard argent, pelleted, sitting on a coronet or.*

Walters of Coomb (par. 80, p. 115)—*Or. on a bend cotised gu. 3 boares' heads of ye first.*

Walters, or Warter (par. 80, p. 115)—*Ar. gouttee gu. a lion ramp^t sa. thrust through with 2 swords saltire-ways arg. ye hilts or.* crest, *a crane proper eating out of a wrinkle shell or.* Hennery Walters, Esqr.

Molford (par 86, p. 119)—*Sa. a fesse ermin between 3 swans proper.* crest, *a demi swan, y^e wings displayed rising out of a coronet.*

Dolbeare (par. 67, p. 103)—The nearest spelling to this in the manuscript is De la bere. *Azu. a bend arg^t cottised or. between 6 martlets ye same.* T. G. SKARDON.

I. Corbelled treatment under the cornice course in the angle.

II. Corbelling from the spandrels of the arcading.

Exeter Guildhall Front.

119. EXETER GUILDHALL FRONT.—The present structure which masks the Guildhall replaced a front and chapel dedicated to St. George and St. John the Baptist. Over the chapel was the priest's apartment.

At the suppression of Chantries (Edward VI.) this chapel appears to have been dismantled, and the utilitarian spirit actuating the minds of the citizens, they resolved, in 1592, to supersede the mediæval chapel, now in a ruinous and decayed state, and to re-edify the forepart of the Guildhall at the city's expense.

They further appointed a committee "to confer with trusty and proper persons as to the plan and expense, and to report to the body the result." We are also informed that John Sampford was appointed overseer of the building, 18th April, 1594, and no time appears to have been lost, for on the 8th October of the same year Mr. Receiver was directed to "planche, plaister, glaze and finish the forepart of the Guildhall." The recent attempt of the Corporation to repair the fabric under review, left all too long by their predecessors for satisfactory results, has enabled those interested in the building to contemplate the decorative features of the design now that the grime and dust have been removed, revealing details not previously discernible.

The bold projecting portico standing in advance of the street line, with its arcade of granite monoliths and semicircular arches spanning the entire path and forming the line of elevation over the path kerbing, with its lavishly-treated superstructure is skilfully arranged to give the occupants of the Council Chamber abundant light, and commanding views up and down the ancient highway. All this is well-known to visitors to the old city, and our American cousins specially delight in studying this quaint fragment.

It may be desirable, before entering into the descriptive portion of this article, to cast a glance at the times during which the structure was presented to the citizens, coming, as it must, as a new creation after the ages of mediæval building, the traditions of which would be sure to linger in a cathedral and decidedly old-world city, averse to changes.

The revival of learning in Italy gave the impetus to the unfolding of the Renaissance throughout civilised Europe, and we marvel now as we look back and consider the wonderful outcome of the invitation which the Signory gave to the learned Greek "Chrysoloras" to come to Florence in 1396. It is hard for us Moderns to realise what we owe to those early painstaking Florentines, and the foundations they laid for all that came afterwards in Literature and Art. For seven centuries Greek was unknown, and when we consider that "except the blind forces of Nature, nothing moves in this world which is not Greek in its origin," we justly turn with grateful interest to that period which followed upon Dante, whose apostle Petrarch, unlearned of Greek, was the first to revive classical latin.

This revival raised Italy to the first rank in painting, in which art she has never been surpassed; and the same revival affected countries in a different way. France reflected the feeling in the influence brought to bear on her architectural designs, whilst England, with her unparalleled age of Elizabethan literature, made her mark.

Comparisons are sought to be made between the Renaissance architecture and that of the Gothic period—each has its votaries, and the older probably the more numerous—but one cannot fail to admire the "golden age" of the fine arts. Amazement follows admiration at the incomparable taste and execution shewn by the designers in every branch at that time, following on an age of stagnation. Italy led the way, and our great designer, Inigo Jones, drew his inspiration from this birthplace of the modern spirit. Milton, too, was influenced by his visit to Italy, and the bringing of Primaticcio, Vignola, and other artists to France gave that country the glorious productions of Fontainebleau, Chambord, Amboise, Chenonceux, Agay-le-Rideau! The leaven spread throughout Europe, beautifying and glorifying each country in turn; for literature, sculpture, painting, architecture, were all revivified.

It would be quite beyond the scope of this paper to attempt to trace the connection of this activity in design with the buildings of this country and of our own immediate neighbourhood. We know that John Shute, "Paynter and Archytecte," went to Italy to study architectural design in 1550, and Thorpe went to France for the same purpose, both eventually giving the world the benefit, through their published writings, of their sojourn in those countries.

Exeter, Guildhall Front.

Representation of the City Arms on the plinth under the shafts facing up

At no great distance from Exeter, near Yeovil, in the adjoining county of Somerset, is a famous house designed on the type of the plans of John Thorpe, and it is possible that when the citizens required their Committee "to confer with trusty and proper persons as to the plan and expenses" for erecting this front in the new style, that a deputation may have journeyed to Montacute to see the great works being carried on there, and to make some arrangement for the production of a design suitable to their requirements. The magnitude of the work at Montacute may be gathered from the fact that it took twenty-one years in building this great house—between 1580 and 1601—and therefore covering the short period when our Guildhall front operations would have been in progress.

There could have been no difficulty for some personage in Exeter to introduce such a deputation to Sir Edward Phelips, Master of the Rolls, the builder of Montacute, who was the younger son of Sir Thomas Phelips, of Barrington, another famous house in the same neighbourhood—who was probably chief builder and supervisor of buildings—appointed by the King in 1539 to act in that capacity in the town and Marches of Calais. It would, therefore, appear that Sir Edward's taste for building was hereditary, and his love for the art may have facilitated the acquisition of a suitable design by the Exeter deputation.

Howbeit, a design was obtained. It was on the "new lines," and modern artists have approved of their selection. No wonder, therefore, that the Corporation recently determined to preserve what was left, for the finish and sharpness of most of the original is gone for ever, and we are grateful for the better preserved portions remaining to indicate to us what the composition, as a whole, must have been.

"Restored," or preserved, as now carried out, we cannot believe but that the crowning feature of the design is lost. Numerous examples of work of this period show that a stately balustrade in harmony with the rest of the design, with a coping, broken at the main vertical lines of the design by characteristic and quaintly shaped terminals, or pinnacles, standing out against the sky in bold assertiveness, like those at Montacute and so many others of this period, completed the structure, instead of the modern painted balustrading, which is beneath criticism.

We have a key to this in the curiously wrought corbels shewn in our illustration, and which construction would be otherwise meaningless; and it is in this quaint feature that we notice in a marked degree, what one modern expert has called "a bold piece of work, but rather overcrowded with mouldings, which are not always in scale with each other and seem to have been introduced in places without adequate reason." In this feature the expansion of the shaft of the corbels is cleverly arranged, while the succession of mouldings and "echinus" ornamentation hide the artifice for securing the necessary "sailing over" of the ogee cornice course.

The elaboration of the oblique leaf-like ornamentation on the shaft between this corbel and the walls of No. 204 High Street, defies description, and, with the diminutive quoin stones placed on the other side of the corbels, leaves the art critic in a maze of questionings as to what the designer actually had in mind. He has certainly gained richness of effect, but the "*motif*" is obscure.

Carrying the eye down to a lower level, and passing the series of large windows, with their lingering mediæval treatment, but with an innovation by the introduction of the interrupted "billet" moulding surrounding them, we observe on the plain space below the sills, that the plinths under the engaged columns have mostly projecting panels with the curious strap-work elaboration of this Elizabethan period, but a departure is made in the return plinth of the side, and shews the effective representation of the Exeter "arms," the triple castle being carved in a sort of Romanesque style, the parapets being unusually heavy, the connecting walls are battlemented, and the portcullis is shewn partially lifted.

The reason for the introduction of the chevron shaped indentations on the face of the side towers is not clear. The result of the carver's skill is decidedly effective and the salient position greets the passer by.

The transition from the plain granite columns through the freestone arcading, with the corbelling in the spaces between the spandrels of the arches had apparently taxed even the ingenuity of the skilful designer, the wealth of mouldings, the frieze decorated with small shields, and the continuation of the keystones to the arches right up into this frieze course shews a fertility for adaptation rarely met with in treating so small a surface.

Our illustration shows only a small portion of all this work, a part of the corbelling to receive the plinths over, before described, the lower part of one of the keystones, with its unique treatment and the panelled work on the soffite of the arch, conveys but a poor idea of the work lavished on this division of the structure.

Much more might be written, technically describing the unusual and rich character of the work. But enough has been said, it is hoped, to show that in a country where ancient town halls are comparatively few, and never of the size and splendour of the buildings of such districts as the Low Countries, Exeter can proudly boast of one of the most picturesque and striking examples, the front of which was so handsomely produced after wise conference and deliberation by the sturdy citizens who merited from the virgin Queen the proud motto of "*Semper Fidelis*."

JAMES JERMAN, F.R.I.B.A.

120. THE FORD FAMILY. MINIATURE OF CHARLES II. WITH SKULL.—This miniature, which has the date of 1664 on the book under the skull, and "Memento Mori" as its motto, was given to a member of the Ford family (Baronet, of Ember Court) by Charles II.; also some gold studs, now lost. The family went to the West Indies (Barbadoes) during the Civil War, being royalists, and lost the link to the Devonshire family to which they belonged, or, rather, did not commit the facts to writing. Sir Francis Ford, second baronet, said his family was a good Devonshire family, and came from near Ford Abbey. Can any of your readers give ideas about this miniature which will help to trace the family? I find in Crisp's "Somersetshire Wills" that Thomas Ford, of Bagtor, Devon, who died 1610, had four sons, Henry, John, Thomas, and Edward. Might not one of these have had a son who went to the West Indies? I find "Memento Mori" on the tomb of Joane, wife of William Leare, and daughter of Edward Ford, in Ilsington Church. She died 24th May, 1663. Also that Sir John Popham held an office to do with the plantations. Thomas Ford, of Bagtor, married a Popham

Or should we look to the descendants of John Ford, of Totnes, who married Anna, daughter of William Upton. If so, where can I find the pedigree of this member of the family. He was buried at Exeter, 1637, and the line is said to have been continued at Ashburton. Can anyone give me any information on this subject. Our pedigree goes back as far as Thomas Ford, of the Ridge, Barbados; his son, Francis, married Martha Barrow, but we have no date until the birth of their son Francis in 1717. I have made enquiries at the Herald's College, but can get no further details.

Kate St. Clair Ford.

121. Drake's Monument in Werrington Churchyard (par. 82, p. 116).—May I suggest that this stone slab having the figures thereon in the costume of the time of Elizabeth, probably applies to John Cottell, of Yeolmbridge, in the parish of Werrington, his wife Beatrix, daughter of Mathew Eyre, of Atherington, and their four sons—they had daughters also. The Cottells were of Werrington, from 130? to 1675, and their burying place would naturally be in Werrington old Church. The late Rev. Mr. King informed me some years ago that the old registers had been lost. I, however, found by a transcript in the Probate Court, at Bodmin, that Thomas Cottell, of Yeolmbridge, was buried at Werrington in 1671. While writing on the question of the old registers is it probable they were removed to the muniment room at Werrington House, and may still be among old documents there, or perhaps they were deposited in the parish chest of some adjoining village during the period when the old church was removed and the present one erected. It would be interesting could these old registers be found. I may add that to the best of my belief, based upon careful research, the portrait of this John Cottell, circa 1560-80, and of Beatrix, his wife, both in Elizabethan costume, were, till within a very few years since, in the old house of the Cottells, at Yeolmbridge, together with other later members of the family. W. H. Cottell.

122. Church Plate (par. 66, p. 102).—I consider the initials of I.P. on church plate refers to Isaac Parkin, working silversmith, Exe Island, whose name appears in *Besley Directories* of 1828 and 1835. J. Jerman.

123. CHURCH PLATE (par. 66, p. 102).—Is J. H. W. sure that the church plate made by I. P. was assayed by the Exeter Office? Cripps, in his *Old English Plate*, 5th edition, has the following note:—

"A spoon bearing three marks, viz.: I. P. twice repeated for maker's mark, and on another stamp the same initials, one on each side of a castle, with the letters BAR above, and V M below it, was made by John Peard, of Barnstaple, he was buried there 15 Nov., 1680."

It would be very interesting to know more about the local assay offices. The records at the Exeter Hall begin about 1701.
J. H. BUCK, New York.

124. LETTER OF MARQUE in the possession of Sir Cuthbert E. Peek, Bart., of Rousdon.

"GEORGE R.

George the Third by the Grace of God of the United Kingdom of Great Britain and Ireland King Defender of the Faith &c. To our Trusty and Wellbeloved John Locke Jun' Commander of the Ship Marchioness of Exeter Burthen Eight Hundred and Twenty Tons and carrying Thirty two guns and One Hundred and two men or to any other the Commander of the said ship for the time being Greeting:

Whereas we are informed that there are several Pirates Free Booters and Sea Rovers which do infest the Seas of India wither you are now going: We have therefore thought fit to Authorize and empower and Accordingly Do by these Presents Authorize and Empower you to apprehend seize and secure the Persons of any such Pirates Free Booters and Sea Rovers being either Our owne Subjects or of any other Nations associated with them as you shall meet with in any of the Ports or Places or upon any of the Coasts or Seas of India or in any other Seas Whatsoever together with their Ships and Vessels and all such Merchandise Monies Goods and Wares as shall be found on Board or with them in case they shall Willingly Yield themselves:

But if they will not submit without Fighting then you are by Force to compel them to yield; and we do also require you to bring or cause to be brought such Pirates Free Booters and Sea Rovers as you shall seize or take to a legal Trial to the end they may be proceeded against with the utmost Severity of the Law—And we do hereby enjoin you to keep an exact journal of your Proceedings in the execution of the Premises and therein to set down the Names of such Pirates and of their officers and Company and the names of such Ships and Vessels as you shall by Virtue of these Presents seize and take and the Quantities and Qualities of all Arms Ammunition Provisions and Lading of such Ships and Vessels and the true value of the same as near as you can judge and also to secure and take care of all Bills of Lading Invoices and Cergners* Charters Parties and all other Papers and Writings of what kind soever which shall be found on Board such Ships and Vessels:—And We Do hereby strictly charge and Command you (as you will answer the same at your utmost Peril) that you do not in any manner Offend or Molest any of Our Subjects or Subjects of Our Friends and Allies their Ships or Goods by Colour or Pretence of these Presents or the Authority hereby granted. In Witness Whereof We have caused Our Great Seal of OUR UNITED KINGDOM of Great Britain and Ireland to be affixed to these Presents.

Given at Our Court at Saint James' the Sixteenth day of January 1802 in the Forty Second Year of Our Reign."

The great seal attached is much worn. P.F.S.A.

❖ ❖ ❖

NOTICE OF BOOK.

125. Mr. PHILLIMORE—his useful "How to Write the History of a Family," and its Supplement having been long out of print—has compiled this capital little volume,† which gives much information as to the proper modes in which genealogical research should be conducted, the sources of knowledge, and many valuable hints for those—an increasing number—persons interested in their own families or in the pedigrees of others, but who are unable to set about their investigations from want of knowledge or training. This book will put them in the right way, and if its directions are observed good work will follow. Its low price puts it within the reach of all. A new date book of the regnal years from William 1 to 64 Victoria is also given.

---

* Query, if not for cargazons—an inventory of goods shipped, a bill of lading.—EDS.

† "Pedigree Work." A Handbook for the Genealogist, by W. P. W. Phillimore, M.A., B.C.L. London: Phillimore & Co., 124, Chancery Lane, 1900. 1/- net.

Samuel Cook, Artist, 1806-1859.

From a Crayon Drawing by Field Talfourd

126. A NOTE ON THREE PORTRAITS OF SAMUEL COOK, WATER COLOUR PAINTER, 1806-1859.—Of the three portraits of Samuel Cook, known to me, the fine drawing here reproduced is the work of the late Field Talfourd, an artist whose portraits, often executed, as in this case, in crayons, are well-known in Devonshire.

Formerly the property of the late Mr. William Eastlake (who mentioned it in his lecture on Cook, read at the Athenæum, 27th January, 1881) it passed, at his death, to Mr. Philip Mitchell, R.I., the well-known Plymouth artist. In Mr. Mitchell's painting room it occupied the place of honour, and I have often heard him speak enthusiastically of its excellence as a likeness of his old friend, and of its merit as a work of art.

Talfourd seems to have seized a happy moment to portray his friend. The sensitive features, the rapt expression, the uplifted hand with pencil ready to record the inspiration of the moment, are thoroughly characteristic of Cook as his friends remember him. And Talfourd had many such an opportunity; he was often in Cook's company, formed one of the little party of friends who went on sketching excursions, arranged by Mr. Eastlake, to North Wales, North Devon, etc., and was a fellow-member of the old Plymouth Society of artists and amateurs, who met at each other's houses once a fortnight to draw and sup and chat.

The second important portrait of Cook was painted in oils by Edward Opie, from life, in 1856, some years later than Talfourd's drawing, and is now hung in the Borough of Plymouth Municipal Museum and Art Gallery. It was described by Mr. Eastlake as "an admirable likeness," and the description is confirmed by many of Cook's friends still among us, and in a striking degree by an amateur photograph which I have lately seen in the Plymouth Proprietary Library. This photograph is in a volume lettered "Plymouth Portraits," and is, I think, but little known. Underneath the portrait is written, "one of three photographs taken by J. Bryant, junr.," and it would be interesting to know if the negatives have been preserved. The artist is seated at a table, on the other side of which is placed one of his own inimitable seascapes, and a comparison of the oil painting and the photograph proves how faithful Opie was to the features and characteristics of his sitter.

It should be mentioned here that, although the whole of his life as an artist was spent at Plymouth, Cornwall claims him as her son. Samuel Cook was born at Camelford in 1806.

This is not the moment to speak at length of Cook as an artist. The only adequate tribute to his genius is to be found in the lecture by Mr. Eastlake, to which I have already referred, but the following excerpts from an obituary notice in the *Plymouth Herald*, written by Mr. George Wightwick, one of Cook's earliest friends and patrons, form, I think, a fitting conclusion to this note on the portraits of the artist :—

" Of all living artists, none, perhaps, ever more realised in his personal appearance, manners, and character, what the expression of his pictures led the observer to expect.

" His works manifested no slashing treatment of Nature, as if she had been merely suggestive of preternatural effects.

" She was his revered deity—whom to look at was to love. To do *her* honour, to regard her majestic grandeur with fearless homage, and to look into her minutest delicacies with the fondest tenderness, such was the spirit of which the pictures of Samuel Cook seem to be illustrative; and when the man himself appeared, the truth of the denotement was confirmed. . . . .

" You saw in his attenuated form and the pallid refinement of his face how the body's substance had been drawn upon by the mind's exaction. . . . . All the marks of superior mental and moral denotement shewn in the pictures of Samuel Cook were equally apparent in the presence of Samuel Cook himself; worthy of being Nature's lover, in that he was one of her own true *gentlemen*." JOHN H. RADFORD.

127. FRENCH FAMILY.—It was stated in the articles on Dartmoor, published in the *Western Morning News* recently, that there were records of the French family on Dartmoor in the reign of Edward III. Can any of your readers inform me where those records are to be found ? Any information regarding this family would be of interest to yours truly,

JNO. WATTS.

128. THE TOMB OF THOMAS CHAFE IN THE CHURCH OF ST. GILES-IN-THE-WOOD (par. 95, p. 129).—Our note on this tomb has been of interest to some of our readers. We have, in the first place, to draw attention to an unfortunate printer's error, which was not discovered until too late for correction in our last issue. The tomb is, of course, in the Church of *St. Giles-in-the-Wood*, not St. Giles-in-the-Heath.

The inscription on the tomb was given in our former note, as well as it could be made out, exactly as it appeared on the monument, but there are clearly errors. The Rev. T. M. Middlemore-Whithard has been kind enough to send us the following as a suggestion as to what the inscription might have been in its original form :—

>In
>Piam
>Thomæ Chafe
>Generosi memoriam
>ex per antiqua Chaforum de chafecombe familia in comitatu Somerset
>oriundi, eq[ue] Collegio Exon[iensi] in Academia Oxon aitium magistri,
>probitate, virtute ac ingenio insignis : qui, in apostolica fide vir
>constanter versatus, in beatâ justorum resurrectionis spe
>animum spiravit 25° die Novemb' Anno Salutis 1648
>ætatis suœ climacterico magno. (*i.e.* 63)
>eXUVIas sUas eXUIt, MeDICUs.
>Uxorem reliquit Margeriam
>filiam Philippi Burgoyne clarissimâ Burgoynorum
>prosapiâ orti, matronam religiosissimam, bonorumq' operum plenissimam,
>quæ et obdormivit in Domino, Anno
>
>à Christo nato 16 ..   ætatis suæ
>Abstulit a nobis miseris quem tempus ademptum
>abstulit e vivis mortis iniqua manus ;
>Nec cecidit solus, namque et prudentia, virtus,
>Candor, amor, pietas interiere simul.
>Teste vel invidiâ, vitâ est letho que beatus,
>Vivus erat Domini, mortuus in Domino.

Mr. Middlemore-Whithard also gives the following as a rendering into english of the elegaic verse with which the inscription concludes :—

>Him, whom t' our loss and sorrow, time has snatched,
>Snatched from the living death's too cruel hand.
>Nor did he fall alone ; but wisdom, worth,
>Uprightness, love, devotion, with him sunk.
>Blessed he, e'en envy owns, in life and death ;
>In life the Lord's, and in the Lord he died.

There is also a manifest mistake in the chronogram. Several of our readers draw attention to this, and point out that the third word in the line " e XVVIas sVas e Xvit MeDICVs" should be "e XVIt," the date would be then correct. Dr. Brushfield writes:—

"There can be little doubt of its chronogrammatic character, and that it was intended to record the year of his death in 1648, as noted two lines above it. If, however, the tall letters forming the chronogram be added together their total is 1642; this alone shows there must be an error somewhere. The Rector of St. Giles-in-the-Wood has kindly re-examined the inscription, and finds the above to be a correct transcription of the entire line. In a perfect chronogram the date, etc., is expressed by letters employed as Roman numerals, and depicted as taller than the rest of the inscription; moreover the whole of such letters must be reckoned, and therein consists the art of the compiler. The stonecutter was evidently unacquainted with these particulars, as in the first place he cut U instead of V. (In chronograms U is always converted into V and W into V V). And in the second place he has incised 'eXvit,' instead of 'eXVIt.' So that the line should be 'eXVVIas sVas eXVIt MeDICVs.'

"If these numerals be added together, they will be found to express the date 1648, the year in which T. Chafe died; as the following will demonstrate;—V = 5. V = 5. I = 1. V = 5. X = 10. V = 5. I = 1. M = 1000. D = 500. I = 1. C = 100. V = 5. total = 1648."

A copy of this chronogram as it ought to be, and not as it is, appeared in *Notes and Queries*, 5th S. ix., 215, but its locality is not stated; from there it was transcribed to Hilton's *Chronograms I.* (1882, 5), where it is translated, "The physician puts off his 'mortal coil.'" The seventeenth century was the great era of the use of chronograms in epitaphs in England, and examples are yet preserved in the churches of this county, *e.g.*, Tavistock, Wolborough, and Ilsington. In an epitaph at Widecombe-in-the-Moor, both the age and the year of death are entered in this manner. By far the most interesting example in Devonshire was contained in the original inscription on the monument of Judge Doddridge in Exeter Cathedral. Three separate chronograms recorded the year in which he died, and a fourth his age. When the monument was removed to its present position a few years since, only a portion of the original inscription was fixed, and this contains two of the chronograms; what became of the remaining stone is unknown. The entire inscription will be found in Prince's *Worthies*, and is given more correctly in the first than in the second edition.

We now give the will of Dorothy Chafe, mother of Thomas Chafe, and hope to print shortly the will of the latter, and of his sister, Pascho Risdon:—

In the name of God Amen. The three and twentieth daye of March in the yeare of our Lord God one thousand six hundred and eleven. I Dorothie Chafe widowe beinge of good and perfect remembrance thanks be to God Doe make and ordeyne this my last Will and Testament in manner and forme following Revoking and by these presents do repeale annihillate renownce and utterly make void all and every former Testament wills legacies gifts bequeathes executors and overseers in any wyse before this tyme made ordyened willed or bequeathed and this herein conteyed to stand for my testament and last will. ffirst I give and bequeath my soul to Almighty God and my body to Christian Buriall.

Itm. I give to the poor people of this City and County of Exeter the some of sixe pounds to be distributed by the discretions of my executor and overseers hereafter named and appointed. Itm. I give to the poor prisoners of the Kings Maties Gaol in the Castle of Exeter five shillings. Item. Whereas Thomas Chafe my husband late deceased by his last Will and Testament did give and bequeath all his silver plate to and amongst all his children to be allotted devided and apporconed unto them by the discretion of me the said Dorothie I doe therefore by this my Testament devise and apporcon the same as followeth. That is to say to my daughter Elizabeth Mules a Tankard of silver, dubble guilted with a cover belonginge to the same and a goblett of silver double guilted. To my daughter Dorothie Bigleston a Tankard of Silver with a cover belonging to the same p'cell guilted a goblett of silver double guilted and six silver spoons. To my daughter Pascoe Risdon a white silver Tankard with a cover a goblett of silver p'cell guilted a little trencher salt of silver double guilted one half a dozen of silver spoones with Appostles heads. To my daughter Richaward Cursane my second best silver salt double guilted with a cover belonging to the same, one ale cup of silver double guilted one little silver Bowle and half a dozen silver spoons with appostles heads. To my son Thomas Chafe a Beer Bowle of silver a little Ale cup of silver and a little goblett of silver. To my son John Chafe during his natural life I give and bequeath to him the use and occupation of my best salt of silver double guilted with a cover belonginge to the same a sacke cup of silver double guilted with a cover belonging to the same and one white Bowle of silver. And after the decease of the said John my son then I give the same salt and cover thereof the sack cup with the cover and the said white Bowle of silver unto the son and heire of the said John my son and for want of such yssue then living I then give and bequeath

the same unto his eldest daughter. Itm. I give and bequeath to the said
Thomas my son my second best fether bed p'formed and two feather
pillows the Bedstead which standeth in the Parlor Chamber with the
cannopie curtains and vallences belonging to the same Bedstead his
Father's signet of gold or gold ringe with his name in the same and all his
father's books wheresoever with a ferr chest in the broad chamber. Itm.
I give and bequeath unto the aforesaid Elizabeth Dorothie Pascowe and
Richawrde my four daughters all the rest of the linen in the great spruse
chest and in the Trunke which standeth in the broade chamber to be equally
divided amongst them. Butt my will is that my said daughters at the
dividing thereof shall deliver to my said sonne Thomas one paire of sheetes
and two pillow ties over and besides the paire of sheetes before bequeathed
to him in the p'formance of the feather bed. Itm. I give and bequeath
to my said son John my great spruse chest in the Broade Chamber. To my
daughter Elizabeth my great spruse chest in mine owne chamber. To my
daughter Dorothie the lesser spruse chest wherein my best lynnen lyeth.
Itm. I give and bequeath unto my said four daughters Elizabeth,
Dorothie Pascoe and Richaward all my best chaires with the workes thereunto belonginge my three little stools with the works to them belonging
two green carpets my two best cupboard cloths being called plate cupboard coverings all my best cushions with the window cushions that is to
say four large cushions and eleven other of my best cushions equally to be
divided amongst them by the discretion of my executor and overseers hereafter named. Also I give and bequeath unto my said four daughters all
best lynnen and wollen apparell to be like wise equally divided amongst
them. Item. I give and bequeath to my son John during his natural life
the use and occupation of my best coverlett my best pair of Curtains and
my best vallences and after his decease I give and bequeath the said
coverlett curtains and vallences unto his daughter Dorothie the younger
my God daughter. Itm. I give and bequeath unto Elizabeth Chafe the
wief of my brother in lawe Mr Robert Chafe my best kertell. Itm. I give
and bequeath unto such women servant or servants wch shall be in my
house dwellinge wth me at the tyme of my death all my old apparell both
wollen and lynnen. Itm. I give and bequeath to Margarett the wief of
Osmonde Lane two sheepe. Itm. I give and bequeath unto Susan
Brimeley two sheepe. Itm. I give and bequeath unto Florence Taylor
my servant two sheepe. Itm. I give and bequeath unto Edmond Chaffe
sonne of my brother in law Mr. Robert Chafe two sheepe. Itm. I give
and bequeath unto Thomas Chaffe my sonne a brasse crocke one little
Caldron a brassen pann a skellett of brasse commonly used to boyle sterch
in a possnet of brasse one paire of plaine brassen candle sticks one payre
of tynnen candlesticks a washinge Bason of Tynne six platters six
poddingers and six sawcers. Alsoe whereas the said Thomas my sonne
heretofore to my great griefe and dislikinge in Ryotous manner hath most
vainly wasted and consumed a farr greater parcon of my goods then my
abilitie was or nowe is able to afforde him for his mayntenance but now
hath faithfully promised unto me reformacon and amendment of the same.
Therefore my will mynde and intent is that my said sonne doe nowe give
over those ill courses and practise wch he hath used wth all other such lyke

misdemeaners and doth henceforth applye him selfe to learninge as he ought to doe. Soe as by reason thereof at the tyme of my death by the opinion and judgment of my overseers hereafter named he shall be by them then adindged and thought worthie uppon his amendment and reformation to have receive and injoyc the benefit of this my legacie hereafter named and not otherwise. That is to weeke *(sic ? wait)* uppon reformcon as aforesaid and their good opinion and judgment of his worthiness thereof I give and doe then bequeath to him the sum of one hundred pounds to be paid three months next after my death. But if by my said overseers he the said Thomas my sonne shall be at the tyme of my death deemed and ajudged unworthie to receive the benefit of my said legacie of one hundred pounds for the causes aforesaid. That then in leeyve thereof I give and bequeath to him but onely fiftie poundes to be paid him in manner as aforesaid. But if it shall happen the said Thomas my sonne to die before he shall be satisfied of his said legacie (wch God forbide) that I then give and bequeath fiftie poundes p'cell of the same unto all my childrens children wch shall be livinge at the tyme of my death to be by equall porcons devided amongst them at the time before appointed and the same to be imployed by their severall parents to their best profitt and behoofe until they and every of them severallie shall accomplish their full adge of one and Twentie yeares or be married. Alsoe whereas M$^{r.}$ Samuell Alford of Exeter merchante doth owe unto me fiftie pounds I give and bequeath the same fiftie poundes uppon the recoverie thereof unto my said childrens children to be devided and employed as aforesaid The rest of all my goods chattles debtes and ready money not before given nor bequeathed I give and bequeath the same unto the aforesaid John Chafe my sonne and him I doe make my full and whole exceutor of this my p'sent Testament requiringe and charginge him in the name of God as he will answer at the dreadfull daye of judgment that he see this my last will and Testament to be trulye executed and p'formed and I doe constitute and appointe Mr. Phillipp Biglestone my uncle and Robert Chafe my brother in law to be overseers of this my Testament. And I give and bequeath to either of them for their paynes takinge in that behalf fortie shillings a peece. Lastly my desire is to be buried in the Church of St. Olave by or neer my late husband if conveniently it may be yf not then to be buried in St Peters Church yarde neer to the graves of my deceased parents. In witness whereof I the saide Dorothie Chafe have to this my present last will and Testament set my signe and seale geaven the daye and yeare first above written. The signe of Dorothie Chafe signed sealed and published by the above named Dorothie Chafe as her last will and Testament in the presence of these ip'sons whoes names are hereunder subscribed By me Robert Chafe the elder By me Robert Hamlyn. Witnes John Paule.

Proved in London 3 Oct. 1612 by John Chafe the son and executor.

P.P.C. Fenney, 181.

J.B.R.

129. DARTMOUTH BOOKSELLER'S BOOK LABEL, 1763.—
The Rev. J. I. Dredge's *Devon Booksellers and Printers* contain but few references to Booksellers in Dartmouth during the eighteenth century, of whom W. Craven seems to have been the principal. The earliest notice of him in this work is of 1703. The following is a transcript of his Book Label, *penes me* (5¼-in. by 3¼-in.), of interest for displaying a wider range of articles sold, than in the earlier Exeter example printed at page 18:—

"Sold by William Craven in Dartmouth, who sells all Sorts of Books; with every Article in the Stationary-way as cheap as in London. He also Binds Books, & Gilds and Letters in the neatest manner.

Likewise sells Greenough's Tinctures, for curing the Tooth Ach, & Preserving the Teeth. Superfine Blacking Balls for Shoes. Stoughton's, Daffy's, Bostock's, Radcliffe's, and Fraunces's ELIXIR. Bateman's drops, JAMES's Fever Powders, Scots' & Hooper's Pills, Turlington's Balsam: Plain & Golden Spirits of Scurvy grass, Balsam of honey, Stomachic Lozenges, Jesuits Drops, Liquid shell, Godfrey's Cordial, British OIL, Cephalic snuff, Corn salve; Curious Liquids for taking out Grease and Jron-moulds, without the least hurt or detriment to either Linnen or woollen.

Jnfallible new Invented Powder, for killing the RATS, which Cats & Dogs will not touch. FINE Durham Mustard, either by the Ounce or bottle; Pomatum, Rhubard, Sulphur, Gauls, Gum, Jvory black, Japan Jnk: The greatest Variety of Mathematical Jnstruments; & Cheaper than at any shop, in the west of ENGLAND.

Books bought of me are Repair'd Gratis.

He has just receiv'd from LONDON, the most Curious and beautiful Assortment of Papers for beds, or hanging of ROOMS, ever Expos'd to the Public in this Country, and very Cheap. He gives the most ready money for any Library or parcel of Books; Exchanges Books; And lends out Second hand Books to read." T.N.B.

130. BALDWIN ACKLAND.—Can any reader give the parentage and ancestry of Baldwin Ackland, of Tiverton, who died there 1732. G. L. DUNSFORD.

Tiverton Castle, 1789.
From a Watercolour Drawing by Swete.

131. TOUR IN NORTH DEVON BY REV. JOHN SWETE (*continued from page* 126).—On Wednesday morning early I left Cross, my road leading through Torrington I proceeded on toward Bideford. The country pleasant, the bottoms and sides of many hills warmly wooded, and varied with gentlemen's seats, among which was Stephenstone another principal seat of Mr. Rolle's. The road was extremely rough, and for five miles I had nothing to do but to ascend and descend but improved as I neared the Town. The prospect also improv'd and at once open'd upon a noble expanse of water over which a bridge of twenty-four arches and six hundred and seventy feet long conducted me to its North side where I found an Inn, not proportionate to the appearance of the Town tho' possess'd by civil people and affording a very good breakfast. The Town itself (Bideford) is very neat, the streets descending a hill rather steep. On the highest point of one of them I had a most delicious prospect. A road led on in front skirted by a hedge row, which as a foreground gave a pleasing relief to the more distant parts of the picture; beneath, a wide marsh spread itself washed by the tide; on the right lay fields above which were the woods and house of Mr. Cleveland, called Tapley—beyond higher yet rose the old family mansion of the Sib Thorpes, and on the banks of the river beneath trended on the little watering village of Instow—the sands which form'd the fine Bason of Barnstaple, the seat of Col^l. Basset, and the high ground beyond terminated this part of the view—but nearer to the eye, on the left presented itself a cliff, behind which lay the town of Appledore and at the extremity close by the shore, the Dane Hubba was slain. On another aspect toward the N. West, the hills rose more elevated and seemingly in several parts artificial; on the conical summit of one tower'd a faint speck of white, in the almost indistinguishable form of a pleasure house, commanding the whole of the prospect described, and the additional one of the Bristol Channel, the surge of whose waters beat against the foundations. Just below was the house of Mr. Hewish to whom this gazebo belong'd and who had called it Cornborough, which I suppose might be a corruption of Hennaborough which Risdon says was the name of a fort in his days about this spot, and indeed there are very considerable intrenchments yet discernible, in the adjacent grounds, these

I was accidentally informed by a gentleman of the town, were called Hengist Castle, a spot, he said, famous in history for the commencement of that battle in which Hengist drove Hubba the Dane from the eminences to the shore, where he was slain and where the barrow of stones was raised over his body. (Here follows a long disertation on the Danish incursions in North Devon).

Ere I quit this town I must observe that the Church is an extremely neat one, decorated with an organ, nor can I again pass over the bridge without thinking how much the town hath been indebted to Priestcraft (a rare instance) for its erection. (The legend of the building is given in Mr. Swete's MS.)

Having now done with the Bridge I proceeded toward Tawstock to which as I nearer approach'd, ere I forded a rivulet, a fine scene presented itself, consisting of woods on the right and left, a charming conical knoll overspread with cattle, who during the midday heat were snuffing in the refrigerating breezes from the sea. Entering thro' a gateway of ancient date, by the stables, I arrived at the front of Tawstock House, the seat of Sir Bouchier Wrey which when completed (for it was now but a shell) will be one of the finest houses in the county. It is seated on an eminence, the grounds gently expanding on each side, covered with wood; beneath, the river Taw flowing through wide-spreading meadows, Tawton on the skirts of them, and hills rising pleasantly above. The Church at Tawstock however at the bottom of the lawn intercepts the middle of the view, and tho' in a great measure conceal'd by plantations, yet cannot but be considered as an object that one would have wished in a less conspicuous situation. Within however it claims particular attention, not only from its form and spaciousness, but from the many highly-wrought family monuments. On the left of the house a new road is forming, leading to Barnstaple circling through a grove with very considerable taste. But on the right above a stately wood, on a projecting eminence rose an obelisk, from whence opened to the eye a scene discriminated and varied beyond anything I had beheld during my excursion; Barnstaple at a distance of two miles had an admirable effect. Returning thro' part of the village, I descended through a wood to a Bridge and thence to

Barnstaple passing along a mound raised above the meadows, cros't the river on a fine bridge of 15 arches, entered the town where the Golden Lion received me and gave me very good entertainment.

Barnstaple doth not as many other old towns discover its antiquity, by its buildings, for they in general seem of modern date and possess a neat and handsome appearance. There are several very good streets, and in them a Church and several Meeting houses for Dissenters from the Church-establishment. The Quays trend by the river, and on the North side of the principal one rises a Portico or Colonnade of 14 Pillars, where the Mayor and corporation were once accustom'd to transact business, but where they now meet (as a person walking in it informed me) not unfrequently to pour out libations to the God Bacchus. Close by was a Religious House founded by Judael de Totness and consecrated to the Virgin Mary or rather Mary Magdalen for Monks of the Cluniae order, this was sometime a cell to St. Martin in the fields near Paris whereof, Robert Thorn was the last Prior, who for his device bare, a Roe-buck leaning to an Hawthorn tree, in an escutcheon with the word *Vert* interposed with this motto, " Caprum cum spina protegat divina potestas ; " in the garden of this Priory was found a figure of a Knight lying cross-legged with his sword and shield. The remains of this house are few, it has passed through various fortunes, for after having been a resorting place for Dissenters it hath since been desecrated and converted to the uses of receiving Merchant's goods, in short a warehouse. More to the North is a vast mount, the Keep of a castle, here built as some say by Athelstan, according to others by the above Judael the son of Alured Earl of Brittany and the lands around given him for his services by William the Conqueror. From hence there is a noble Prospect, including most of the points I have noticed before and others to the East beneath it. On the banks of the River I found an exceeding pleasant Terrace, of very considerable length, and kept gravelled in most excellent order, which however seem'd to fail in attraction for the Ladies of the town, who universally give the preference to a promade on the Bridge, which was not only a rough *pavè* without any causeway, but was very subject to the inconviences incident to every common frequented passage of cattle, carriages, etc., possibly the ladies of Barnstaple may have a peculiarity of taste, or possibly they may have a predeliction for the Bridge that was in part indebted to their own sex for its erection, for tradition hath handed it down, that when the rest of the Bridge was rais'd by the beneficence of one Stamford of London, three of its Pillars or Piers were built by the bounty of Maids. The trade of this place is of late very much reduc'd, specially in the woollen manufactory, for whereas it formerly maintained forescore combers, it now possesses but four; its other commerce consists of the conveyance of coals and coasting voyages of but littte import or advantage.

The next morning passing over another bridge I rode through the village of Pylton, at the end of which I observ'd a Pillar, 10 feet high and about 6 in circumference, standing on a rising ground on the right of the road. The people of the place could give me no account of its erection, or for what purpose it was thus form'd, all that I could learn, was that from time immemorial it had been called " long stone " and that the current opinion was, that it had been hewn out of the solid rock, the circumjacent parts having been removed. About four miles further on, I perceiv'd another of pretty nearly the same dimensions, now convertèd to the use of a Gate-post. The appropriation of these huge stones cannot at this day be ascertain'd without they are found erected on Barrows, when there can be no doubt of their being Sepulchral tokens of honour.

From the summit of an ascent which brought me to Swannon down about, seven miles from Barnstaple, I had a a most charming and extensive prospect, commanding the island of Lundy, Hartland Promontory, Bideford, Appledore, Barnstaple and the fine reach of waters spreading onwards to either town. A mile or two ere I came to Ilfracombe, a scene extremely romantic, of wild mishapen rocks, towering to the skies presented itself, soon after the church appear'd, seated on an eminence above the town, of which riding thro' a long descending street for near a mile I at length reach'd the Quay where the Inn was, and having breakfasted I under the guidance of a ropewalk was led to a hill on the S. West of the town, from whence I had a delightful view of the sea. The trade of this town consists for the most part in coasting voyages from Wales, carrying coals to Cornwall and bringing back copper and tin. Within a few years indeed hath been revived another article of commerce, which for forty years hath been unaccountably disus'd. I allude to the capture and seasoning of Herrings, which at periodical times are here taken in vast quantities, and being cured are afterwards exported to the Continent. They have two ways of curing them, one by a common pickle of salt, and a second by salting and smoking. These latter which from their colour are call'd Red Herrings are all number'd into barells which hold about 900, of the number of which an oath is taken, a duty being exacted by Government; the former, which are white, are prest as close together as possible, and the Barells hold from 12 to 1400. These are sold from fifteen shillings to twenty four shillings per barrell, but the red, tho' less in number, have produced the sum of 50 shillings. There is also a manufactory for rope and cordage, which finds ready sale among the numerous vessels which frequent this Port. The Harbour having the advantage of a Lighthouse, and being secured by a strong and handsome pier, built by the ancestors of the present Sir Bouchier Wrey to whom the Manor belongs.

Repassing part of the town, and ascending a steep hill I had a charming farewell view of the town, the lighthouse, the harbour and the wild mountainous Rocks which environ it, forming a most excentric and very picturesque scene. The road, which was rugged and intricate, brought me to the village of Berry, or Berrynherber, of no note saving that it was the *natale solum* of John Jewel, Bishop of Salisbury; here turning round by the Church, which is a very handsome building, descending into deep and wild dells, and again mounting aloft to the clouds, at length I reach'd the long scattering dilapidated village of Coombe Martyn, lying in a fine vale or coombe, and bearing the adjunct of its ancient Landlords the Martyns, whose inheritance it was many ages past, and whose principal Mansion was at Oxton from whence I set out on this excursion.*

The hills in this parish were in former times much noted for Mines of Copper and tin—tho' more so for the silver which

---

* The Rev. John Swete inherited Oxton as the representative of the Martyns of Dartington, and from the above also of Coombemartin. See introduction to these transcripts, p. 89.

it produced, being discovered in the time of Edward I, so great was the ardour of enterprise that no less than 337 miners were engag'd, from the Peak of Derby, to work there. In the reign of Edward III it yielded that King great profits towards carrying on the French Wars; from that period they were neglected till the days of Queen Elizabeth, who was presented a cup here made, by the Earl of Bath with this Inscription :—

> "In Martyn's coombe I long lay hid,
> Obscure, depres't with grosser soil,
> Debased much with mixed lead,
> Till Bulmer came, whose skill and toil
> Reformed me so pure and clean
> As richer no where else is seen."

Since that period they have been again discontinued working, till within a year or two, when another attempt was commenc'd by some gentlemen of Cornwall who however seem not very adventurous, the mines being limited to four.

The valley in which the village is situated is pleasant, its meadows fertile, and its wild hills charmingly wooded. At the Western part the tide flows up to a little Quay and vessels of small burthen moor close to the houses in a shelter'd creek.

From Coombe Martyn, slow and not devoid of apprehension from the steepness and ruggidness of the road I pass'd on to Parracoombe, a small village, the church of which stands unaccompanied by any building saving the Clergyman's. As the road often ran on the summits of very elevated hills, I was often gratified with the views of the Sea, and of the coast of Wales, tho' the latter thro' the haziness of atmosphere was but dimly seen. From Parracombe I journey'd pleasantly over downs till within a mile of Linton, from whence a rapid and stony descent brought me to the village.

Nothing can well exceed the scenery of this place. Mountains closing upon mountains, deep hollows, sometimes rude and bare, at others, soft and rich in woods, and through their gloomy bottoms rivulets ran rumbling on, and at their base extended to the sea a green-sward plain of a few acres on which was very pleasantly situated a Gentleman's house and a few fishing cotts. From the borders of the Churchyard, as I sat on a projecting rock at the close of day, my eye ran over one of the most grand, wild, and most picturesque scenes conceivable—such delicious scenery had a most pleasing effect on my sensations :—

"They lull'd my Spirit, while they fill'd my mind."

"Such sweet composure waits upon the roar
Of distant floods—or on the softer voice
Of neighing fountain, or of Rills that slip
Throught the cleft rock, and chiming as they fall
Upon loose pebbles, lose themselves at length
In matted grass ; that with a livelier green
Betrays the secret of their silent course."

The next morning I started forth in quest of the Valley of Stones, considered as the chief attraction of the place. The scenery of this spot was of a different kind from any I had ever met with, (Then follows a charming description of the wonderful valley, but too long to give here and too good to be condensed). The several parts however of its composition are so intricate, so various and so complicated, that they seemed to mock all art and to rise superior to imitation. My pencil therefore lay untouch'd ; it certainly requires a Master's hand to give an idea of the whole. Returning to the village from whence (being thro' a trifling accident unable to walk) I on horseback *descended gradation* and with the utmost caution a very bad Alpine road all but perpendicular—for the road makes many traverses so close, that at every flexture it seems almost to return into itself. As I gained an angle where the way was wider, I stop't, being enabled without apprehension to gaze around. (From this point the author describes the valley and Waters meet with Linmouth just below). There is a little public house at Linton, called *The Crown*, where the people are civil and attentive, though the accommodations are indifferent. It cannot but be an object of request that a better Inn, and even lodging-houses were built on the plain at Lin-mouth, for as the Beach is very tolerable for bathing, seemingly much superior to Ilfracombe, I know no place more likely to be resorted to—for none in Great Britain, I think, can exceed it in the beauty and magnificence of its environs.

(To be continued.)

132. REYNELL, SAINTHILL, &c. (par. 77, p. 112).—Examination of the original Letters of Administration quoted by Vivian show him to have been in error here. Instead of John Snell and Richard Reynell administering (by grant dated 14 Feb., 1675) the estate of Elizabeth, widow of Samuel Sainthill, it was that of Elizabeth (with will annexed), mother of Samuel and relict of Walter. Samuel appears to have died unmarried, administration of his goods being granted in Prin. Reg. Exon., 7 Feb., 1666, to Elizth. Sainthill, widow, "mother of said deceased." A floor slab in N. aisle, St. Stephen's Church, Exeter, confirms this: "Dormitorium Samuel Sainthill mercatoris filii Gualteri Sainthill generosi et Elizabethæ uxoris obiit 20 die Decembris Anno Dom 1666 ætatis suæ 37. Also here lyeth the body of Elizabeth Sainthill ye mother of ye above named Samuel Sainthill who died ye 2 Feb., 1675."

(Item 12, p. 112).—The marriage license dated Jany. 31, 1664, should be to Henry Reynolds and *Elizabeth* Sainthill, of Totnes, widow.   REYNALL UPHAM.

133. TORRINGTON (par. 31, p. 48).—Although no further information has been gleaned respecting the occurrence here recorded, the following report of a similar accident, that happened seventeen years earlier, is of interest as containing fuller particulars:—

" Laſt Week a melancholy Accident happen'd at the Seat of Sir Robert Barbutt, Bart., near Barton upon Trent in Staffordſhire, where a Pack of Hounds, lately preſented to him, quarrelling in the Night-Time, the Huntſman roſe from his Bed, and went into the Kennel to quiet them, but they fell on him (tho' he fed 'em every Day) tore him in pieces, and devour'd him." (*Universal Spectator*, Sept. 17th, 1743).
    T.N.B.

134. BRIDFORD SCREEN (par. 108, page 137).—It would be interesting to know whether the Bridford screen is really *in situ*, since the arcade pillar shows no sign of having been used as a corbel; one of the proofs would be whether the staircase door opens into air or over it; if it is not, that would account for the very odd spandril flaps tacked on to the side, which would be needed elsewhere.   F.W.

Clock in the Tower of the Church of St. Mary Steps, Exeter.

135. EXETER CLOCKS.—Few places probably can show more interesting relics of primitive horology than Exeter. "From the patent rolls of Edward II.," the late Mr. Britton observes, in his description of Exeter Cathedral, "it is evident there was a clock in this church in 1317. In the fabric roll under the year 1376-77, the sum of 119s. 9d. is set down for expenses '*circa cameram in boreali turre pro Horologio quod vocatur* clock—(this appears to be the earliest mention of the word)—*de novo construendam.*' The whole charge in the roll '*novæ cameræ pro horologio*' is £10 6s. 5½d. In the same rolls we find repeated entries relative to the clock. In 1424-25, two men were sent off on horseback to fetch Roger, clockmaker from Barnstaple."

Whatever its construction, no trace of the original horologe can be found, but of its successor, stated to have been presented by Bishop Courtenay in 1480, the wrought-iron framing and the great wheel are preserved, and were quite recently to be seen in the Chapter House. It is stated that this clock was made by Peter Lightfoot, but if the date of its construction (1480) is correct, this cannot be true, for Lightfoot had then been dead some years. The dial which still does duty bears a resemblance to one of Lightfoot's at Glastonbury, from which it was possibly copied. It shows the hour of the day, and the age of the moon; upon the face or dial, which is about seven feet in diameter, are two circles, one marked from one to thirty for the moon's age. the other figured from I. to XII. twice over for the hours. In the centre is a semi-globe, representing the earth, round which a smaller ball, the moon, painted half white and half black, revolves every month, and in turning upon its axis shows the varying phases of the luminary which it represents; between the two circles is a third ball, representing the sun, with a *fleur de lis*, which points to the hours as the sun, according to the ancient theory, daily revolved round the earth. Underneath it is the inscription, *Pereunt et imputantur* (they [the hours] pass and are placed to our account). In 1760 the clock was thoroughly repaired by William Howard, when an additional dial to show the minutes was provided and placed on the top of the case as shown in the illustration. The movement was re-placed by a modern one in 1885.

The hours are still struck on "Great Peter," a fine-toned bell in the north tower. This bell was the gift of Bishop Courtenay, and was brought from Llandaff (1478-1486). According to Worth's excellent Guide to Exeter Cathedral, it was recast in 1676 by Thomas Perdue. Its weight, as computed by the Rev. H. T. Ellacombe, is 14,000 lbs., its diameter at the mouth 76 inches, and its height 56 inches.

In the tower of the Church of St. Mary Steps, near by where once stood the old West Gate, is a most curious clock, which is probably a production of the sixteenth century. The dial is embellished with basso-relievos representing the four seasons. In an alcove over the dial are three automatic figures. The centre one is the statue of Henry VIII. in a sitting posture, which, on the clock striking the hour, inclines the head at every stroke. On each side is a soldier in military attire, holding a javelin in one hand and a hammer with a long handle in the other. The soldiers strike the quarters by alternate blows on two bells beneath their feet.

The three figures are termed by many Exonians "Matthew the Miller and his two sons," from the fact that "Matthew the Miller," who resided in a place known as Cricklepit Lane, was remarkable for his integrity and regular course of life. His punctuality of going at one hour for and returning with his grist led his neighbours to judge with tolerable exactness the time of day from his passing. By this the statue received its vulgar name.

Some years ago the following distich used to be current in Exeter:—

> Matthew the Miller's alive,
> Matthew the Miller is dead.
> For every hour in Westgate Tower
> Matthew nods his head.

Another old clock is contained in the tower of St. Petrock's Church, in the High Street. This timekeeper is believed to date from 1470. In the tower also is a peal of six bells, the oldest of which bears the arms of Henry V. or VI., not later than 1425.

136. LOVELACE'S CLOCK.—Jacob Lovelace was born in the city of Exeter, where, in 1766, at the age of sixty, he ended his days in great poverty, having been thirty-four

Ancient Clock in Exeter Cathedral.

Lovelace's Clock.

years engaged in constructing the monumental clock shown in the accompanying engraving. The mechanism is enclosed in an elegant cabinet ten feet high, five feet wide, and weighing half a ton, ornamented with Oriental figures and finely executed paintings, bordered by richly carved fretwork. The movements are: 1. A moving panorama, descriptive of day and night. Day is represented by Apollo in his car drawn by four spirited coursers, accompanied by the twelve hours; and Diana in her car drawn by stags, attended by the twelve hours, represents Night. 2. Two gilt figures in Roman costume, who turn their heads and salute with their swords as the panorama revolves, and also move in the same manner while the bells are ringing. 3. A perpetual almanack, showing the day of the month on a semi-circular plate, the index returning to the first day of every month on the close of each month, without alteration even in leap years, regulated only once in 130 years. 4. A circle, the index of which shows the day of the week, with its appropriate planet. 5. A perpetual almanack, showing the days of the month and the equation of time. 6. A circle showing the leap year, the index revolving only once in four years. 7. A timepiece that strikes the hours and chimes the quarters, on the face of which the whole of the twenty-four hours (twelve day and twelve night) are shown and regulated; within this circle the sun is seen in his course, with the time of rising and setting, by an horizon receding or advancing as the days lengthen or shorten, and under is seen the moon, showing her different quarters, phases, age, etc. 8. Two female figures on either side of the dial-plate, representing Fame and Terpsichore, who move in time when the organ plays. 9. A movement regulating the clock as a repeater, to strike or to be silent. 10. Saturn, the god of Time, who beats in movement when the organ plays. 11. A circle on the face shows the names of eight celebrated tunes played by the organ in the interior every four hours. 12. A belfry with six ringers, who ring a merry peal. The interior of this part of the cabinet is ornamented with beautiful paintings, representing some of the principal ancient buildings in the city of Exeter. 13. Connected with the Organ is a bird organ, which plays when required. Beside the dial is the inscription, "*Tempus rerum Imperator.*"

According to an advertisement in the *Flying Post*, June 5th, 1821, this clock was about to be publicly exhibited; and in the same publication for September 8th, 1834, it was announced that "Lovelace's celebrated clock," which was for several years was in the collection of Mr. James Burt, had the previous week been sold by auction for 680 guineas by the noted George Robins.

At the International Exhibition, 1851, it was a prominent feature in the Western Gallery. It then belonged to Mr. Brutton, who had it put in order by Mr. Frost, of Exeter, after it had been deranged for some years. In 1888, a suggestion was made in the Exeter Press that the clock should be purchased for the Imperial Institute, but nothing came of it, and the clock was afterwards acquired for the Liverpool Museum, where it remains.

NOTE.—The Editors are indebted to the courtesy of Mr. F. J. Britton in permitting the reprint of these Notices of Exeter Clocks from his valuable work, entitled, "Old Clocks and Watches and their Makers, being an historical and descriptive account of the different styles of Clocks and Watches of the past in England and Abroad, to which is added a list of eight thousand makers, *with four hundred illustrations*. London : B. T. Batsford, 1899," and also for the use of the illustrations.

136. FORD FAMILY (par. 120, p. 157).—The motto "Memento Mori" is one very generally found on sepulchral monuments, memorial rings, and the like, during the seventeenth and early part of the eighteenth centuries, so that nothing in the way of evidence can be deduced from its occurrence on the miniature and tomb mentioned, to show a connection between the Edward Ford whose daughter Joane Leare is commemorated in Ilsington Church. I have some notes on the Ford family, but, unfortunately cannot now put my hand on them, but think it very unlikely that a pedigree of this younger line will be found. It will have to be worked out from original evidence, such as wills and parish registers. The Somerset Wills of the Rev. F. Brown, edited by Mr. Crisp, is a most useful work, but, unfortunately, omits a great deal, being, in fact, a large selection from the Principal Probate Registry, Somerset House, some from the Probate Registry at Wells, Somerset, and a few from the Taunton Registry.   ARTHUR J. JEWERS.

137. PRISONERS IN DEVON, TEMP. RIC. II.—I lately came across, at the Record Office, London, a document concerning Devonshire which appeared to me very interesting, but which, owing to the worn state of the parchment, the peculiarities of the hand, and my own scant knowledge of Latin, I was unable to decipher satisfactorily. The Rev. Oswald J. Reichel has most kindly, however, corrected my imperfect transcript, and I send it in the hope that it may induce someone to explain the circumstances of the case.

The description in the catalogue runs:—*2nd Richard II., Bund. 40, No. 2, Excheq. Q.R., Ed. Courtenay, Earl of Devon, Admiral of the West and others . . . . to enquire as to goods seized, and prisoners taken, with inquisitions in pursuance.*

Sciatis quod . . . . . nos et consilium n[ost]rum monemus et . . . . . . vos, octo, septem, sex, quinque quatuor, tres aut duos . . . . . ad informandos vos sive ad inquirendum per sacramentum proborum et legalium hominum de comitatu Devon tam infra libertates quam extra per quos rei veritas memorari poterit, de quibuscunque manibus bonis aut prisonariis quae per potestatem maritimam usque portum de Plimuth infra regnum nostrum Angliae nuper agitata fuerunt, ac ad prisonarios bona et catalla praedicta in quorumcunque manibus fuerunt vel ex nunc inveniri poterunt et in . . . . . prisonarios qui in manibus Johannis Sampson, Stephani Derneford, Willelmi Cole, Johannis Hamekyn, Thomae Bull, Reginaldi Hill, Willelmi Holyman, Willelmi Noyter, Johannis Machonn, Ricardi Foley, water-bailiff, Jacobi Hore, Johannis Buvee, Thomae Langrake, Willelmi Hirward, Johannis Blakston, Johannis Charwetton et Adae Gunter nuper fuerunt vel nunc inveniri poterunt nomine nostro arrestandos et eadem bona in manus certarum personarum per nos ad hoc assignandarum ponenda, et ad omnes et singulos, quae . . . . . hac parte indicari contigerit, ad plenam restitucionem bonorum predictorum si extent, vel valorum eorundem [si] non extent tam per incarceracionum corporum suorum quam arrestacionem bonorum suorum ac capcionem terrarum et tenementorum suorum in manum nostram compellendos aut compelli faciendos. Et ideo vobis mandamus quod ad certos dies et loca, quos vos octo, septem [sex, quinque quatuor, tres aut duo] ad hoc indica veritas inquisiciones super praemissis faciatis ac praemissa omnia et singula faciatis aut . . . . . . in forma predicta et cum prefato vice-comite ad certos dies . . . .

The Commission was to 1, Courtney; 2, Botreaux; 3, Aasthorpe the Sheriff; 4, Denyle; 5, Passour; 6, Bere;

7, Thorp; 8, Bonrewe; and 9, Jayvalt. Without the Sheriff these were 8 only, and either 8, 7, 6, 5, 4, 3 or 2 were authorised to act.

Then, on a long strip, is a list of names of prisoners (that of *Willm. Wykes* occurring twice), with account apparently of their belongings and the value thereof; in one or two cases wearing apparel seems to be specified, in many the word *huch*. ETHEL LEGA-WEEKES.

138. EFFECT OF STRONG WIND ON FERMENTATION AND SPRINGS (par. 112, p. 144).—" Eolus " asks three very puzzling but interesting questions, and, in doing so, appears to put forward the subjects of them as facts. Are they really facts or merely old women's tales? Can others corroborate such statements? Referring to (*a*) " Why strong wind causes cyder to begin to work again after having apparently stopped fermenting?" Supposing it to be a fact that it does so, I should suggest the cause arises from an increase in temperature and a reduction in atmospheric pressure, accompanying a wind probably from the south-west and, perhaps, a slight disturbance in the electrical equilibrium, due both to variation in temperature, and to the friction of the air on the surfaces of the ground, trees and houses. (*b*) " Why must cyder, to be bright and clear, be bottled during weather when the sky is bright?" Is this always the case, or only so when there is no wind blowing? Probably the best time to bottle cyder is when it is not working, and that time is according to the statement (*a*) when there is no wind. A fall in the barometer would be almost certain to be followed by some evolution of bubbles of gas in the new cyder. (*c*) " Why do water springs diminish in volume before rain, and increase their flow with wind, not necessarily accompanied by rain?" The question is especially interesting, supposing the statements contained therein are correct. Do all springs act in the same way? It would be useful if readers of *Notes and Queries* would kindly communicate their experiences. Some people say that one spring flows faster and another slower during wind. Any explanation of the phenomena is difficult to arrive at. Instead of wind, it might be termed a variation of barometrical pressure. If the pressure were increasing, then the air in cavities in the earth would be slightly compressed, and so

afford storage for water that would otherwise travel towards the mouth of the spring, and thus the flow would be reduced. On the other hand, if the barometer were falling, the pressure being less, the air in the cavities would expand and the flow be temporarily increased. Doubtless in some subterranean water-courses the water is generally only conveyed by means of syphonic action. In these cases a reduction of atmospheric pressure might in some few instances cause the syphon to be temporarily thrown out of action and cause the flow to cease. From the same cause a pump, when the barometer is low, cannot suck water from as great a depth as usual.

CIVIL ENGINEER.

139. LOCAL TUNE OF CHRISTMAS HYMN.—The accompanying tune to " While Shepherds watched their flocks by night" appears to be purely local.

I should be glad to know if it is to be found in any printed collection, and also to have the original harmony of the air, if known. I understand it ought to have a violin accompaniment. It has been used for many years in Buckland Brewer Church.

ROUGE-ET-NOIR.

140. FITZWARREN OF TOTELEY (par. 111, p. 144).—The armes of Fitzwarren of Toteley are given by Pole as *Gules ten bezants and a quarter argent*. This is really Zouch, but Pole, 358, says Sir Almarick le Zouch's daughter and heir (perhaps some I.P.M. or deeds, may give Christian name) married Walter Fitzwarren. The canton or quarter would show most likely a junior branch, but, of course, he bore it as an escutcheon of pretence, which his descendants would quarter. I think Matilda, the wife of Sir Ivo Fitzwarren, was the third daughter of John Argenton.

F.W.

141. HOOKER'S DISCOURSE OF DEVONSHIRE.—The following account of this Manuscript was written by the late James B. Davidson, M.A.:—

"The manuscript (Harl. MSS., No. 5827) is in the handwriting of John Hooker, or Hoker (*alias* Vowell), and was concluded by him in 1599 (42 Eliz.) It bears the following title, 'A Discourse of Devonsh and Cornwall, with Blazon of Arms, &c., the Bishops of Exeter, the revenews of the Deneries and parsonages, and other Gentlemen.'

"John Hooker, who was uncle to Richard, the famed ecclesiastical writer, was made first Chamberlain of Exeter in 1555, and sat in Parliament for that City in 1571. He was the author of a number of works, enumerated for the most part in this MS., which was the last of the series, and contains an autobiographical sketch and notices of many Devonshire worthies. Prince has a life of John Hooker, compiled mainly from this MS., of which he says (Ed. of 1810, p. 506) : 'This book was never printed; but goes up and down the country in MS. from hand to hand; which upon the author's death was put into Judge Dodderidge's hands (who was a learned antiquary) to correct and fit it for the press.' Prince describes a copy he has seen 'wherein that great lawyer (Dodderidge) had marked many things which he thought fit to be expung'd,' and this Harleian MS. is found to contain several erasures with marginal notes, amongst which is one at leaf 52, suggesting the omission of a passage which might not be pleasing to Sir William Peryam, then Chief Baron of the Exchequer, making it little less than certain that this is the MS. which was corrected by Dodderidge, and, as Prince adds, 'delivered, by Hooker's executors, after his death to Sir Walter Raleigh.'

"Risdon, writing in 1630, made large use of this MS., and printed from it, apparently, one document (List of Places priviledged and free from Tax and Toll: Ed. of 1811, App: p. 17), if not more; and Westcote, whose work was published by Dr. Oliver and Pitman Jones in 1845, borrowed largely from the same source, adopting Hooker's arrangement and division of the subject, his ideas, even when erroneous, and sometimes his language The original, however, up to the present time, as in Prince's day, has never 'come under the press.'

"Four or five leaves are wanting at the beginning of this MS., and one in the middle, between leaves 56 and 57 of the last numbering. The first unbroken sentence relates to 'The nombre of the market townes.' From this the writer passes to 'The nombre of parkes,' the 'forestes,' the 'nombre of the sweate waters,' the 'abundance of fyshe,' and the 'salmon of the Exe.' He shews that the country is 'evill to be travelled,' then describes the 'commodities' and the 'nature of the people,' being of four degrees, the 'gentleman,' the 'merchantes,' the 'yeomanrye,' and the 'laborer.' Then comes a description of Dartmoor, mixed up with a number of charters of Elizabeth's reign, for the most part very incorrectly copied. Soon after comes thirty-one pages of biography, from which Prince and others have largely borrowed. This was in all probability the germ of Prince's Worthies. Next a few pages are devoted to armory; then a great many to the Exeter trading companies, to the lives of the Bishops of Exeter, the materials of which were worked up by Godwin in the (English) edition of the De Presulibus, and to the monuments in Exeter Cathedral Church. Next follows a list of valuations of Ecclesiastical Benefices, both in Devon and Cornwall, with tables of tenths, aud having in the margin, inserted by another hand, the names of the patrons. Then are given, incorrectly, copies of well-known charters relating to the disafforesting and perambulation of Dartmoor, and then an account of the local customary rights—existing to this day—known as the Fenfield or Venville tenures. In his account of these tenures, Hooker has fallen into a singular mistake, the origin of which has been discovered. (Devon Association Transactions, Vol. VIII, p. 410). He also gives a pen and ink sketch of his (erroneous) identification of certain boundaries existing in an Old English (Anglo-Saxon) hand in Exeter Cathedral library, and which he fancied were boundaries of the Venville parishes. In his identification of the boundaries, Hooker was followed by Risdon, and in the sketch map by Westcote—on either occasion without acknowledgment.

Next occurs the list of valuations of parishes, arranged in hundreds, for Devon and Cornwall, and interspersed amongst these, descriptions of market towns in Devon, which possibly are (now) the most valuable portions of the MS. Then comes a list of names of gentlemen bearing arms, 'by way of a

Catalogue or Alphabett,' with the names of their residences in the margin; then a list of the 'Parkes,' of the 'Market Townes,' of the places exempt from Toll or Tax, of the 'Monasteries,' and finally of the 'Castles,' with which the MS. ends."
J.B.R.

142. LOCAL TRADITIONS, NORTH BOVEY AND ITS NEIGHBOURHOOD.—Can anyone throw more light upon certain reports which have reached the ears of the rector of North Bovey, as follows?

It is said that about fifty years ago a somewhat masterful churchwarden and farmer of the parish enclosed a piece of waste land by the roadside near Bughead turnpike gate, on the Princetown road, just where the Thorne lane branches off from the main road; that he blocked up a footpath and ancient right of way which led from this point to Sloncombe across the farm he occupied, and, while so doing, removed and destroyed a flat stone which was in the waste land at the junction of the two roads. The stone was engraved with the initial letters "J. F." and old people say that these letters indicated "John Fall," and that in their youth they dared not pass the stone after dark. Who was John Fall? What was his end? Where is his stone? Can anyone throw further light on the subject?

What grounds are there for the tradition that the last, or one of the last, malefactors who in this neighbourhood were hung in chains, was executed at Beetor Cross, just where the old cross has been recently re-erected?

What were the circumstances which attended the death of the poor girl who occupies, or occupied, Jay's grave, at the point where the Heatree Common lane joins the Chagford and Ashburton road? Local tradition declares that she was a maidservant at Manaton Ford farmhouse, and that she hanged herself, and was buried at night on the down above the house. It is also asserted that the grave has been opened and no remains found. They had either been previously removed by friends, or the burial must have taken place long ago. The grave is still distinct, and the mound of earth over it is decently kept. Can anyone assign a date to the tragedy?

A parishioner assures me that a great-uncle of his was murdered at the head of the Trenchford lane, near to the spot where it joins the lane which leads to Christow. This ground will probably soon be submerged by the new Torquay reservoir. The murdered man was named either Cornish or Cuming, and the place is not very far from where Jonathan May was murdered in the year 1837.

Can anyone add to the number of these occurrences or throw further light on those now alluded to.

W. H. THORNTON.

143. LITTLE SILVER.—May I direct attention to this name of frequent occurrence in Devonshire? There are Little Silver's in Shobrook, Cadeleigh, Crediton and Dunsford, not to mention a dozen others, which suggest that the name must have reference to some feature of general occurrence. There seems every reason to accept Mr. Elworthy's suggestion as to the second part of it—that *Silver* is none other than the Latin *Silva*, a wood. But what about the prefix *Little*? We find in Domesday a Liteltune, a Litel Racheneford, a Litel Toreland, a Litel Were, and, in later documents, a Litel Totnes, a Litel Torington, a Litel Remston, a Litel Washford, etc. Now, Litel Washford, which is an outlier of Witheridge, is certainly not little, but bigger than the manor which bears the name of Washford, and Mr. Amery (Trans. Dev. Assoc. XII, 189) has stated that Litel Totnes is the part *without* the walls, Litel Torington is outside Torington, Litel Hemston outside Broad Remston, Litel Racheneford outside Rachenford. I ask, then, is not *Litel* in this connection analogous to the Middlesex *Without*, as in the name Bishopsgate Without? And may not Litel Silver mean the Wood Without, *i.e.*, the Wood outside the limits of the agricultural unit or liberty within which the villagers had rights?

OSWALD J. REICHEL.

144. REGNE LODBROG.—In Lockhart's "Life of Scott" appears a statement that in one of two note-books inscribed "Walter Scott, 1792," was "a translation 'by a gentleman in Devonshire' of the death-song of Regne Lodbrog." Can any of your readers say who this "gentleman in Devonshire" was, and where this translation is to be found? Tradition, I believe, points to Regne Lodbrog as the ancestor of the west country family of Lethbridge.

W.L.

145. NORMAN TYMPANA IN DEVON (par. 106, p. 136).—
I may state that there is a fine example, in very good
preservation, in the south wall of Bishopsteignton Church,
near Teignmouth. This tympanum, which is outside the
church, is semi-circular—or, rather, semi-elliptical in form,
and is divided into four niches, in each of which is a subject
figure, the whole representing the adoration of the Magi. The
eastern-most niche contains figures of the Blessed Virgin, and
a child and the kings occupy the three other niches. The
treatment is archaic, but strangely reminiscent of Byzantine
work. It is, I should imagine, even earlier than the western
doorway of the church, a fine example of a Norman arch.

MORRIS DRAKE.

146. LITELCOTE, COPLESTON, AND MORRIS FAMILIES.—
In the Visitation of Hampshire under Thornburgh (see
Berry's Hampshire Families), Robert Thornburgh, of Tropes,
marries Alice, daughter and heir of Simon Litlecott, of Kent,
by Jane, daughter and heir of Thomas Copleston. In Vivian's
Visitations of Devon, Jane, daughter and co-heir of Thomas
Copleston, of Luckcombe, co. Somerset, marries Gilbert
Litilcot. Which is correct, and where can I find more about
this Litelcote family?

Simon Litelcote was a younger brother of Edward, and
son of Ralph Litelcote, lord of the manor of Orchestone-moor,
co. Wilts, which manor was held by John Litelcote in the
time of Henry IV. by knight service.

William Morys, elder brother of Evan Morice, Chancellor
of the diocese of Exeter, 1594, was apparently—from his arms
on an ornamental fire-back, still to be seen at the entrance to
the Cock Tavern, Billingsgate—a member of the Grocers'
Company, and no doubt is the "Mr. Morys" whose name
occurs with George Lytelcote in a list of Freemen for 1537.
The arms are: *(Gules) a lion rampant regardant (or)*, Crest
over the helmet with mantling, *on a wreath a bird*, apparently
a cock, certainly not a falcon on a perch; the crest attributed
to Sir William Morice, his nephew. Between the mantling
and the shield are the initials "W. M." and below the date
"1586," and on each side of the shield is a pineapple. This
William, I believe, married the daughter of Simon Litelcote,
and was father of Simon Morris, who died at Newton St.

Cyres, 16th September, 1609; and the Christian name of Simon was kept up for some considerable time in the family. William Morys is also, apparently, the Morrice of London, whose daughter was married to Hannibal Slader, of Bathe, and their daughter, Johanna, married Brooking, of Newton St. Cyres (see Vivian's Devonshire Visitations). I should be glad, however, of confirmation on these points.

On 12th June, 1550, John Cowper, of St. Magnus, London, was married to Alice Litlecote, of St. Martin's, Outwich, London, widow (? of Simon Litlecote).

G. F. WINDYER MORRIS.

147. SIR RICHARD WHITTINGTON AND TORRINGTON (par. 111, p. 143).—Through the omission of two words, and the transposition of a comma, the second paragraph of my note on Sir Richard Whittington, is unintelligible. It should read as follows:—

"The note in question states that Sir Hugh Fitzwarren was of Torrington, in Devonshire, and from the will *of Whittington*, and by the ordinances of his almshouses, the author points out, we are informed that his wife's name was Alice Fitzwarren, daughter to Sir Ivo Fitzwarren, and Dame Molde" (*not Maude*) "or Matilda, his wife."

GEORGE M. DOE.

148. CHARLES CHURCH, PLYMOUTH.—In Mr. W. F. Collier's entertaining book, "Country Matters in Short," one of his subjects is "Great Towns—Plymouth," p. 124, etc. After referring to the erection by Charles II. of the Citadel there, he goes on to say, p. 124, "He at the same time built Charles Church as a sort of pious set-off to the Citadel, the men of Plymouth fully appreciating at the time his royal motives for these additions to the glory of their town." Is there any well-founded authority for this statement? If so, where is it to be found? A CHARLEY BOY.

[The statement that Charles II. built Charles Church, Plymouth, is absurd. In 1634 the mayor and inhabitants petitioned the King for permission to erect a new church on land given by John Hele, of Wembury. Letters Patent were granted, and in 1640 an Act of Parliament passed. The church was certainly roofed in in 1643, and in use, and there is an entry of a baptism in it in that year. EDS.]

149. ARTHUR FAMILY (par. 104, p. 135).—Collinson says the Arthur coat was probably borne in allusion to Robert Consul, of whom they were dependents. Now, Robert Consul bore *Gules three clarions (or rests) or*, and he married Mabel, daughter and heir of Robert FitzHamon, whilst Richard de Grenville was a younger brother of the same, so this would seem to prove that this coat was really the FitzHamon's, and that Robert Consul bore it, as he ought to have done as an escutcheon of pretence. This would not prevent the FitzHamons bearing another coat, though this one represented the Lordship of Granville. This *may* help "Quisquis" in his query.
F.W.

150. BERNARD FREDERICK TAYLOR.—Can anyone give me the parentage of Bernard Frederick Taylor, who married Frances Duke, one of the co-heiresses of Otterton, on October 2nd, 1753, at St. Leonard's Church, Exeter, and died at Antony on December, 17th, 1783, aged 59, as appears by an inscription on his tomb in that churchyard?
COLERIDGE.

151. CLOTH WORKERS OF EXON.—In the Carew Scroll, No. 520, is a coat '*Arg a chev. gu. betw. three pair of sheares sa.*' with also a drawing of a pair of shears, called the arms of the Cloth-workers of Exon, and stated to be on the old pulpit in Buckfordeslee (Buckfastleigh) Church. Perhaps some correspondent may have seen a drawing of these, and can describe them, as well as give some account of this Guild, which is one I have not been able to discover the existence of.
F.W.

152. EGGWORTHY NEW BRIDGE.—In Falcon's "Dartmoor Illustrated" the beauty of the plates is remarkable, but I should like to know why and when the bridge, which Mr. Falcon calls Eggesford New Bridge, received that name. I have gone over the *old* bridge, before it was washed away, scores of times, and have always heard and seen it called *Ward* Bridge. See Mrs. Bray's Works, etc.
W.S.B.H.

[Eggesford Bridge, Plate 67 in Falcon's "Dartmoor Illustrated," is evidently mis-named for Eggworthy Bridge, marked on Ordnance Map Ward Bridge. EDS.]

153. CHURCH PLATE (par. 123, p. 159).—John Peard, of Barnstaple, 1650-1680, silversmith, must have been a fairly large maker of silver plate for a small provincial town, for I have seen impressions of at least three sets of punches used by him. The largest is on a silver chalice cover at Parracombe Church, weight about 3-oz. 3-dwt.; it fits a chalice, date 1661. The others were on spoons, large and small sizes. There was also another silversmith, with initials " I. P.," but certainly earlier than 1828. I saw it on an alms-dish at Arlington, a rather curious shape, with arms of Chichester, and inscription in embossed letters, " Benedictus deus in donis suis et sanctis in omnibus." Much of the Church Plate in this neighbourhood is of Exeter make, the earliest being several chalices with covers, the work of Mathew, of Exeter, 1575-6.

J. F. CHANTER.

NOTICES OF BOOKS.

154. TEIGNMOUTH.*—This is a well written and prettily got up little volume. Teignmouth has not much of a history, and that little is not of much consequence, and probably it was never so important a place as it is at the present time, when its attractions of coast, river, and beautiful surroundings bring many visitors to sojourn in it for longer or shorter periods. Piratical invasions in the middle ages, and the descent of the French in July, 1690, wrought much damage on the little place. The appeal to the public, as was the custom then and before and after, for help in re-building the town, made by means of a royal letter or brief, said to have been read in ten thousand churches, brought in a considerable sum of money, which was used in the re-building of the houses after the descent of Tourville. We hope we shall not have to wait long for a similar account of another Devon town by Miss Cresswell, as pleasantly written as this one is. Our fair authoress must, however, enlist the services of someone who will prevent her making such a mistake (pp. 92-93) as to

---

* " Teignmouth : Its History and its Surroundings," by Beatrix F. Cresswell. Illustrated by Gordon Home. Small 4to, London : The Homeland Association, Ltd. 1901. 5/-.

suppose that the surname of the Vicar of Kingsteignton, who died in 1670, was Huish, it was Richard Adlam. Mr. Gordon Home's illustrations add much to the attractiveness of the book. Of the large paper edition three hundred copies only are issued.

155. DARTMOOR.†—We ought to have referred to the publication of this interesting volume in our last number. Although the subjects for illustration are inexhaustible, we doubt whether any better selection of typical Dartmoor scenes and places could have been made than those Mr. Falcon has presented us with. The reproductions of the original photographs are very good. This collection of views should be in the possession of everyone owning a large or small paper copy of Rowe's Perambulation, with which it ranges in size and general appearance, although we believe the whole of the large paper edition has been already sold.

156. BARNSTAPLE.‡—It is a great thing to have the papers on the Municipal Records of Barnstaple, by the late John Roberts Chanter and Mr. Thomas Wainwright, collected and reprinted. These appeared in the *North Devon Journal* some twenty years ago, and their value and interest were immediately recognised. We could have wished that the very competent editor had seen fit to annotate the articles, and to have given his readers more information here and there; no one could have done this better. But Mr. Wainwright has contented himself with a little re-arrangement and some corrections, and has printed an additional article on the Town walls by the late Mr. R. W. Cotton. There is, by-the-bye, a very interesting paper by this gentleman, whose decease is so much regretted, on the Beaple Tomb in Barnstaple Church, which might well have found a place in these volumes. And Mr. Wainwright! oh, Mr. Wainwright! where is the Index?

---

† "Dartmoor Illustrated." by T. A. Falcon, M.A. A series of one hundred full-page plates of its scenery and antiquities, with some short Topographical Notes. Exeter: James G. Commin. 1900. Royal 8vo and demy 8vo.

‡ Reprint of the Barnstaple Records, published by J. R. Chanter and Thos. Wainwright, with corrections and additions by Thos. Wainwright, 2 vols. Barnstaple: A. E. Barnes, High Street. 1900. 15/-.

JOHN CRANCH,
Born at Kingsbridge in Devonshire, 12th of Octr 1751 Aged 44.

157. JOHN CRANCH.—John Cranch was born at Kingsbridge, Devon, 12th Oct., 1751, and having when a youth evinced unusual quickness and understanding and great skill in writing was engaged by Mr. John Knight, a land surveyor of Axminster, the steward of Lord Petre's estates, as a writer in his office at a salary of fifteen pounds a year. While there the Rev. William Sutton, a Roman Catholic priest, gave him instruction in Latin and other branches of learning, to which, as well as to his employment with Mr. Knight, he attended with the greatest diligence. The beauty, rapidity and correctness of his writing were extraordinary, and in addition to his severer studies he made considerable progress in music and drawing. His peculiar talent for the last mentioned art was manifested in a circumstance quite consonant with his decisive and original style of thought and action. During the absence of his employer from the office on a winter's day Cranch amused himself in front of the fireplace by executing a design on the panels of a large oaken chimney-piece with the pointed end of a red-hot poker, producing an effect by the boldness of style and execution which was greatly admired. At the end of five years Cranch engaged himself with Mr. Simon Bunter, an attorney in Axminster, who gave him his articles of clerkship and so highly esteemed his character that he left him by will more than two thousand pounds and made him his trustee and executor. Cranch then settled in London, where, for a time, he followed his profession with such assiduity that if it had been continued would have secured him a handsome independence. He published a work on the " Economy of Testaments " (1794) which attracted attention, but prosperity became his ruin, and his taste for the fine arts led him to neglect his business and to desert the interests of his clients for the more agreeable occupations of music and painting. The latter he is said to have practised under the instruction of Sir Joshua Reynolds, who used to say that Cranch was the best critic and possessed the greatest judgment in painting of any man he ever knew. His picture of the death of Chatterton, and others of less consequence attracted public notice. He also painted some portraits. The D.N.B. says that he failed to get a place on the walls of the Academy, but he was more successful at the Society of Artists to which he contributed " Burning of the Albion Mills," and at the British

Institution to which he contributed eight pictures in 1808. There is a picture of his at South Kensington. He also executed many poker pictures, but stability of character was not one of his qualifications, and painting was neglected for the still more hazardous profession of authorship. He projected a series of periodical essays in the style of the *Spectator*, some few of which were published, but not even the title of them has survived. He was a diligent transcriber of remarkable epitaphs, of which he had a large manuscript collection, but which failed in teaching him the folly of a misspent life and the misery of its close. In 1811 he published " Inducements to promote the Fine Arts of Great Britain by exciting Native genius to independent Effort and Original Design." The versatility of his genius and the variety of characters with whom his talents brought him into association led him into irregularity of habits, and a deficiency of right principle suffered him to become the slave of intemperance. He lived many years at Bath, and died there unmarried in the year 1823, in his seventieth year, in almost the extreme of poverty and wretchedness, too indolent to exert himself for his own support, and too proud to accept relief when proffered by the hands of those who had known him and esteemed his character in early life—a melancholy instance of the little value of natural genius and elegant acquirements, when not under the correction and control of proper principles or sound judgment. It is probable that John Cranch was related to John Cranch, of Plympton, died 1772, who assisted Reynolds so materially. His father, also John, was of Modbury. J.B.R.

158. OXENHAM TOMBSTONE.—The following extract from Epistolæ Ho-Elianæ, The Familiar Letters of James Howell, may be of interest to readers of *D.N.&Q.* Can any one say where the tombstone referred to is now? W.L.

"As I passed by St. Dunstans in Fleet-Street the last Saturday, I stepped into a lapidary or stone cutter's shop to treat with the master for a stone to be put upon my father's tomb; and casting my eyes up and down, I might spy a huge marble with a large inscription upon't, which was thus to the best of my remembrance:

Here lies JOHN OXENHAM a goodly young man, in whose Chamber as he was struggling with the pangs of death, a bird with a white breast was seen fluttering about his bed and so vanished.

Here lies also MARY OXENHAM the sister of the said John who died the next day and the same apparition was seen in the room.

Then another sister is spoke of.

Then, Here lies hard by JAMES OXENHAM the son of the said John who died a child in his cradle a little after, and such bird was seen fluttering about his head, a little before he expired, which vanished afterwards.

At the bottom of the stone there is : Here lies ELIZABETH OXENHAM the mother of the said John, who died sixteen years since, when such a bird with a white breast was seen about her bed before her death.

To all these there be divers witnesses both squires and ladies, whose names are engraven upon the stone. This stone is to be sent to a town hard by Exeter, where this happened.

Were you here, I could raise a choice discourse with you hereupon So hoping to see you the next term to requite some of your favours, I rest your true friend to serve you. J.H.

Westminster 3 July 1632.

[The question of the whereabouts of the stone seen by Howell has been often discussed. See Notes and Queries at various times—Devon Assoc. Trans., vol. XIV, 1882, p. 221; vol. XXVIII, p. 90 ; vol. XXXII, p. 85. We insert the note of W.L. in the hope that some of our readers may be able to help. EDS.]

159. SAMUEL FARLEY.—Can you tell me anything about Samuel Farley, a printer in Exeter in 1689-1702. He was located over against Guildhall, later owned by Gilbert Dyer, now a heap of ruins (1901), and in May, 1723, he started the *Exeter Journal*. He left for Bristol about 1724, and his son Edward took the paper. Sam went in with his brother Felix on the *Bristol Journal*. In 1713 Samuel Farley started the *Bristol Postman*, and on his death his niece Sarah, daughter of Felix, took the paper. Now, is there any way of getting at the family record of these men, who their father was, who he married, and the names of other children. F.

160. CELT FOUND NEAR THE TAMAR.—On 25th February, 1864, Mr. Richard Peter, of Launceston, exhibited to the Society of Antiquaries a drawing of a bronze socketed celt, 5 inches long and 2 inches broad, with three parallel ribs on the flat surface. It was found in 1857 on the surface of a field about 200 yards from the River Tamar by a man cutting grass, whose scythe struck against it. Can anyone say whether it is preserved in any public collection, or where it now is ?

T. CANN HUGHES, M.A., F.S.A.

161. ROLLE FAMILY RING.—On 10th March, 1864, the late Edmund Waterton, F.S.A., exhibited to the Society of Antiquaries a gold signet ring, with a coat of arms, *on a 'fesse dancetté between three billets, each charged with a lion rampant as many roundels, in chief a mullet for difference.* Within the ring were the initials C.R. It was suggested this related to Christopher Rolle, third son of George Rolle, the purchaser of Stevenstone. Where is the ring now? Can it be procured for illustration in *D.N.&Q.*?

T. CANN HUGHES, M.A., F.S.A.

162. EGGWORTHY NEW BRIDGE (par. 152, p. 190).—It was a curious mistake of Mr. Falcon to call an old bridge over the River Walkham, I believe, originally the Stour (see Risdon) always known as Ward Bridge, the Eggesford New Bridge. Sir M. Lopes built a shooting-box near some years ago on an estate called Eggworthy, but the bridge never bore that name. Ward Bridge, which had resisted the floods for 300 years, was a beautiful old bridge, beautifully situated. The County Bridge authority widened it, and by so doing weakened the foundations, the consequence of which was the that extraordinary flood in July, 1890, carried it away, and the present new bridge had to be built. W. F. COLLIER.

163. DAVID LONG, SHERIFF OF DEVON, 1704.—In the MSS. of the Duke of Portland, preserved in Welbeck Abbey, and calendared in the 15th Report of the Hist. MSS. Com. (App., pt. iv.), is the following anecdote of a former Sheriff of the County:—

"We have a comical High Sheriff here, Mr. David Long, who was bred a farmer, but with £30,000 or £40,000. He is very honest and generous, and drinks to the Queen (Anne) by the name of 'the good old gentlewoman, two times with all my heart.' He does not drink out of bottles, but pulchers as he terms them, that is great jars of claret, and that is his usual way of living." (219-20).

This is transcribed from a letter addressed by "Robert Price, Baron of the Exchequer, to (Robert) Harley, at Whitehall." David Long was Sheriff in 1704, the third year of the reign of Queen Anne. T.N.B.

164. SQUIRREL AS A FIELD NAME (par. 114, p. 14).—
In a recent issue Mr. Amery mentions a field in connection
with Burleigh Dolts called Squirrel, which he considers
a puzzle. In the manor of Hulham, within the parish of
Withecombe Raleigh, two adjoining fields (Nos. 566 and 601
on the Tithe Map) also bear the name of Squirrel, or, as
it is locally pronounced, Scörrel. It has seemed to me that
Scörrel may be the local pronunciation for Score-hill, a name
which is found thus written in the parish of Gidleigh. In this
connection *score*, which appears also in the word landscore,
may be the hard form of the better known *share*, just as in
field names the word *scot* seems to be the hard form for *shot*.

OSWALD J. REICHEL.

165. BOUNTIES TO SEAMEN AT ASHBURTON, 1793.

Ashburton, February 16th, 1793.

The undersigned Inhabitants of the Town of Ashburton
desirous of shewing their attachment to their King and
Country by promoting the present armament:—

Have resolved to give such of their Parishioners who shall
enter with Captain Hill or Lieutenant Cuming of this place
or with any other Officer of his Majesty's Navy on or before
the first day of March next, the following Bounties (in
addition to the Allowance made by Government) viz.:

To every able Seaman two Guineas.

To every ordinary Seaman one Guinea and half.

To every able bodied Landman one Guinea.

The Money to be paid by the Ashburton Bank upon the
production of a proper Certificate. And the Surplus of the
Subscription which shall be raised and not be paid by way of
Bounty, with the Interest to accumulate thereon till the Close
of the War (after deducting the incidental Expences) to be
divided among the Widows and Children of any such Seamen
who may be killed during the War.

They likewise take this Opportunity to declare that
considering the present War with France as both unjust and
unprovoked they would see with Pleasure a Subscription
begun in any of the great Cities of the British Empire for the
purpose of assisting his .... Majesty to carry it on with vigour,
and to avenge in a signal manner the Cause of Justice and
humanity which has been so cruelly insulted.

A Consciousness that it would come with greater weight from a more considerable place prevents their beginning such a subscription but they will chearfully follow if any of the Great Towns will take the Lead. Resolved that

A Committee be immediately named, any five of whom shall constitute a Meeting, and that Copies of these Resolutions signed by Mr. Abraham as Secretary shall be transmitted to the Chancellor of the Exchequer, The first Lord of the Admiralty and the Secretary of State for the Home Department, and that the same shall be published in the London, Sherborne and Exeter Papers.

Richd. Eales	Joseph Sunter	T. Metherell
Jas. Mogridge	Edwd. Bovey	Richd. Litterell
Revd. J. Palk	Edwd. Bovey, junr.	Wm. Ireland
Thos. Soper	Mrs. Caunter	Jas. Bidgood
Richd. Preston	Ste. Taprell	Jno. Mitchell
Richd. Berry	Wm. Monday	Robt. Dawe
Mrs. Winsor	Geo. Monday	Richd. Hill
Miss Woodley	J. Higgins	Wm. Cuming
Mrs. Jerman	J. Higgins, junr.	Geo. Winsor
Miss Adams	Robt. Pitts	Henry Gervis
Wm. Bickford	Jno. Stenteford	Revd. J. White
Jas Lloyd	Robt. Vans Agnew	Thos. Tucker
Henry Callard	Walter Palk	V. Langworthy
Miss Lowndes	Rev. R. V. Willesford	T. S. Cookesley
Joseph Widger	John Caunter	Saml. Tanner
Wm. Widger	Wm. Soper	T. Serle
Walter Palk, junr.	Peter Cockey	J. Hurst, junr.
John Winsor	Miss Dunning	T. Brown
Rev. Wm. Cockey	Wm. Cookesley	T. Ireland
Solomon Earle	Henry Lyde	T. Widdecombe
Wm. Sunter	Allen Perring	Richd. Widger
Richd. Soper	J. Gribble	Richd. Glanville
Wm. S. Young	Jas. Foster	Jno. Taprell

Robt. Abraham, junr., *Secretary.*

FRANCES B. TROUP.

166. A NOTED PLURALIST.—Samuel Partridge, M.A., Rector of Skyness, 1780; *Vicar of Cockington,* 1781; Rector of Leverton, 1782; Chaplain to the Bishop of Bristol, 1785; Vicar of Boston and Surrogate, 1785; Justice of the Peace, 1787; Chaplain to Brownlow, Duke of Ancester, 1792; Chaplain to Peter, Lord Gwyder, 1797; Vicar of Wigtoft cum Quadring, 1797; Fellow of the Society of Antiquaries, 1800; Proctor in Convocation, 1806 and 1807; and Chaplain

to the South Lincoln Militia, 1809. He is also said to have been Chairman of the Quarter Sessions for the hundreds of Kirton and Skirbeck, and to have died in 1817. Is the Cockington referred to the parish lately amalgamated with Torquay, and, if so, is anything known of him during the time he held the living? A complete list of the vicars of Cockington would be of great local interest. A. J. DAVY.

167. LICENCE FOR PAPISTS TO LEAVE THEIR HOMES, 1679.—By statutes of Queen Elizabeth and King James I., Papists were forbidden to depart above five miles from home without licence from the Privy Council, or under the hands and seals of four Justices of the Peace. The licence quoted below, granted to certain members of the Arlington branch of the Chichester family, shows that the statute was by no means a dead letter in North Devon. The Arlington branch of this family professed the Roman Catholic religion until about the year 1795, when John Palmer Chichester read his recantation in Exeter Cathedral. This gentleman was the great grandson of the John Chichester to whom the licence was granted, and great grandfather of Miss Chichester, of Arlington Court, the present representative of the family.

" Devons:

Forasmuch as John Chichester of Arlington in this County of Devon Esq. did come this day before us and did take his corporall oath that Ursula his wife and Prudence his daughter are in a very ill condition of health and strength and that they are advised by there Physitions for the recovery thereof to make use of the Bath Waters. We, therefore John Gifford, Richard Coffin, Edward Lovett and Arthur Ackland Esq^{rs} foure of his Maj^s Justices of the Peace for this County do hereby upon the request of the said John Chichester and by Virtue of a Statute made in the 3^d yeare of King James of blessed memory, so farr as in us lies licence the said John Chichester together with Ursula his wife and Prudence his daughter and such Servants as are for there necessary use not exceeding the number five to travell the direct way from Arlington where they now dwell to the City of Bath in the County of Somersett so as there journey be not of longer continuance than two months after the date hereof and then to return to there said habitation of Arlington aforesaid. Praying you and every of

you nott to molest or trouble the said John Chichester or Company in there said travell but to permit and suffer them peaceably to pass so as they show themselves in no respect offensive to his Maj^{ts} Laws. In Witness whereof We have hereunto set our hands and Seals the 18th of June in the 31st year of his Maje^s Reign, Anno Dom^i 1679.
To all Justices of the Peace
Mayors Bailiffs Con^{bles}
and all other his Maj^{ties}
officers and Ministers whatsoever.   THO^s WAINWRIGHT.

168. BARNSTAPLE MECHANICS' INSTITUTE (par. 74, p. 108).—The Mechanics' Institute in Barnstaple was started on Oct. 30th, 1830, with Mr. S. Westacott, Treasurer, and Mr. J. Barry, Secretary. It ceased to exist on Oct. 19th, 1837.

The Barnstaple Literary Scientific Institution was established in March, 1845, mainly through the influence of the late Mr. W. F. Rock, with the assistance of the late Earl Fortescue. Mr. Rock from first year subscribed £100 per annum providing free admission for a hundred members and students.

The first President was the late Rt. Hon. Earl Fortescue, the late Mr. J. R. Chanter was the first Secretary, and the late Mr. H. K. Thorne the first librarian.

Mr. W. F. Rock was elected President on the death of the late Earl Fortescue and continued so until March 27th, 1873, when the present Earl Fortescue was elected and who continued to occupy the position until 1888, when the institution was merged into the North Devon Athenæum. The library, which was a good one, was removed from the house in High Street to the North Devon Athenæum, where Mr. Rock had provided a permanent local institution, devoted to literature, science and art, for the benefit of Barnstaple and district.

When Mr. J. R. Chanter retired from the Secretaryship he was followed by Mr. J. G. King, who was succeeded by Mr. Richard Cotton, Mr. J. B. Pascoe, Mr. J. Dunstone aud Mr. W. H. Toller. In 1872 Mr. Wainwright was appointed Secretary. He discharged the duties until 1888.

Mr. H. K. Thorne, Librarian, resigned in 1855, when Mr. Knill was elected Librarian and continued so until the Institution was removed to the Athenæum, where he also discharged the duties until 1890, when Mr. T. Wainwright was appointed to that position.   J.H.

HIC · IACET · HENRICVS · ROBERTI
1650
PARSONII · FILIVS · QVI · EXIIT · ANNO
ÆTATIS · SVÆ · CLIMACTERICO
ΔΕΥΤΕ ΡΟΠΡΣΤΣ

Brass, Sidbury Church.

169. TWO INTERESTING EPITAPHS.—In Sidbury Church, is the following inscription on a small brass, as shown in the illustration:—
1650.
Hic iacet Henricvs Roberti Parsonii filivs qvi exiit anno ætatis svæ climacterico. ΔΕΥΤΕΡΟΠΡΩΤΩ.
What age does *climacterico* represent? and the Greek word?

In Holy Trinity Church, Exeter, commemorating a former Rector:—
M. S. Thomæ Wight, A.M. S. Sta Trinitatis Exon Rectoris, nec non Societatis militans ibidem sacellum; qui obijt 11º die February, Anno Ætatis 40. Dom. 1682.
Fortis eras Probus (et quod rarum est) Fidus amico, Doctus item (sed quod rarus est) Humilis.

Will some correspondent contribute translations? Q.R.

170. CHARLES CHURCH, PLYMOUTH (par. 148, p. 189).—The editors say the statement that Charles II built Charles Church, Plymouth, is absurd. It was an old tradition told me in my youth that Charles II took care to have guns in the Citadel, commanding the town, in memory of the part the town took in the war against his life. Also that he built Charles Church as a pious counterblast. This part of the tradition appears to be incorrect, but I do not see the absurdity of it. It was a tradition, and traditions even have some interest. I was brought up in it. W. F. COLLIER.

[We are pleased to insert Mr Collier's note. Traditions are frequently of the greatest value and interest, but we should hardly call this a tradition. It was only gossip. The slightest enquiry would have shown that the merry monarch could have had nothing to do with the building of Charles Church. A real tradition in connection with it is that the spire was originally a wooden one. This is now proved to be the case. The present stone spire was erected in 1766. EDS.]

171. RALEIGH OF FARDELL. P.C.C. 20, Cobham.—Will of George Raleighe of ffardel, Co. Devon, Esq. To be buried where yt please God to visit me with death. To poor of Withecombe Raleigh 20s. To poor of Cornwood where ye house of ffardel standeth 20s. To poor of Littleham where my other house is in Exmouth 20s. To wife Dorothie a round table which her father Mr. Walter Snedall gave me. To said wife all corn standing in my barton of ffardell and all oxen horses &c. and the use of the household goods for life, but she to give bond to George Blake *als*. Raleigh the son

of Margaret Blake, of Withecombe Raleigh or his assigns for all such goods to go to said George Blake or in default his children if he have any within six weeks after the death of the said Dorotye and if said Dorothie refuse to give such bond then said goods to go immediately to the said " George Blake *als* Raleigh " or his assigns. To Henry Snidall my shippe called the " Lion " of Exmouth with all furniture belonging. To said Henry a bed and bedsteed &c. with one Island chest and a fflanders chest in the same chamber over the hall at Exmouth and the hall furniture, all brewing vessels great and small two great andirons with garnish of pewter and all wood and iron at Exmouth. To Margaret Drake and Thomas Drake of Harpford £50. To Thomasine Hodder my woman servant £3. Mawdlin Rogers my woman servant 40s. Margaret Medland ditto 40s. Itm. I give to George Blake *als* Raleigh the *daughter* (*sic*) of Margaret Blake of Withecombe Raleigh all lands rents &c. in Ilsington, Newton Abbot and Newton Bushell as follows. All those closes of land called Clappes Park now in the tenure and occupation of Wm Binmore, a tenenement in Newton Abbot in occupation of John Granfield, a tenenement in Newton Abbot in occupation of John Seller, a tenement in Newton Bushell in occupation of Andrew Ray which said tenements and closes my brother John Raleigh purchased of Nicholas Carswill Esq. and a meadow of the ffeoffees of Wolborough aud one other meadow of Philip Stidson and Jone his wife all of which I give and bequeath to George Raleigh *als* Blake the sonne of Margaret Blake of Withecombe Raleigh. The said George Blake *als* Raleigh sole executor. Dated 25 Mch. 1595. Witnesses : Robt. Hill, John Gribble. Pvd. 18 Mch. 1596. P.C.C.

REYNELL UPHAM.

172. THE COPY OF THE WILL of George Ralegh, the elder step-brother of Sir Walter, is of much interest, inasmuch as it serves to corroborate some of the important points of information concerning the Ralegh family, contained in my paper " Raleghana " that appeared in the *Trans. Devonshire Association*, vol. xxviij., pp. 272-312.

It is noteworthy that he left similar amounts to be distributed to the poor of Withycombe Raleigh, where he occasionally resided and probably died ; and was interred in the Parish Church. To the poor of Cornwood, in which parish the ancestral home of Fardel was situated. And to the "poor of Littleham where my other house is in Exmouth." This last named residence is now known for the first time, as hitherto his sole connection with that parish has consisted in the knowledge of his having served the office of Churchwarden in 1586.

The will is dated March 25th, 1595, and was proved on March 18th, 1596 (7), he having died on the 16th of the previous month, according to the inscription on the tombstone in the churchyard of the Church of St. John in the Wilderness, as copied by Dean Milles in the 18th Century. (The stone was removed probably when the greater part of the church was taken down many years since.) It demonstrates that his wife "Dorothie" survived him; and that she was the daughter of Walter Snedall, "of Exeter," according to Westcote. In the Holland pedigree of the Ralegh family in *Harl. MS.* 1500, he is named John Snedall. It is curious that Mary, George's step-sister, married Hugh Snedall at St. Mary Arches Church on Oct. 13th, 1563.

Some authorities affirm Dorothy to have been his second wife, but whether or not this be correct, it is certain he left no legitimate issue. "George Blake, *alias* Raleigh, the son of Margaret Blake of Withecombe Raleigh," was in all probability his illegitimate son, who, very soon after his father's death married Margaret Drake, apparently the one of that name in the will who was left a legacy of £50. He evidently assumed the name of Ralegh and in that name his six children are registered in the parish books of Withycombe Raleigh.

Another item in the will deserves notice, viz., "To Henry Snidall (*sic*) my shippe called the "Lion" of Exmouth with all furniture belonging." It is known that George's father had some interest in shipping, and in the time of Q. Mary possessed a bark. It was this circumstance that led Edwards (in the *Life of Sir W. Ralegh*, I, 12) to conjecture this as the reason of his leaving Fardel for Hayes Barton, so as to be nearer the sea. George's name appears in a list of "Sea Captaynes" on Jan. 5th, 1585-6. As a shipowner he is alluded to in a remarkable letter from Sir F. Walsingham to the Mayor and Aldermen of Exeter, dated Nov. 26th, 1588, preserved in the City Records, that is well worth transcribing here:—

"I am geven to understand that at suche tyme as ther was geven this last sommer for the settings forthe of certain shippes out of your Citie yet apperethe that emongst others you tooke a man of warre, beinge a shippe appertayning unto Mr. George Rawley, making agreement wth him for the furnishing and setting of her fourthe for her Maties Service, but now you refuse to make him satisfaction for the same." Prays them to pay him without more delay. "I have saved him from acquayntying their Lordships wth your slackness herein uppon the perswasion I have that this my own letter shall sufficientlye prevaile wth you." (*Notes and Gleanings*, ij, 106.)

T. N. BRUSHFIELD, M.D.

173. COAL IN DEVONSHIRE.—The following advertisement appeared in "Andrew Brice's Old *Exeter* Journal; or the Weekly Advertiser." Exon, Friday, August 16th, 1754":—

"THE PROPRIETORS of the Work, in carrying on the present Search after **Coal**, near this City of EXETER, were quite sensible of what Advantage such a Discovery would be to this Age, as well as to Posterity; which did induce them to begin this laudable Undertaking, But, after Twelve Months Tryal, the large sums they had expended as *private Adventurers* did somewhat deter them from *so vigorously pursuing* such a favourable Prospect of Success, as perhaps some may think might have been done. But if they look back on the last long cold Winter, they will find, that in Hail, Rain, Frost, or Snow, the work was carried on both Day and Night; which did not show a Want of Spirit in either Adventurers or Workmen. However, the Proprietors, having taken into consideration the Arguments and Proposals publish'd in Mr. *Brice's* Journal, and finding the Inhabitants of both City and County adjacent thereupon ready and willing to aid and assist in raising up **this valuable Fossil**, which, if obtained, can be deem'd no less than A TRIPLE BLESSING: Therefore, the Proprietors do hereby acknowledge, they are willing to accept the Offer made them, in the Manner and Form which has been set forth, viz.:

"*For every Guinea raised by Subscription, they will in Return, oblige themselves to render Four Quarters of Coal (as soon as it is in their power to do so) containing the same Measure as at the Kay of Exon; and so in proportion to every other sum subscribed.*

"And the Proprietors do hereby also acquaint the Public, that a Subscription is already opened, and that Books are placed at *Moll's and Swale's*, Coffee-houses, and also at Mr. *Barnabas Thorn's*, Bookseller, in the *Churchyard*, *Exon* ; and they also give Notice, that the said Mr. *Barnabas Thorn* has accepted of the Office of TREASURER for that Purpose.

"And that, upon Receipt of the Subscription Money, he will deliver to each Subscriber a Ticket, which shall intitle the Bearer to the Proportion of Coal Subscribed for.

"And further : The Proprietors do consent, and agree, that every Subscriber shall have their Quota of Coal according to their Subscription, previous to *any Sale whatever*. And to Convince, and fully satisfy, the Subscribers that the Money raised by Subscription shall be used and wholly expended, in their *'future* Search, they do also consent, that every Gentleman subscribing the sum of Five Guineas (whose Proportion of Coal will be Twenty Quarters) shall have Access to, and Free Liberty, weekly, or monthly, to inspect and audit their Papers and Books of Account.

   By Order of the Proprietors
      J. TAYLOR
      Clerk to the Company.

Is anything known of the situation of the Mine or the promoters of it ? What was the weight of a "Quarter" of Coal according to the Measure of the *Kay of Exon ?*

          A. J. DAVY.

174. TOUR IN NORTH DEVON BY REV. JOHN SWETE (*concluded from page* 175).—On Sept. 11 (1789), taking a guide to conduct me over the downs, I quitted Linton and proceeded to Paracombe on my way to Castlehill, the seat of Lord Fortescue. Quitting the Ilfracombe road I attain'd the high ground of Rowleigh Common, and after proceeding over it for three miles, I perceiv'd on the West of the track, a large Burrow which had been opened in several places, and was in diameter about 100 feet, its situation was contiguous to the lonely farm of Carbrocken burrow, deriving its name from the adjoining tumulus. From thence I mounted Bratton down, where I had the finest riding imaginable, the turf as smooth as that of a bowling green and nearly as level. The circular survey of the circumjacent country was extensive, including Youlston, the seat of Sir J. Chichester, on the N.W. and nearer Arlington,

Mr. Chichester's, the tower of Bratton, Hartland point, and toward the East receiving its bounds from Exmoor. On many of the eminences I discovered Beacons, at times several together; all of them in the form of Burrows, saving that they were not conical, but having, as it were, the cone inverted, being hollowed out in the middle. Some of them were of considerable magnitude—being in diameter no less than 50 or 60 feet. To what uses these hollows were applied, I am at loss to say, excepting as fire beacons to give a wide alarm of an enemy.

Having quitted this beautiful plain, I rode up a steep ascent to the top of Mockham down, where I discovered a Danish encampment, the vallum of which was very thick and high, and the fosse, in particular parts deep. Its diameter was 300 feet and its situation was such as to give it considerable strength, and the view commanded a vast extent of country. Four miles from thence brought us to Castle Hill, The gardener attending. I rode through Lord Fortescue's grounds, passing before the front of the house, of no extraordinary beauty, very little taste hath been displayed in spreading out before it a wide space of gravell'd terrace. I was pleased with the information that this old stile was to be abolished, and that the lawn was to ascend gradually with Nature's best embellishments to the front door. I visited the dog-kennel situated on the beautiful slope of a hill, and after skirting a wood and ascending a hill, arrived at a Spa, a chalybeate water of considerable strength and colour. The middle front of this building is encrusted with old roots of trees and moss in good stile, and the cell is of similar construction, having in its center a reciptacle for the mineral water. (Mr. Swete continues to give a full description of various points in the Park and woods, he mentions the Triumphal Arch and a Temple dedicated to the memory of Earl Clinton, by his brother, the late Lord Fortescue, in the the year 1772; also the Hermitage, which he remarks "had been constructed with taste and propriety.")

In the way to South Molton I past a fabric of elder days —the ruins of which denoted former worth, though the only part now habitable be converted to a farmhouse, belonging to Lord Fortescue. South Molton hath nothing apparently to attract a stranger's notice, its streets are but of mean appearance, a walk leads to the church thro' a range of trees, and the Church itself, large and handsomely built, rises on an eminence and appears an object of importance. The road from hence to Tiverton, passing by Bishops-Nymet and Rackenford, was very stony, very hilly, and afforded a view of a very tame and meagre country, till within two or three miles of Tiverton, when it assumes a more verdant and fertile aspect. In the West suburbs through which I entered, I was struck with an uncommon building of a very antique form, having a turret at one end, where a bell seemed to hang—an inscription in old characters was painted throughout the whole length of the front, which was composed of two stories of Galleries, in which several old Paupers (for it was an Almshouse, built by John Waldron, 1579) were walking, as under Porticos, and gazing over the meadows opposite. Several Images were in alto relievo on the walls, which, with the old Chantry, contributed to the giving it an air of reverence and antiquity.

On the North-East end of the town is the old Church, covered over with arms, and with a variety of emblematical devices—a large venerable Pile, which hath attached to it, a grand tower, of considerable thickness and height—on the Northern side of the Church, which is otherwise of Gothic Architecture. is an arched doorway of Norman Architecture, ornamented with the wonted embellishments of the stile, fretwork and zig-zag mouldings. Contiguous to the Churchyard are the remains of a Castle, placed on an eminence, falling precipitately on the North, toward the river. At the West end it hath a square tower, another on the South-East of a rounded form, enriched with ivy, which hath a fine effect when contrasted with the stone of the Building, which is of reddish tint. Between these towers, appears a long range of walls, which, from the peculiar turn and ornamental frettings of the windows seem'd to have been the Chapel. The battlements have been destroyed and roofs of slate usurp'd their places, and on the front, near the tower, in the sketch (*see illustration*, p. 169), are the vestiges of machicolations. The whole occupied the space of about an acre and an half, in the quadrangle hath risen a modern built house, inhabited by a farmer, who rents the estate of Sir Thomas Carew, amounting to £300 per annum. It once belonged to the Courtenays, Earls of Devon—from thence it pass'd by a female to the Trelawneys.

The Free school is entered by a Porter's Lodge, and over the gateway, on a tablet, an inscription told me that it was built by Mr. Peter Blundell, in 1604, *ætatis suæ* 81.

The following morning was Sunday, Sept. 13th. I attended divine service in the old church. After prayers, I observ'd a number of handsome modern monuments and two very ancient tombs on each side of the altar, over this a large modern painting of " Peter's release from Prison," which was painted and presented to the town by Richard Cosway, Esq. (a native of the town), in the year 1784. I noticed what devistation hath been repeatedly made on the old buildings by a succession of fires. As I rode out of the town on the opposite side of the river, along whose banks the road tended, Colly-priest offered itself to my view, and the bridge thrown over the Exe about a quarter of a mile down the stream, adds to its beauty. At the five mile stone from Exeter, I stop't to admire a very noble, antient, and vast Oak, whose circumference at the height of two feet from the ground, I found by measurement, to be 21 feet, and whatever might be its age, it was yet in a state of growth. Thus I made my way homeward through Upton Pyne to Exeter, and thence to Oxton House. P. F. S. AMERY.

175. THE ALTAR AT ST. TORBRYAN CHURCH.—This fine work of art is, I rather fancy, filling at the present time a different rôle from the one originally intended, as although I know of no documentary evidence on the point, I cannot help having a strong conviction that it was once a pulpit and has been altered and converted to its present use.

I may, however, be entirely wrong, and it may be now fulfilling the purpose for which it was originally designed.

It is rather a curious mixture, as regards the cornice and base mould, which appear to me to be different from the remainder and the result of the supposed conversion. The carving, which is the chief beauty, is the work of a real artist who scorned repetition, the bane of so much modern work; the crockets and finials, although following the same general outline, being entirely different from each other in treatment and style of foliage; whilst the pilasters, which are wholly composed of vine branches, leaves and fruit, shew a fresh design in each case, a sure mark of true artistic feeling. A. L. TATE.

Church-yard Cross, Plympton St. Maurice.
From a photograph by C. Aldridge, M.D

176. CHURCHYARD CROSS AT PLYMPTON.—We give an illustration of the recently re-erected cross in the graveyard of St. Maurice, otherwise St. Thomas of Canterbury, Plympton. In 1861 alterations were being made in the Guildhall of the town of Plympton. In the removal of a wall running east and west, separating the court from the lock-up or clink, a fine granite monolith, upwards of nine feet long, was found built into it lengthways. This stone was brought out so that it might form a part of the face of the wall, and to make the latter quite smooth, one of the chamfers, where the upper part of the square base runs into the elegant tapering octagonal of the shaft, was hacked off by the mason. This stone proved to be the shaft of a cross. The iron dowell projected for a foot or so above the top, and was so firmly fixed as to resist all efforts to remove it to shorten it to take the new head. The wall in which this shaft was found was probably built in 1680, certainly not later, so that the stone had remained where it was placed for nearly two centuries. It was purchased of the builder, and it has been carefully preserved until the opportunity for its restoration,—now happily arrived nearly forty years later,—should come. There is a question whether this was the shaft of the cross which at one time stood in the Market place of the town, within a very few feet from where the cross is now re-erected, or whether it was the churchyard cross. In either case it would have been dedicated to God, and its present position is an appropriate one. The approximate date of the shaft is A.D. 1380, which is also about the date of the chapel of St. Maurice, in the church. The cross has been re-erected close outside the south porch. The restoration was completed under the direction of Mr. James Hine, F.R.I.B.A., and was re-dedicated by the Bishop of Crediton 27th Nov., 1900.   J.B.R.

177. SHILLINGHAM, BARABERGA, ALBERICA.—Can any one locate the following places?—

Shillingham. In Harleian MS. 3,874, fol. 14, Ferrers holds the manor of Bere (Bere Ferrers) with the hamlet of Shillingham.

Baraberga. In Round's Calendar of Documents in France, p. 235. In 1096 William de Poillei gave to St. Martin's Abbey at Sees the tithe of Lenga (Chellonsleigh) as he had already granted at Bocheland (Buckland Monachorum) and a certain manor named Baraberga, a part or member of Bocheland with its own hall in that township.

Also the tithe of a mill called *Alberica*. Mr. Round suggests Melberry, but Melberry was waste in Domesday, and this is only ten years later. Is there a mill of that name in Stoke Rivers?   OSWALD J. REICHEL.

178. LITTLE SILVER (par. 143, p. 187).—In support of the suggestion in the Rev. O. J. Reichel's note on the origin of the above, I may instance a place of this name within the borough and parish of Great Torrington. It lies just on the border of the parish about a mile *without* the town itself, thus bearing out the suggested derivation of the first part of the name, and with respect to the second part, it is, I think, more than a mere coincidence that the parish which Little Silver adjoins, is that of St. Giles-in-the-Wood.   G.M.D.

179. COBLEIGH OF BRIGHTLEIGH.—It will be interesting if any of your readers can throw light on the pedigree of this family. Several pedigrees are given by different authorities, and each differs from the others.

I. Sir William Pole* gives the following descent (pp. 420, 421):—

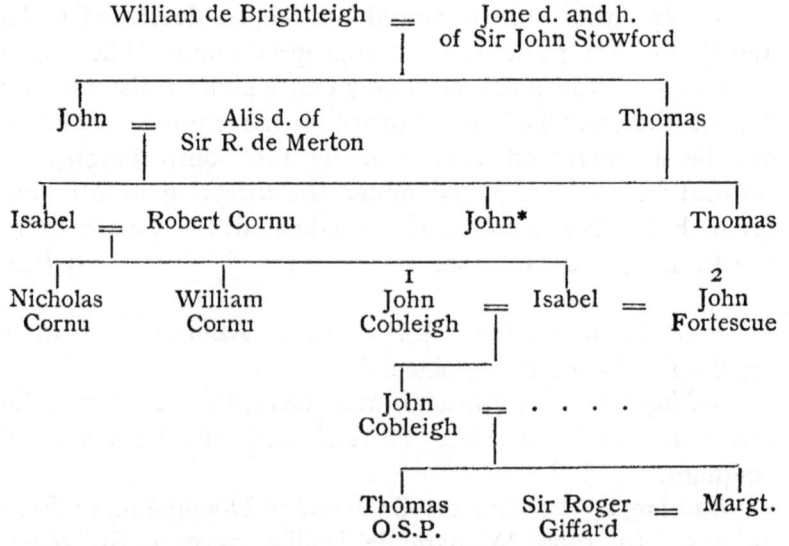

* It does not appear whether this John was father or brother to Thomas, the father of Isabel.—H.F.G.

II. Westcote gives the following pedigree (pp. 286, 287):—

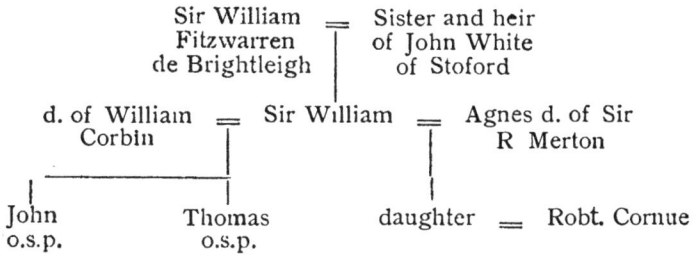

III. The pedigree of Cobleigh recorded in the Heralds' Visitation of Devon, 1564, is thus given:—

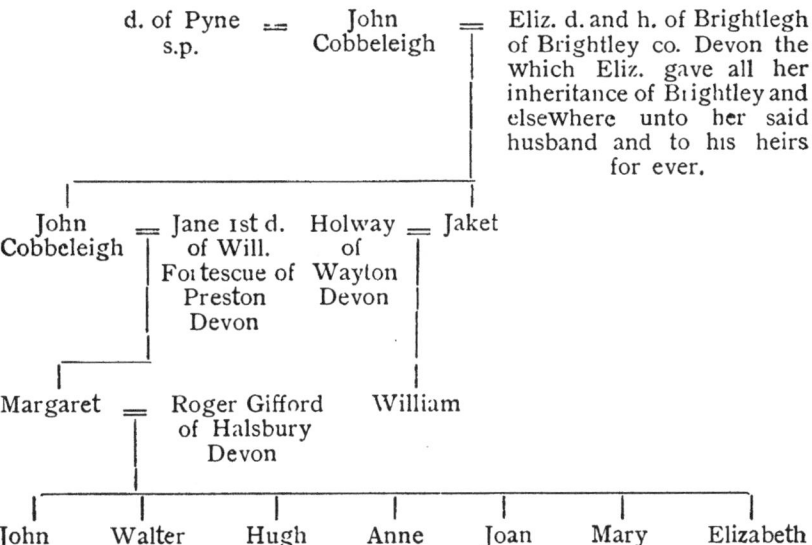

IV. Harl. MS., 1538, folio 154b, contains the following pedigree:—

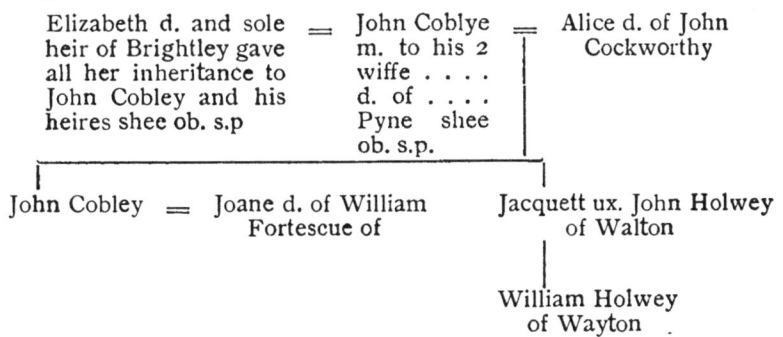

Excluding pedigree No. II. (Westcote's) which does not include Cobleigh descents, it is curious that the three others are incorrect when tested by the monumental brasses in Chittlehampton Church and by the P.M. Inquisition held on the death of " John Cobele of Bryghtele," in 1492. Thus, Sir Will. Pole's pedigree (No. I.) would appear to be inaccurate in that he makes Isabel, wife of Robt. Cornu, a different person from the Isabel who married John Cobleigh. The brass, however, at Chittlehampton, proves that Cobleigh's wife was Cornu's widow. The inscription is as follows:—

Hic jacet Johannes Coblegh et Isabella uxor ejus ; nuper uxor Roberti Cornue, armigeri, quæ quidem Isabella obiit 21 Oct., A.D. 1466.

Again, the pedigree of the Herald's (No. III.) cannot be correct, because *if* there were only two John Cobleighs, the second of that name could not have been the son of the heiress of Brightleigh, but must have been the son of the other wife. This is proved by the P.M. Inquisition held on John Cobleigh, in 1492, which establishes the fact that *then* John Cobleigh, the son of the deceased John Cobleigh, was thirteen years old. It is clear, therefore, that Isabella, who died in 1466, could not have been the mother of a boy who was thirteen years old in 1492. *Assuming*, therefore, that there were only two John Cobleighs, it is clear that the mother of the second John must have been the " Johanna uxor predictis Johannis Coblegh obiit ultimo die mensis, Sep. A.D. 1480," because the younger John Cobleigh must have been born in 1479, that is the year prior to that in which Johanna, second wife of John Cobleigh, the elder died.

Thirdly, it is also clear that the Harl. MS. pedigree (No. IV.) is faulty, because, assuming that there were only two John Cobleighs, the younger of that name must have been, as I have just demonstrated, the son of the *second* wife, Johanna, who was living for nearly a year after the boy's birth, and not the son of the third wife, Alice Cockworthy, as stated in the Harl. MS. In view of the fact that the three pedigrees are wrong, it is legitimate to attempt to reconstruct it on the known facts, and I cannot but think that all the errors are owing to the assumption in each of the pedigrees that there were only *two* John Cobleighs. Careful comparison has induced me to arrive at the conclusion that there were *three* John Cobleighs, and, if I am correct, the pedigree would stand thus:—

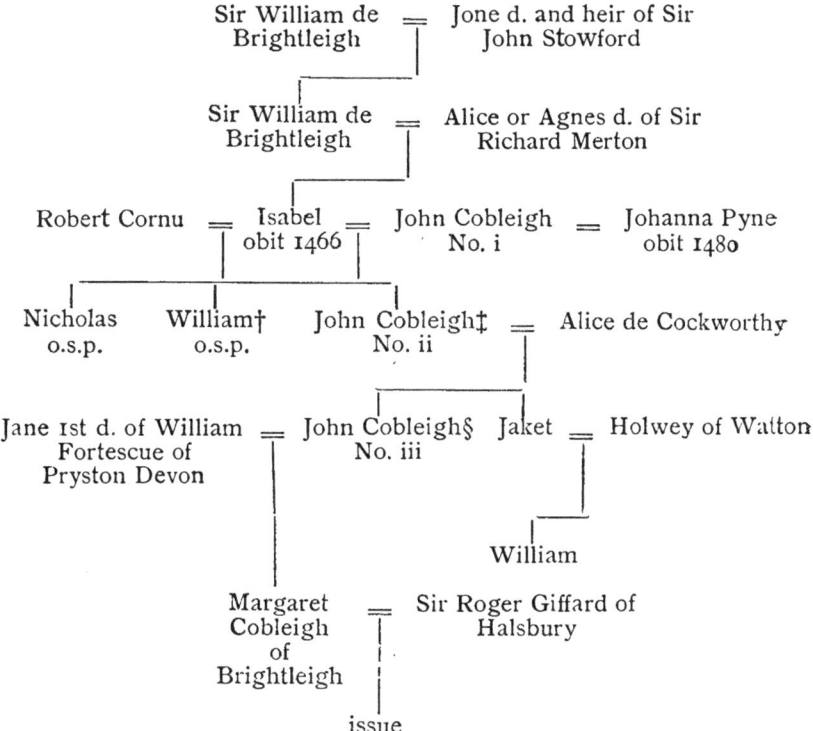

My reasons for thinking that there were *three* John Cobleighs are as follows:—

1. It appears to be the only way in which to reconcile the several pedigrees to each other.

2. It appears to me to be improbable that John Cobleigh, the husband of Isabella de Brightleigh, whose first husband is believed to have died in 1415, should have survived till 1492.

3. It is more probable to suppose that it was John's and Isabella's son who married Alice de Cockworthy, than to suppose that John, the husband of Isabella and Johanna, married *three* times. It is a fact that John Cobleigh, who died in 1492, left a wife, Alice, mourning him.

4. It is scarcely probable that Isabel de Brightleigh would have left her estates to her second husband and his

---

† Mentioned in P.M. Inq. 1492 as having been seized with John Cobleigh of Brightleigh—H.F.G.   ‡ Cobleigh of the P.M. Inq. obit 1492. ?   § 13 years old in 1492 ?—H.F.G.

issue *by another wife* over the head of her own offspring, and it is significant that in the P.M. Inq., 1492, William Cornu and John Cobleigh are described as having been seized of Brightleigh.

5. Upon an ancient domestic screen for many centuries in Brightleigh Manor House, and now in my possession, are painted certain shields of arms. Three of these are Cobleigh impalements, the arms on the man's side in each case being those of Cobleigh, which, though faint, can be recognised. On the female side of one shield are the Brightleigh or Fitzwarnie arms, but on each of the other two shields it is impossible to say what the arms are on the female side. The fact remains, however, that the three shields represent the marriages of *three male* Cobleighs.

In conclusion, let me say that it will be of great interest to me if any of your readers can aid in constructing, upon certain foundation, the Cobleigh pedigree.

HARDINGE F. GIFFARD.

180. REGNAR LOTHBROG THE DANE, AND HIS DEVONSHIRE DESCENDANTS.—The query of W.L. in the April number of *D.N.&Q.* relates to a tradition that has been handed down through every branch of the ancient Devonshire family of Lethbridge, that the family is so named on account of its descent from Regnar Lothbrog, or Leather-breeches.

Prince, in his *Worthies of Devon*, gives the life of Christopher Lethbridge, Mayor of Exeter in 1660; and therein narrates the legend at considerable length :—

"This name and family derive themselves from Lothbroke, *alias* Lethebrich, the Dane, and their coat armor seems to declare so much this day ; whose history, for the rarity thereof, and the honour it may bring to some surviving flourishing branches of it, I shall here insert, as I find it related by that excellent antiquary Vestigan* in these words :—

"'Lethbroke, a noble Dane, hawking on the sea-shore, his hawk took her flight sea-ward, and he taking a little cock-boat to follow her, was driven by contrary winds to the coast of Norfolk, and there landed at Rodham ; where by K. Edmund he was well entertained. But this Beric, the said King's falconer, greatly envying, he murdered him in a wood ; and the body by his spaniel being found out, Beric was convicted of the murder, and by sentence of justice being set in Lethbroke's boat, without sail or tackling, was by the wind and tyde driven over into Denmark, even there where Lethbroke himself had taken boat : The boat there

---

* Restitution of decayed Intelligence in Antiquities, p. 173.

being known to have belonged unto Lethbroke, Beric was laid hands on and examined; but very falsely and maliciously he told them, that K. Edmund had murdered the aforesaid Lethbroke; which being made known, the K. of Denmark, glad of the occasion, raised an army and sent it over into England, under those two famous captains, Hunga and Hubba, the two sons of Lethbroke †; whom, the rather to encourage to revenge, their sisters wrought with their needles, in an ensign, the proportion of a raven, or rather an eagle, which they did bear as no small sign of their good luck.'

"This, with the story of a rape committed upon the body of the lady Frea, as a late gentile pen (Sir Winst. Churchill, Kt., in his 'Divi Britain,' p. 161, 162, father of the present right honourable the Earl of Marlborough, whose birth at Ash, in the parish of Musbury, hath greatly honoured our county of Devon) informs us, are the fancies of melancholly monks, not more ignorantly written, than maliciously mistaken; the truth (to mention only what relates to Lethbroke) he says, is thus: 'Harold, K. of Denmark, quarrelling with Reigner, K. of Norway, beat him out of his dominions; who thereupon turned pyrate, and infesting the northeast parts of this isle that lay nearest to his country, was, after sundry inroads made upon them, driven into Norfolk, by the violence of foul weather; where the rabble, accustomed always to cruelty, but then most barbarous when a noted enemy is given up to their mercy, fell upon him and slew him: And to shew that it was not in the power of death to give them a full revenge, they abused his carcass by dragging it up and down in derision, calling him in scorn Lothbroc, which was as much as to say, Leather-breech. He leaving behind him a numerous issue by several wives, three of the younger sons, Ivor, Hungar, and Hubbo, came into England, with purpose, as they pretended, to revenge the ghost of their murdered father; but rather to provide for their own livelyhood being banished according to the custom of their country, which always forced their younger children to prey for themselves abroad: Wherein, being like young rooks drove from their nests, they took that bird for their cognizance, which being embroidered by their vestal sisters in a banner, consecrated after the horrid rites of their paganish superstition, (which rendered it, as the vulgar believed impossible to be taken) they sate it up as the royal standard, calling it by the name of the reafan, *i e.*, the raven. What the ground of this portraicture was, is not certain; but this is, that it drew great numbers to them, who supposing the genius of the nation was wrapped up in that flag, exposed themselves to all desperate attempts with so little caution, that the English, daunted with their more than humane courage, gave ground; till fortune was pleased to undermine them by that unexpected success at Kinworth in Devonshire, (called by our antiquaries Kenworth-Castle, which with Hubbaston, now Whibblestone, they place near Appledore, in the north-part of this county, *vid.* Risd. and Weste. MS.) where the reafan was taken, and Hubba slain; from whom the place is since called Hubbleston. As to the truth of those two different relations, I shall leave the historians to agree among themselves, and go on."

---

† Risdon's Survey.

There is an earlier reference to this tradition, in the tablet, in Faringdon Church, near Exeter, erected to the memory of Frances, the daughter of the Rev. John Lethbridge (the eldest brother of the above-named Christopher), erected by her husband, the Rev. Lewis Burnett, B.D., Sub-Dean of Exeter Cathedral, and Rector of Faringdon. The Rev. John Lethbridge, M.A., of Exeter College, Oxford, born at Bow in the year 1608, was the well-known Royalist Rector of Ashprington, whose life is given in Walker's *Sufferings of the Clergy*, and who was ejected by a troop of Parliamentarian horse, under the orders of the Westminster Assembly, in the year 1647. We give a *facsimile* of the inscription on this tablet, in which Frances Burnett is described as the youngest daughter of " John Lethbridge, Clerk, of Bow in this county, head of this name and family *of Danish origin*."

Regnar Lothbrog was the favourite mythical hero of the Norse Sagas. Otté's *Scandinavian History* gives so much of the life of this hero as may be regarded as historical, in connection with the great Battle of Bravalla, in which Odin was fabled to have aided Sigurd Ring against Harald Hildetand, which was to the Scandinavians what the siege of Troy was to the Greeks, or what Kurukshetra was to the Sanskritic races of India :—

" The battle of Bravalla is supposed to have been fought some time in the eighth century, and it probably gave Denmark to the successful young King of the Swedes, whose son, Regnar Lodbrog,* is a great favourite among all the early writers of Scandinavia. . . . . His nickname of Lodbrog, or Leather-leggings, he owed to the fact of his having adopted the fashion of wearing these leg-protectors when he was making court to the Gothic princess, Thyra, a young lady who lived in a bower defended by a venomous serpent, which had the very inconvenient habit of biting at the legs of all her suitors. After a long course of viking, Regnar of the Leather-leggings met his death at the hands of Ælla, King of Northumbria, who, having seized him in the act of invading his country, caused him to be thrown into a pit filled with adders, as he would not declare his name and the cause of his appearance on the Northumbrian coast. Regnar bore the torments of his slow death without complaint, simply remarking that 'the young pigs at home would grunt aloud when they found out what had become of the old boar their father!' According to the old sagas, his sons certainly did cry aloud when they heard of the death he had suffered, and never rested till they had taken a still more

---

* Lodbrog was said to have sailed from the Lofoden Isles on the coast of Norway.

Hujusce Sub Introitu Sacrarij jacent FRANCISCA cum Infantulo LUDOVICO
Cui moriendo quadrimestrem cum dederit vitam,
Sibi ipsi adepta est Immortalem. JOANNIS LETHBRIDGE De Bow
In hoc Comitatu Clerici (Nominis et Familias (Origine Danicæ) Principis)
Filia natu Minima – Et LUDOVICI BURNETT S.T.B.
Hujus Ecclesiæ Rectoris Uxor Dilectissima

Cur(heu) quid Saxa dabunt moritura aut Sepulchrales mutiles nugæ
Quæ Sinceræ erga Deum Religionis Officiosæ in Parentes Pietatis
Illibatæ erga Maritum Fidei Urbanæq; erga omnes Conversationis
Famâ are ipsô aut marmore perenniori, Vivum Supererit Monumentum
Hoc tamen quale quale (ne officio erga optimam Uxorem,
Filiolum et Seipsum deesse Videretur) poni curavit

Nat: fest: Nat: 1651
Nupt: 7mo Idus Nov^{ris} 1682   Conjux Moestissimus.
Denat: Idibus Sept^{ris} 1683

Quem cum optata dies cum fors extrema peremptum
Reddet in amplexus (vmbra beata) tuos.
Una Marritos cineres Sociale Sepulchrum
Misceat atq; idem conteget ofsa lapis

23° Die Julij Año. D$\bar{n}$i 1704 voti Compos Factus
Fuit Ludovicus Burnet Ecclæ B^{ti} Petri Ex^{on} Subdecanus, et
Hujus Ecclæ per 25 Años Rector Dignisimus

cruel revenge on Ælla. We are told that these sea-rovers landed in Northumbria, some years later, with a large fleet and a great number of other *vikingar*, and over-ran and pillaged the country; and that they took the king captive, and killed him by cutting open his back, tearing out his heart, and after thus torturing their victim, ended by carving the figure of an outspread eagle on his back, shoulders, and loins."

It is this "outspread eagle"—which is borne on the coat-of-arms, and also as the crest of every branch of the Lethbridge family—as shown in the brass in the floor of the south transept of Exeter Cathedral, dated 1610, thus:—

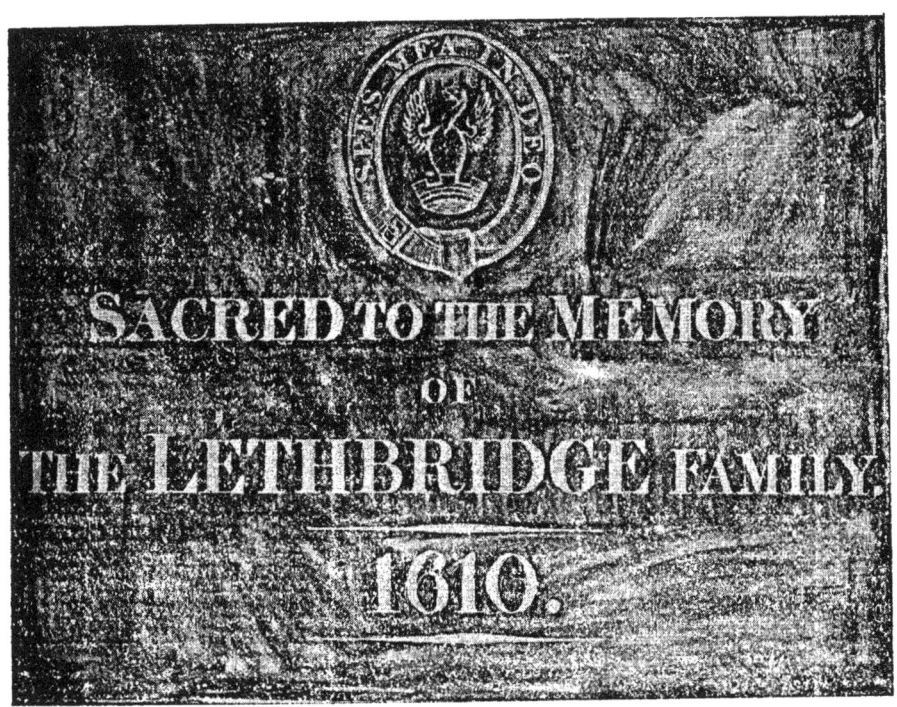

that suggested Prince's remark quoted above. And furthermore, the head of the family was granted the special heraldic distinction of "supporters"—those "supporters" being two ravens, to commemorate the "Reafan" flag of Lothbrog.

In addition to the evidence of the family tradition, dating at least from 1608, given above, there are some coincidences of nomenclature that seem to corroborate the legend. The earliest ancestor of the Lethbridges of whom there is any record was Oger of Lethebroke,* who lived at Lethebroke, and was seised of lands there—almost certainly the farm now called Lydbridge or Lefbridge, in the parish of Hatherleigh, belonging to H. M. Veale, Esq., of Passaford—in the reign of King John. His name recalls " Oger le Danois," the famous paladin. His descendants remained at Lethebroke, in Hatherleigh, till Henry VII.'s reign, when one branch went to live at Deckport in Hatherleigh, and Innerleigh (now Ingleigh Green) in Broadwoodkelly, and the other went to Exbourne and Dennisland (now Dunsland) in Jacobstowe. All these are adjacent parishes; and it is noticeable that many of the local place-names are clearly Norse in origin. Verstegan, quoted above by Prince in his *Worthies*, noticed that Swanston in Exbourne was originally Svend's Stone; and that Inwardleigh (*vulgo* Ingarleigh) was Ingvar's-leigh. Innerleigh in Broadwoodkelly was probably another Ingvar's-leigh. Whibblestone near Appledore was Ubba's-stone —Ubba and Ingwar being the two sons of Lothbrog who were defeated by the Saxons at Kenwith Castle near Appledore. This cairn (Whibblestone) is referred to in the *Malmesbury Chronicle, circa* A.D. 1321, known as the *Eulogium Historiarum*—in which, however, the death of Ubba is placed at Chippenham in Wiltshire, and attributed to King Aluredus (Alfred the Great), although his tomb, said to be at that time existing and called " Ubbeslawe," is distinctly stated to be "*in Devonia.*" The passage in the *Eulogium Historiarum* runs thus :—

Rex [Aluredus] vero ista nova audiens, ad Exoniam cum parvâ manu hominum et cum obsidibus se direxit. Dani eventum regis audientes reversi sunt in Estsax, Aluredus autem Danos præivit et ad Chippenham congressi sunt ; ibi enim occisus est Ubba rex Danorum et Buerna dux Deiræ ot Bogardus Danus, et multa millia ceciderunt ex utrâque parte sed victoria Danis remisit. Dani vero corpora suorum occisorum sepelientes et corpus Ubbæ invenientes magno mærore perculsi sunt. Ipsum vero sepelierunt more Paganorum ; fecerunt magnum struem lapidum, vel quod in vulgo dicitur congeriem, quod usque in hodiernum diem vocatur Ubbeslawe quod est in Devoniâ. R.L.

---

* There were several Domesday Manors named Lethebrok, Lochebroc, Lachebroc—notably, the modern Ludbrook in Ermington, the modern Lashbrook in Bradford, and possibly the modern Lydbridge in Hatherleigh, Lashbrook in Jacobstowe, or Brook in Sampford Courtenay. But whether these were at all connected with the name of Lodbrog, the Norseman, is quite uncertain.

181. RALEGH FAMILY (par. 39, p. 63).—A letter has been received from Capt. A. Young, Chief Secretary to the Government, Cyprus, enclosing a long and extremely valuable report from Major Chamberlayne, as the result of his examination of many sepulchral slabs in the ancient Cathedral of Saint Nicholas at Famagusta (miscalled ' Santa Sofia ' Mosque) and elsewhere, without, however, discovering any sculptured arms of any of the branches of the Ralegh family, although he found several that belonged to some other English families of note. T.N.B.

182. LITTLE SILVER, MANATON (par. 43, p. 137).—A most picturesque little thatched cottage, situated in the dense woods adjoining Foxworthy Bridge, where the parish boundary against Lustleigh crosses the stream which it has followed for some distance and apparently goes out of its way to embrace a bit of woodland that should belong to Manaton. P.F.S.A.

183. THE APPRENTICES' WARNING-PIECE.—The accompanying reprint of a tract or chap-book, with a ʾfacsimile of its title page (unknown to bibliographers), and is of much interest as recording a murder which took place in Exeter just prior to the commencement of the Civil War, with the justice meted out to the one who committed it.

In what parish in the city Humphry Bidgood, Apothecary, lived is unknown, but he kept an open shop and supplied many drugs to John Hayne, a resident in the parish of St. Mary Arches, whose MS. Diary, *penes me*, contains many entries relating to such purchases. He must have been well known, as his name appears in the list of bailiffs for the year 1628. The following extract from the Diary evidently refers to him :—

" 1638-9. March 13. More paid x^s paid Dr Vilvaine for his advice in writing wth a Byll to direct an Apothecary. 10. —."

Dr. Robert Vilvaine was the principal medical practitioner in the city, at that date, and was the author of the well-known lines in Izacke's *Memorials of Exeter*, under the year 1640, descriptive of "twelve Doctors of several Professions born within this City." The last entry in the Diary in which Hayne refers to him runs thus :

" 1640. Dec. 16. More vij^s I paid m^r Bidgood in his owne shopp, viz, for pilles twice, for a Cordiall for my Wife in March last, for fumus pectoralis, and some other very small things, amounting in all to x^s odde mony, but I paid him this in full of all demands to this day, and saw him crosse his booke being a long thin paper booke. I say paid him. . . . 7. —." (There is an evident discrepancy in the account.)

This shows the murder to have been committed most probably early in 1641, by his apprentice, Peter Moore, who " put powdred white mercury " (probably corrosive sublimate) into his Master's " messe of pottage," and so poisoned him. Moore was taken, " upon a sledge, " to " the common place of execution " at Heavitree.

There can be little doubt that any remarks that may have been made by him immediately prior to the completion of the sentence, have been considerably expanded in his so-named confession ; and the attempt to throw the onus of the act upon others is a feature by no means uncommon in such cases.

Other members of the Bidgood family were residents of the city. Another Humphry Bidgood, most probably a son of the Apothecary, was an actor in Monmouth's Rebellion, and although one of those who received sentence from Lord Jeffries, he escaped with his life. Nevertheless the *Treasury Letter Book*, 1684-6. III. 189, records the following as one of seven names under the heading of " Prisoners fined at Exeter for Words and other Misdemeano[rs] " :—

" For speaking seditious Words severally fined and Whipt. Hum. Bidgood repreived."

A later note states he had been recommended "to his Ma[ty] for his gratious pardon."

Another son was Dr. John Bidgood, a man of considerable eminence in his profession. He is thus referred to in a MS. book belonging to the Sainthill family (for which the writer is indebted to Mrs. Dymond)

"1664. Ap[l] 25. To M[r] G. S. Hill for Physick   -   11 0
                To him for the D[r] Bidgood   -   10 0
      May 4. To D[r] Bidgood for him by G. S. Hill   11 0 "

He died on Jan. 13th, 1690, and was interred in Exeter Cathedral. By his will he bequeathed £600 to St. John's Hospital. A long memoir of him will be found in Dr. Munk's *Roll of the Royal College of Physicians* (1878), I.348-350.

Prince (*Worthies*, 1810, p. 74) asserts the poison to have been intended for Mrs. Bidgood, but this tract disproves this.

T. N. BRUSHFIELD, M.D.

THE
Apprentices VVarning-piece.

Being
A Confession of *Peter Moore*, formerly Servant to Mr. *Bidgood*, Apothecary in Exeter, executed there the last Assises, for poysoning his said MASTER.

Wherein is observed such lamentable expressions proceeding from him, as may produce a trembling to all who reade or heare thereof, and be a warning to such leud servants who walk the same steps, lest they receive the same punishment.

LONDON,
Printed, and are to be sold by *Henry Walker*.
1641.

THE APPRENTICE'S WARNING-PIECE.

To heare good counsell is not sufficient, but to make use of it is the thing which is required of al men. Here is example prescribed for al young men, that they may learne to rule themselves according to Gods holy Statutes; let them marke well the relation of this penitentiall confession, and by him which made it bee sure to take warning. But first of his parents, which are a very sufficient couple; their chiefe delight was in him their sonne *Peter Moore.* Whilst he was young they sent him to Schoole, where he proved an indifferent good proficient. At length he grew to such ripenesse of yeares, that they bound him as an Apprentice to Master *Humphrey Bidgood,* an Apothecary in Exeter; with whom for a certaine space he lived very well, and was willing to obey their commands in every thing. But the devill (which doth envy the happinesse of all mankinde) was vext to see him tread the paths to goodnesse, wherefore he by his alluring bait, called pride, provoked him to forsake piety, and imbrace iniquity; as you shall now perceive by his confession writ with his owne hand.

The confession of Peter Moore *at the place of Execution.*

Being brought to the common-place of execution upon a sledge, bowing his body to the people round about him so wel as he could, he spake after this manner.

All you good Christian people which are come hither to see me dye, let me desire you to give attention to what I shall now declare, who have now scarce one quarter of an houre to live: my parents are scarce unknowne to any here present: but as for my unhappy master, (the more wretch I for making him so) he was better knowne to you. I was an Apprentice to Master *Humphry Bidgood,* Apothecary, too good a master for so ungracious a servant; notwithstanding, for a time my service was not disliked of, neither had it still, had I not wanted grace. Being in the prime of my youth, the devill by his allurements and wicked inticing, made me partaker of each damned vice, so that my heart being puffed up with ambition, I began to scoffe at Gods holy Minister, prophaning Sabbaths, and taking Gods holy name in vaine. But yet still was I provoked further to evil courses, so much alas, that you could scarce name a sinne wherein I had not beene an actor. Pride waxed daily more and more strong in me, in so much that I beganne to kicke at service, my time seeming too long and tedious to me, wherefore in all haste I did run to my parents, that they out of hand might buy out my time, which they rebuking me denyed, saying, I made more haste then good speed, in so much as I had not skill enough as yet to manage a shop of any consequence. Then went I againe to my master, seeming to be contented to serve out my Apprenticeship, and so had done, had not my mistresse beene too cruell toward me; never permitting me to remaine quiet; for daily she was cause of such strife, that I grew desperate, and as one weary of life which makes me now to pray that never any young man may have so bad a mistris as she was to me.

Dayly was my heart more and more filled with discontent, still meditating of nothing but mischiefe, which at length thus did worke my fatall overthrow, for being still greedy to bee freed from my Apprentiship, I acted a deed which now doth make each Artery to quake, and totall body to tremble: for I seeing a messe of pottage about dinner time provided for my Master, I most unnaturall servant put powdred white Mercury into it, so privately that no man could perceive me, which so soone as he good man had tasted, presently began to swel, and a while after died.

Thus *Iudas* like traterously did I betray my master unto death, but yet was not found out, but yet the Lord whose judgments are alwaies just and true, caused many towards me to have a great mistrust, and layd the fault to my charge, which I most impudently denyed, which so soone as my father and mother did heare, upon their knees weeping with brinish teares came and desired mee to confesse the truth, which I denied, notwithstanding my conscience told mee that I lyed; in the same minde I went to my fathes [*sic*] house and received the Sacrament, still denying the hainous murder committed upon my Master, but God at last revealed it, and I was sent to prison, to answer for the Death of my Master, where I thought my selfe to be secure from being found out, because I did the act unseene. All the while I lay in prison, I had the keies thereof in my own custody, with which I might have both freed my selfe and others; the divell daily tempted me to runne away, but God hee would not have it so, for to goe thence I had not the least of power, until such time as the Assizes did begin, that I should answer the death of my

Master, where I was most justly judged to die, my conscience still telling mee no man did the deed but I. One there is in this City whom I pray that the Lord may forgive, God he knowes that I speake nothing concerning him at this present for any malice I beare to him, but to clear my owne conscience.

His name is *White* a Papist, who did often times seduce me to abuse Gods Ministers, and to spend my time in that Diabolicall study of reading Magicke, in which I tooke too much delight, which now doth very much oppresse my soule: All young men which are here present, and did behold me drawne hither upon a sledge, take warning by me, and let your study be, first, to please your heavenly Master, and then your Masters upon earth.

Contemne the divell, despise the world, and abhore lust; Hence, hence, with pride which is the devils darling, away with lust which is the divells chiefe attendant, away with magicke spells which lead unto the divell.

When I am dead let the cause of my dying bee engraved upon a stone that all may know wherefore I did die, and thereby take example. Pray, pray for my soule good christian people, that notwithstanding my horrid offence, the gate of heaven may not be barred against me: Againe, againe, and againe I earnestly intreat your prayers

Now farewell dear father, a thousand times farewell O mother also farewel to all my dear friends and kinsfolks.

Wipe, wipe, your eyes, and each one cease his mourning, for I am now exchanging a lump of mortall clay, for immortall blisse; which that I may receive, grant, grant most mercifull father. O receive me, receive me into thy bosome, for behold I come, I come, I come; so soone as which words were spoken he was turned off the ladder and so died.

Finis.

184. WEST COUNTRY BALLADS.*—The perusal of these verses and ballads will be a pleasure to many of our readers. The author's muse does not soar to a great height, but his is true poetry. His descriptions of scenery are very good. The ballads in the Devon dialect are well written and with much humour. "The Parish Clerk" is a clever satire on the ignorance of the old Church official, and the fox-hunting parson of a past generation.

---

* West Country Ballads and Verses by Arthur L. Salmon, 2nd ed. W. Blackwood and Sons, 2/6.

Cadhay House.

185. HAYDON, OF WOODBURY AND OTTERY ST. MARY, ETC., DEVON. Among the old Devonshire families whose ancestry lead us back to the twelfth and thirteenth centuries, the descent of Haydon, located in south-east Devon, and who flourished in influential estate there for about six centuries, finds conspicuous and honourable place Of them their first recorded representative appears to have been :—

JOHN DE HAYDON, who is thus spoken of by Prince :—

"He was a Judge in the first year of the reign of King Edward I (1272), according to the ensuing record, taken out of the Tower of London by Henry St George Richmond *(Ex ahutogr. in Man. Gid. Haydon Armig, M.S.)*

Herbertus de Mortles. Johannes de Haydon, Willielmus de Bikbur and Guido de Nonaunt constituuntur justiciarii ad Gaolam Exon. diliberandam 24 Jul. I. Edw. I, 1273.

This gentleman was a younger branch of a Knightly stock so called that flourished in the eastern parts of England."

Referring probably to the Heydons of Kent, but with no authority.

In the following descent the *Visitation* of 1620 is principally followed.

ROBERT HAYDON, probably a son of *John*, was of Boughwood, an estate in Harpford, near Ottery St Mary. This appears to have been their earliest recorded settlement, which their descendants held for four succeeding centuries. He married JOAN, and resided there 19. Edward I, 1291. They left three sons, *Henry*, *Roger*, who was of Nether-Stowford, and left a son *John*, who died s.p.,—*Peter*, heir to his brother *Roger*, and a daughter *Meraud* (Maud ?)

HENRY HAYDON, 1291, married JULIAN, and left a son *William*.

WILLIAM HAYDON, left two sons *Robert* and *Thomas*.

ROBERT HAYDON, 12 Edward III, 1339, left a son *John*.

JOHN HAYDON, left two sons, *Henry* and *John*.

HENRY HAYDON, of Bowood and Ebford, being the first named of that place, 20 Richard II, 1397, left a son *John*.

Pole thus notices Ebford, and the Haydon family :—

"Ebbeford lieth in this parish (Woodbury), and in King Edward I time—1272-1307,—Ralph de Ebford was the owner thereof, and it hath been divers descents in the name of Haydon, which name I find often, and very ancient, as witnesses to the grant of lands in these parts. It is now (1630) the land of Gedeon Haydon, Esq., who dwelled there in his father's lifetime, as other his ancestors had formerly done."

JOHN HAYDON, of Bowood and Ebford, 8 Henry IV, 1417, left a son *Richard*.

RICHARD HAYDON, of Bowood and Ebford, 15 Edward IV, 1476, left two sons *Richard and John*, and one daughter *Jane*, married to *Robert Gilbert*, of Powderham.

RICHARD HAYDON, described as of Bowood, Ebford, Lympstone, and Woodbury, 13 Henry VIII, 1522, appears to have been the first influential member of the family. Speaking of his gravestone at Woodbury, Dr. Oliver enquires:—

"Is it not the tomb of Richard Haydon, gent, who was Steward to Bishop Veysey, and by his will dated 2 April, 1533, desires to be buried in Woodbury church, near his wife Jane?"

He died the 16 October following. He appears to have been thrice married. First to JOAN, daughter of *Morris Trent*, of Ottery St Mary, who bore for their arms—*Argent, a chevron between three eagles displayed gules*. By her he had three (or four) sons, *Thomas*, his heir; *John*, of Cadhay, in Ottery (to be further referred to); *George*, of Hornshayes, Northleigh; and probably *Peter*, of Poltimore, Farway; and one daughter, *Joan*, married to *John Coram*, of Ottery, with descent given in the *Visitation*, 1620, and arms *Argent a cross sable, between four eagles displayed gules*; crest: *a beaver passant or*.

Secondly to AGNES, daughter of . . . . *Merifeild*, probably of Huish, near Crewkerne, whose arms were, *Or, on a 'fess cotized azure, between three crescents sable, as many roses, argent*. By her he had one son *John*.

Thirdly, he appears to have married ELIZA, of what family does not appear, but stated on his gravestone to be there buried with him; with no issue recorded.

Richard Haydon, died 16 Oct.; *Inq. p. m.* 24 Henry VIII (1533), No. 8.

The north, or Haydon aisle, of the church of St Swithin, Woodbury, was with little doubt, either wholly or partially erected by the Haydons, with a mortuary chantry at the east end, beneath which they were interred. This is attested by the character of the architecture, which dates towards the conclusion of the fifteenth, or early in the sixteenth century, the period at which Richard Haydon lived. The Chantry at the east end was screened off from the aisle, but opening toward the chancel, is an enriched panelled arch, lower than the rest of the arcade, and apparently designed to become a monumental canopy, where, beneath, the gravestone of Richard Haydon, was with little doubt originally placed, and himself and wife interred below it. This gravestone is now outside, and has probably been moved more than once; the Chantry continued to be the burial place of his descendants. Shields with alliances of Haydon, apparently recently emblazoned, are on the capitals of the pillars of the aisle.

The gravestone of Richard Haydon was originally very handsome. It is of Purbeck marble, and consists of an incised ledger line inscription, and in the centre is the indent

of a gentleman, in long gown, his feet on a dog, and below it, a square, on which was probably an elegiac Latin inscription. Above the figure is a long label, at the corners of the stone four shields, and a central one in the base, all with labels over them, and six other labels, three on each side are inserted between the words of the inscription. All the brasses are now gone, the stone has been broken, and is greatly denuded and decayed, the inscription considerably obliterated, but can be satisfactorily made out, (the upper portion appears in the illustration) and is to this effect :—

Here liethe Richard Haydon, esquier, and Eliza his wyfe, the which Richard dyed ye 26 day of October, an'o dom'i 1533, on whose soules God have mercy.

John Haydon, fourth son, and only child by his second wife, married *Martha*, daughter of *Nicholas Rose*, of London, where he appears to have settled, and became a wealthy and influential man, a Mercer by vocation, an Alderman and Sheriff of London, 1582-3; and according to Stow, was buried " in the fair parish church of St Michael, called Paternoster Church in the Royall, and Ward of Vintry," and apparently died s.p. He left large legacies for charitable purposes, mentioned by Stow, and thus summarised by Prince :—

"He gave more than £3,000 for the relief of the poor, to 100 poor so many gowns, and 12d. apiece in money; to the Company of Mercers, in London, £600 to be lent to young men at £3 6s. 8d, per cent.; £400 more to the same Company, to be lent at the same rate, the interest whereof to go to the maintenance of a lecture in St Michael, Paternoster; to Christ's Hospital £500; to the eleven Worshipful Companies £1,100; to Exeter £200; to Bristol and Gloucester £100 each, to be lent to young tradesmen at the before-named percentage; to the Company of Mercers, which was his profession, for a cup, £40; to his servants £240, etc."

and the following donation to the poor of Woodbury, as set forth on a tablet in the church there :—

In Memoriam Perpetuam.

John Haydon, Gent., Merchant and Citizen of London, gave by will in 1579, Three pounds, six shillings and eight pence, to be distributed to three poor inhabitants of this parish (Woodbury) every Sunday in the year, viz :—four pence in money and one penny in bread, the remainder to be distributed by the Churchwardens for the time being, payable for ever by the Wardens and Masters of the Company of Mercers, of the City of London.

THOMAS HAYDON, eldest son and heir of Bowood and Ebford, aged 23 at his father's death, and heir to his nephew *Edward Haydon*, of Hornshayes, who *ob*. 1562. He married JOAN, daughter and sole heir of *Richard Weekes*, of Honichurch, by *Alice*, daughter of *Henry Kelly*; their arms, *Ermine, three battleaxes sable*. By her he had one son, *Thomas*, and three daughters, *Jane*, married first to *Richard Williams*, secondly to *John Gove*, third son of John Gove, of Bridge, Woodbury, 11 Feb., 1588-9, died 1627, s.p. On a flat stone in the Haydon aisle :—

Here lieth the bodie of John Gove, gent., who died ye xxix day of June, An'o D'ni, 1627.

Arms of Gove : *Argent, a cross lozengy between 'four eagles displayed sable;* and thirdly to *John Towell; Mary,* married to *Walter Leigh;* and *Margaret,* to *Thomas Browning.*

Thomas Haydon died 27 June, and was buried at Woodbury, 17 July, 1576. *Inq. p.m.*, 18 Elizabeth (1576), P^t I, No. 23.

THOMAS HAYDON, eldest son and heir of Bowood and Ebford, aged 30 at his father's death. He married CHRISTIAN, daughter of *Robert Tytherleigh,* of Tytherleigh, in Chardstock, Dorset *ob.* 1578, and Johanna his wife.

Arms : *Ermine, two glaziers irons in saltire gules,* By her he had three sons : *Robert; Thomas,* buried at Ottery, 20 Jan., 1609-10; *Peter,* of Netherbury, Dorset, will 18 June, proved 4 Oct., 1627, s.p., and four daughters : *Amy,* wife of *Edmund Huntly,* son of John Huntly, of Milborne, St Andrew, Dorset, *Margaret,* unmarried, her administration 27 Jan., 1634-5; *Joan,* married at Woodbury, 5 Feb., 1589-90, *Erasmus Broughton,* son of *Thomas Broughton.* of Sandford-Bickford, in Wembdon, Somerset. Arms : *Sable, a chevron between three bucks' heads cabossed argent.* Crest : *a spaniel sejant ermine;* and *Bridget.* He died 25 Sep., buried 6 Oct, 1589, *Inq. p.m.* 32 Elizabeth (1590) No. 211. His wife was buried 30 Oct. 1600, and both were interred at Woodbury. *Bridget* marrried as his first wife, *John Sherman,* of Knightstone, Ottery, and died, *s.p.*

ROBERT HAYDON, eldest son, of Bowood and Ebford, also of Cadhay, in Ottery, which had been left him by his great uncle *John,* of that place, aged 29 at his father's death. He married *Joan,* eldest daughter of *Sir Amias Paulet, Knt.,* P.C. to Queen Elizabeth, and Governor of Jersey, of Hinton St George, Somerset, by Margaret, only daughter and heir of Anthony Harvey, of Columb-John, *ob.* 23 May, 1564, whose fine renaissance tomb is in the north choir aisle of Exeter Cathedral.

By her he had three sons : *Gideon, Amias,* buried at Ottery, 12 Jan. 1614, with this inscription on a stone to his memory—:

Epitaphium Amicii Haydon filii Roberti Haydon, Armigeri, qui obiit 12 *Januarii, An.' Dom.'* 1614.

> *Quis jacet hic, quæris, percussis vulnere mortis ?*
> *Virtutis socius nobilis, alter Ajax:*
> *Mortuus, ah ! dixi ? revoco, sic esse videtur*
> *In cœlis vivit nescius ille mori.*

Drewe, living 1621, and two daughters, *Margaret*, wife of *William Every*, of Cotthay, Somerset, son of John Every of Weycroft, Devon, and Frideswith, daughter of William Jervice of Hemiock, arms, *Or, four chevronels gules,* crest, *A demi unicorn, couped gules, armed, unguled and maned or,* and *Sara*, buried at Ottery, with this inscription on a stone, now utterly decayed:—

Sara Haydon, filia Roberti Haydon, Armigeri, quæ obiit 24 *Aprilis, An' Dom'* 1620.

> *Apollo moist this tomb with tears,*
> *For such great loss in tender years,*
> *Virtue's hope now is dead.*
> *And fro' earth to heaven fled,*
> *Wits perfection with pure spirit,*
> *Doth an Angel's place inherit,*
> *Stay in that celestial skie,*
> *Where thou shalt live, and never die.*

Robert Haydon, died 10, and buried 15 Dec. 1626, at Woodbury. Will, 12 Jan. 1620-1, proved 14 Dec. 1627. On a flat stone in the Haydon aisle, Woodbury is this inscription:—

Here lieth the Bodye of Robert Haydon, Esquire, who died the Xth of December, An'o d'o, 1626.

Arms: Haydon, impaling, *three swords in pile, points in base,* (PAULET).

GIDEON HAYDON, son and heir, of Ebford and Woodbury, aged 40 at his father's death. He married MARGARET, daughter of *John Davie* of Sandford, Crediton, and *Margaret* daughter of *George Southcote* of Calverleigh, their arms *Azure, three cinquefoils 2 &·1 or, on a chief of the last a lion passant gules*. By her he had nine sons, *Robert, John*, baptised 2 Nov. 1606, at Ottery, *Gideon*, heir to Robert, *Thomas*, baptised 23 June, 1611, at Sandford, *George*, of Houndsbeare, Woodbury, baptised 11 Sep. 1614, he was probably unmarried, and buried at Woodbury. On a marble stone in the pavement of the Haydon Chantry is this inscription :—

Here lyeth the Body of George Haydon, sonne of Gedeon Haydon of Ebfford, Esq. who Departed this life the 26th Day of February, Anno Dom'i, 1685.

Arms : Haydon, with helmet, crest, and motto, IE·AY·PRISE ·MON·PROYE.* *Amias*, baptised at Woodbury, 30 April, 1618, *James*, baptised 17 May, buried 18 July, 1619, at Ottery, *Nicholas*, baptised 19 May, 1620, he married *Anne*, daughter of *Henry Trosse*, of Exeter. He was buried at Woodbury, beneath a high tomb in the churchyard, outside the Haydon aisle, with this inscription :—

---

* This appears to be the only example of the Haydon motto, found on their memorials except the FIRM·EN·FOY, on the Haydon tomb a Ottery. In Prince (1810) it is given as JEO·AY·PRIS·ET·MORIER. The illustrations to this account are from original sources.

Here lyeth the Body of Mr. *Nicholas Haydon, eighth son of Gideon Haydon of Cadhay, Esq, who departed this life the 26 of January,* 1676. *Aged* 56 *years.*

Arms: Haydon, impaling, *Gules, three cutlasses barways in pale argent, the hilts or* (TROSSE). She was buried at Ottery, 16 Feb. 1652-3. A flat stone in the north choir aisle thus commemorates her:—

Ita hoc sub marmore deposita sunt reliquia Anna filiæ Henrici Trosse Exoniensi Armigeri, ex uxore Rebecca uxoris Nicolai filii Gedeon Haydon de Cadhay, Armigeri, ex uxora Margareta, qua obiit VII Februarii A. D. CIƆIƆCLII.

Arms: much obliterated, apparently Haydon impaling Trosse.

They had two sons, *Walter*, Rector of Talaton, buried 19 June, 1680, at Ottery, aged 32, *Nicholas*, baptised 6 Aug. 1651, at Ottery, he married *Mary*, daughter of *(William?) Martyn* of Woodbury, 5 Dec. 1673, and she remarried at Woodbury, 30 Nov. 1678, *John Hall.*

A flat stone in the Haydon aisle, thus probably commemorates Martyn

Dormitorium Guilielmi Martyn de Ebford, Generosi, qui vicesimo secundo die Februarii Anno salutis 1670, *ætatis suæ* 75, *multum desideratus obijt.*

    Da veniam quis quis terræ possessor es hujus
    Amborum cineres urna ut condantur in una
    Cum Christus judex super æthera venerit orbis:
    Corpora divisim tumulo conjuncta resurgent.

Arms: *three bars, a crescent for difference* (MARTYN) impaling *two bars, in a chief three cinquefoils pierced.*

This was William Martyn, second son of William Martyn, of Oxton, Kenton, Recorder of Exeter, by his wife Susan, daughter of Thomas Prestwood, Mayor of Exeter, 1576; he was baptised 6 Oct., 1596, at All-Hallows Church, Goldsmith Street, Exeter, a date that would agree with his age on the stone.

And two daughters, *Rebecca*, buried at Ottery St. Mary, 8 May, 1652; and *Anne*, baptised at Ottery, 20 Dec., 1652.

Richard Haydon, ninth son of *Gideon*, before named, baptised at Woodbury, 22 May, 1623, married at Ottery, June, 1658; *Elizabeth*, daughter of *John Ware;* and six daughters making fifteen children in all.

Of these, *Johanna*, married at Ottery, 13 June, 1629, John Coke, of St Erme, Cornwall. Polwhele records:—

"In S Erme church, in Cornwall, in the window of Tregasso aisle, I found this inscription:—

"*Joanna filia Gideonis Haydon de Cadhay, armigeri, uxor Johannis Coke de Tregasowe armigeri, obiit* 28 *die Decembris, a'no do'mi* 1630 *corpus*

"Court of the Kings," Gadhay,

hic deponitur. Filiam uxorem nurum qualem quis obtaret mulierum denique probatissimam præsentis seculi testimonio posteritas credat."
He was the son of John Coke, of Trerice, and Prudence Godolphin, who was the son of Christopher Coke, of Thorne, Ottery, and Margaret Garland. Thomas, his son was Sheriff of Cornwall, temp. Charles I; Thomas, his son, sold the estate to Boscawen. Tregasow House was built, but left in an unfinished state, by Thomas the younger; it is now a farmhouse."

Maria, married at Woodbury, 1 May, 1624, *George Raleigh*; *Margaret*, buried 13 June, 1634, at Woodbury; *Frances*, baptised 1 Sep., 1612, at Woodbury; *Dorothy*, at Woodbury, 9 May, 1616; *Elizabeth*, buried at Ottery, 12 Nov., 1644. In Ottery church is this inscription, probably to one of these daughters:—

Heere lieth the bodyes of William Coke, of Thorne, Esq. who died the 26th day of July 1652; and alsoe Margaret his wife daughter of Gedeon Haydon, Esq. who dyed the first day of January, Anno Domini 1667.

ROBERT HAYDON, of Cadhay, eldest son and heir, baptised 17 Aug., 1604, at Sandford. He married ELIZABETH, daughter of *William Gould*, of Hayes, near Exeter. His will 29 Sep., 1634, proved 10 May, 1635, he died 12 Nov,, 1634, *s.p.* His wife married secondly at Woodbury, 26 Jan., 1637-8, Arthur Upton, of Lupton, South Devon, *ob.* 1661-2, by whom she had two sons and two daughters, and was buried with her second husband at Brixham, 17 Dec., 1685.

Arms of Gould: *Per saltire or and azure, a lion rampant counterchanged.*

GIDEON HAYDON, of Cadhay, third son and heir to his brother *Robert*, baptised at Sandford, 25 June, 1609, buried 20 Aug., 1680, at Ottery. He married ELEANOR . . . . , buried 29 Jan., 1690-1, at Ottery, by whom he had three sons: *Gideon; Robert*, buried 2 July, 1648, at Ottery; *William*, *ob.* 7 April, 1722, aged 80, buried at Ottery; he married June, 1680, *Dorothy*, widow of . . . . *Lee*, by whom he had a daughter, *Dorothy*, married 6 July, 1704, at Ottery, to *Nicholas Fry*, son of Henry Fry, of Buckerell, *ob.* 1697, he died 16 March, 1714, buried at Buckerell, and she married secondly the Rev[d.] Gilbert Yarde, of Bradninch. The inscription to his memory is on the pediment of John Haydon's tomb, at Ottery, facing the aisle:—

Here Lyeth the Body of William Haydon, Gent., Son of Gideon Haydon Esq. of Cadhay, who Departed this Life in ye 80th year of his age, 1722.

Polwhele gives this inscription to four of their children, as then found in Ottery church :—

"*Near this place are buried the bodies of Robert Haydon, who died 2 July.* 1652 ; *Jane Haydon, who died 2 April,* 1653 ; *Elizabeth Haydon, who died 3 April,* 1653 ; *and Eleanor Haydon, who died 2 April,* 1658, *the son and daughters of Gideon Haydon, Esq. and his wife Eleanor Haydon.*"

GIDEON HAYDON, of Cadhay, son and heir, buried 2 March, 1702, at Ottery, married Feb., 1660-1, CATHERINE, daughter of . . . . *Stokes*, of Colyton, buried 3 June, 1697, at Ottery. by her he had four sons : *Gideon ; William*, buried at Ottery, 10 Dec., 1670 ; *Thomas*, baptised at Ottery, 24 Jan., 1671-2 ; *John*, buried at Ottery, 5 March, 1677-8 ; and four daughters : *Catherine*, her gravestone at Ottery, thus inscribed :—

Here lyeth ye Body of Catherine eldest Daughter of Gideon Haydon of Cadhay, Esq. and of Catherine his Wife, who deceased the XXVIII of July, Anno Domini MDCLXIII.; ætate sua dii tertio.

Arms : Haydon in a lozenge. *Eleanor*, baptised at Ottery, 17 March, 1664-5 ; *Margaret*, at Ottery, 1 Nov., 1666 ; *Mary*, 20 July, 1676.

GIDEON HAYDON, son and heir, of Cadhay. Baptised at Ottery, 26 July, 1666. buried there 17 Mar., 1706-7. He married ALICE, daughter of *John Fitch*, of Henbury and Sturminster-Marshall, Dorset, *ob*. 1705, son of Sir Thomas Fitch, of High Hall, Wimborne-Minster. Arms : *vaire on a chevron or, between three leopards 'faces of the second, three crosses patée fitchée*. By her he had three sons : *Gideon ; John*, died in London, buried at Ottery, Feb., 1701-2 ; *Thomas*, baptised at Ottery, 18 June, 1705, living 1707. The inscription to *Gideon Haydon* is on the pediment of John Haydon's tomb at Ottery, facing the altar :—

Here Lyeth the Body of Gideon Haydon, of Cadhay, Son of Gideon Haydon Esq., who departed this Life in ye 41*st year of his age* 1706.

GIDEON HAYDON, of Cadhay, son and heir, baptised at Ottery, 6 Oct., 1696, named in his father's will, 1707.

HAYDON OF CADHAY, OTTERY, S^{T.} MARY. JOHN HAYDON, the first of Cadhay, was the second son of *Richard Haydon* of Woodbury, *ob*. 1533, and whose gravestone is in the church there.

Pole thus describes the demesne, and its acquisition by Haydon.

" Cadhay, lieth west, over the river Tale, which there unladeth itself into the river of Otter. It was the land of the name of Cadehay, and not of any great quantity. It came after unto one Robert Grenvill, whose daughter and heir Jone, was married unto John Haydon, Esquire, who builded there a fair house, and enlarged his demesnes. The said John Haydon and Jone his wife conveyed it unto Robert Haydon, Esqr, son of Thomas Haydon, his nephew, whose dwelling was at Cadehay, and hath left it unto Gedeon Haydon, Esq, his son. The said John Haydon before mentioned builded a fair bridge of (three) arches over the river Otter, betwixt his house, and the town of Ottery."

This circumstantial account of Cadhay, and its acquisition by Haydon through a daughter of Robert Grenvill, is apparently the correct one, although the inscription on his tomb states she was "*consanguinea et hœres Johannæ Cadhay, quæ fuit uxor Hugonis Grenvile, Generosi*," but in either case it became his *jure uxoris*.

Prince in his inconsequent way, says he was one, —

"whose genius inclining him to the study of the common law, he became eminent for his skill and knowledge therein. He was first a member, and after that a bencher of Lincoln's Inn. Although I must confess I don't find him mentioned by that name in Sir W. Dugdales *Origines Juridicales*"

and mixes his name up with the Heydons of Kent.

That he was a man of large generosity and social influence, which he dedicated to the welfare of the town, there is ample evidence. He appears to have been considerably interested in procuring 37 Henry VIII, 1545-6, Letters Patent from that monarch, granting a Charter of Incorporation for Ottery, and founding "*the King's New Grammar School of Saint Mary of Ottery.*" Prince speaks of him as its first Governor, a statement apparently confirmed by the inscription on his tomb, but this was scarcely the case, four names are given as the first Governors, of these John Haydon stands first, and with his are associated Hugh More, William Trent (probably his cousin, Haydon's mother having been a Trent) and William Sherman, gent, subsequently of Knightstone. He also built the bridge mentioned by Pole, and apparently erected the south porch of the Church, as specified, with other his good deeds, in the long elegiac ode thereon, found over the door, inside the south aisle of the Church. He appears to have extended his charitable bequests to Exeter, by augmenting the endowment of the Alms House of Simon Grendon, thrice Mayor of Exeter, 1395, 1398, 1405, and founded 1406, thus mentioned by Izacke,—

"By his (John Haydon's) deed indented dated 6 *Martii*, 32 *Elizabeth*, *Anno Domini*, 1590, he *(inter alia)* gave the poor of the aforesaid Alms-house, the yearly sum of Forty-six Shillings and eight pence, to be bestowed in bread for them, at two feasts of the year at Christmas and Easter for ever."

Relating to the bridge built by John Haydon over the river Otter, Powhele observes :—

"The following inscription was on this bridge :—

> John and Joan built me,
> Pray, good people, repair me.

it was very ungraciouly destroyed on the repairing of the bridge," and he further notes :—

"At this place (Cadhay) there was, some years since, a curious picture of John and Joan of Cadhay, where *John* is represented on one side of an altar, together with his sons, kneeling, and *Joan* on the other side of the altar, with her daughters, in the same attitude. There is a taper burning, on the altar. This picture is said to be, somewhere, in the possession of the descendants of the Haydons."

The picture could not have represented John and Joan Haydon of Cadhay, as they had no children. It probably pourtrayed his father and mother, Richard of Woodbury and Joan Trent of Ottery, and their five or six children. He presumably built the north or Haydon aisle, with mortuary Chantry at its east end, in Woodbury Church, where they and their descendants are interred,

Cadhay House is a large and picturesque structure about a mile north west of Ottery. It is of quadrangular shape with an inner court, and the architecture characteristic of the Elizabethan era during which it was erected, but of comparatively plain character. The most striking portion is the inner court or "Court of the Kings," as it is designated, from the circumstance that the effigies of Henry VIII, and his three children Edward VI, Queen Mary and Queen Elizabeth during whose reigns John Haydon lived, are represented standing in enriched niches, one on each face of the quadrangle. They are clad in royal robes, with sceptres, and crowns on their heads. The niches consist of ornamented brackets, with Corinthian pillars by the sides, supporting pediments with finials, the canopies, domed and fluted. The walls of "dice-work," chequered courses of squared black flint and white stone. The building has been well cared for, and although considerably modernized, the repairs have been carried out in harmony, as far as possible, with the original characteristics.

John Haydon and Johanna his wife, are buried on the north side of the high altar in Ottery church, and over them is a large high tomb, of commanding character, with a pyramidal canopy. On the Purbeck marble table is this inscription :—

Hic iacet Johannes Haydon de Cadhay, Armiger, et Johanna uxor eins consanguinea et heres Johannæ Cadhay quæ fuit uxor Hugonis Grenuile, Generosi qui quidem Johannes fuit primus Gubernator incorporatus huius Parochiæ ac obiit sine exitu nono die Martii Anno Domini 1587, *dicta autem Johanna obiit sine exitu decimo nono die Decembris Anno Domini* 1592, *pro quibus laus sit Deo.*

Arms: in the pediment, an escutcheon with helmet and mantling, *Quarterly of four*, 1 and 4, Haydon, 2 and 3, *per saltire sable and argent, in the sable divisions two lions rampant argent, and in the argent two bulls courant sable*, also for Haydon, being the device of their crest borne as a charge, below is the motto FIRM·EN·FOY, and the date 1587, Under the table of the tomb in quatrefoil panels is a shield, *Gules, three clarions, or rests or* (GRENVILLE), and in another the crest of Haydon.

In the south porch, which presumably he erected or re-edified, on the ironwork of the door is "J. H.—1571." Over the doorway the royal arms are sculptured, and above them is inscribed :—

He that no il will do
Do nothyng yt lang yto.

and below is :—

In te Domine speravi,
Non confunder, in æternum.

on a tablet above the door within the aisle is the following :—

In obitum ornatissimi viri Johannis Haydoni, armigeri:
Vita defuncti carmen.
Dicite mortales, quis fructus divitiarum
Hinc quum demigrans vita petita fugit?
Dicite quam multum dives sit paupere major
Quum fera mors una tollit utrumque die?
Omnis homo fænum est, levis et vanescit ut umbra ;
Nulla est, et fœdis vermibus esca manet.
Indicat hæc nobis tua mors, Haidone, dolenda,
Quæ siccas hominum non sinat esse genas.
In patriam benefacta tuam primaque supersunt,
Quæ poterant multi multa referre viri.
A Rege Henrico primus Diploma parasti
Floreat ut literis læta juventa bonis ;
Ludus et erectus fiat et Rectoria clara

> Effecit studium sedulitasque tua.
> Sparsit ubique tuam pietatem Pons novus infra,
> Inque Dei monstrat Porticus ista fidem.
> Legem cultor eras, semper dilectus egenis.
> Impia devitans jurgia, pacis amans ;
> Vos igitur pueri, juvenes propeiate senesque
> Et mecum Haidoni tradite corpus humo.
> Illi, qui meruit prœconia reddite justa,
> Famam et elegiis concelebrate suum
> Dicite, livor abi ; tandem post funera cessa
> Spiritus Haidoni nam loca sancta tenet,
> Qui multa in terris vivens benefacta locavit,
> Cum Christo sedem, jam capit ille suam.
> 1618.

This inscription is given as approximate only. It has been somewhat differently read by the older authorities, and appears to have been renewed of late years.

He also gave to the poor of Woodbury as recorded there —:

1590.

John Haydon. of Caddy, Gent, gave five nobles per annum to the poor of this parish (Woodbury), payable by the Chamber of Exeter, for ever.

Cadhay appears to have been alienated by Haydon, early in the eighteenth century to William Peere Williams, Esq., and is now the property of his descendant, Sir George Ralph Hare, Bart., of Stow Hall Norfolk.

HAYDON, OF HORNSHAYES, NORTHLEIGH, AND FARWOOD COLYTON. GEORGE HAYDON, third son of *Richard Haydon*, of Woodbury, *ob.* 1533, was of Hornshayes, Northleigh, and the adjoining estate of Farwood, Colyton. He married SUSAN, daughter of . . . . *Parke,* of London, by whom he had a son *Edward.* He died 28 Aug. 1558, and was buried at Farnay, *inq. p. m.*, 2 Elizabeth (1560) p^t 1. No. 38. His wife married secondly Richard Yorke.

EDWARD HAYDON, son and heir, was of Lincoln's Inn, Co. Middlesex, aged 18, 22 June, 1560, died 12 May, 1562, s. p. *Inq. p. m.* 9 Elizabeth (1567) No. 202. His uncle *Thomas,* of Woodbury his heir, *ob.* 1576.

" Farwood," says Pole, belonging to the Abbey of Quarr, in the Isle of Wight, was purchased by George Haydon of Hornshayes, and from him descended unto Thomas his nephew, and from Robert his son, unto Gideon Haydon, whose now it is." Earwood house was burnt down, several years since, but an escutcheon of painted glass, in one of the windows although considerably mutilated, was fortunately preserved, and exhibits:—

Quarterly of six:—
1.—*Argent, three bars gemels azure, in a chief gules a barrulet dancette or* (HAYDON). 2.—*Ermine, three battle axes sable* (WEEKES). 3.—*Argent, within a bordure engrailed, two chevrons gules.* 4.—*Ermine, two glaziers irons in saltier gules* (TYTHERLEIGH). 5.—*Argent, within a bordure engrailed gules, two chevrons azure, a martlet for difference* (TYRELL). 6.—*Argent, ten torteaux, 4, 3, 2, 1, a label of three azure* (BABINGTON), Crest, *a lion argent, seising a bull sable.* In Northleigh Church there was formerly a small squires pew, with the Haydon arms carved on it, as given below.

HAYDON, OF POLTIMORE, FARWAY, DEVON. PETER HAYDON presumably a son of *Richard Haydon* of Woodbury, ob. 1533, and his wife JOAN *Trevill*, query *Trent*, was of Poltimore, with a separate descent given in the *Visitation*, 1620, left a son *William.*

WILLIAM HAYDON, of Poltimore, married JOAN, daughter of . . . . *Hales,* co. Kent, left a son *Thomas.*

THOMAS HAYDON, married GRACE, daughter of *Thomas Collins* of Colwell in the adjoining parish of Offwell, a reputable family originally of Ottery S Mary, whose arms were, *Azure, three torches or, enflamed proper,* crest, *A cubit arm erect, the hand holding a torch proper.* They had two sons *William* and *Francis,* and she married secondly 21 Oct. 1611, Clement Southwood of Crediton. *Francis,* of Poltimore, married, and had a daughter, *Anne.*

WILLIAM HAYDON, of Poltimore. He is described as being Rector of Honiton, Dr. Oliver does not include him in the succession of rectors, his incumbency was apparently during the Commonwealth. He married 29 Jan. 1609-10, at S⁺ Martin's Church, Exeter, EBETT, daughter of *John Searle*, of Honiton. She was buried at Farway, 12 May, 1647. They had three sons, *Thomas, John* who married *Agnes* .... and left a son *John* baptised 21 Sep. 1641, at Farway, *Simon*, baptised at Farway, 1 Apl. 1625, and two daughters *Ann*, buried at Farway, 1622, and *Grace*, baptised 14 June, 1622.

THOMAS HAYDON, eldest son, baptised at Farway, 1 Nov. 1610. Poltimore is an estate of some size in this parish. Inscriptions almost obliterated are found on some old tombs in Farway churchyard to members of this descent.

W. H. H. ROGERS.

186. TWO INTERESTING EPITAPHS (par. 169, p. 201).—Owing to imperfect light, the darkness of the little tablet—black marble—and obscurity of the lettering, three words have been wrongly transcribed in the Trinity church inscription; a rubbing has been taken and the correction is: for *militans*, read *militaris*, for *sacellum, sacellani*, and for *rarus, rarius*.   Q.R.

187. I suggest the following interpretation of the words "*climacterico*" and "δευτεροπρωτω." Climacter means a critical period of life. The word with its adjectival variations was often used as an English word—*vide* Sir T. Browne (Vulgar Errors), Massinger ("The Old Law," act I, sc. I), Burke (Reflections on the French Revolution), Richardson, Cotgrave and others.

The word refers to the 7th, 9th or 63rd years of life, all presumed to be dangerous, but the last most so. The person referred to in the epitaph probably died at one of these ages. The Greek word "κλιμακτηρ" means a step in a ladder. Climax is a cognate word (*vide* Skeat's Philological Dictionary). The other word "δευτεροπρωτω" is probably intended to convey the meaning that the person died on the first sabbath after the second day of the feast of unleavened bread, *vide* Liddell & Scott's Greek Lexicon *tit* " δευτεροπρωτον σαββατον," where that meaning is given and attributed to Scaliger. In the epitaph the word sabbath is presumed to be understood.   WILLIAM DAVIES.

188. If this word "*climactericus*" is used in its ordinary English sense, *i.e.*, as the Latin representative of "climacteric," it would mean the "critical" year of life, *i.e.*, the 63rd year; but in that case "δευτερόπρωτω" seems without meaning. I, therefore, prefer to think that the writer was a Greek scholar who knew that "κλιμακτηρ'" meant the round of a ladder, or the step of a staircase and then a step or stage in life. The ancients held that owing to waste and repair the constituents of the body were entirely changed every seven years, each period of seven years being consequently known as a stage in life. Infancy was one, childhood another, youth a third, early manhood a fourth, and so on.

The word "δευτερόπρωτω" is a word which occurs once in the New Testament, in St. Luke vi., 1 (if, indeed, as Dr. Field suggests, it is not a mistaken reading altogether) and in the authorised version is rendered " on the second [sabbath] after the first." Liddell and Scott, however, describe it as on "the first [sabbath] after the second [day of unleavened bread.]" If we assume that this meaning was present to the mind of the epitaph-writer, the combination of the word with *climactericus* will give us "the first [year] after the second [stage in life was passed]." This will be the 15th year. The epitaph might then be rendered :—

1650
Here lies Henry, son of Robert Parsons, who passed away in the year of his age, reckoned by life-stages, the first after the second.

Epitaph-writers of the seventeenth century were fond of providing puzzles for their readers. OSWALD J. REICHEL.

189. THE Rev. F. B. Dickinson writes:—When I saw the July number of *D.N.&Q.* and read the inscriptions on p. 201, I felt convinced that the one from Holy Trinity Church, Exeter, was incorrectly given. I wrote to my old friend, Mr. Bazeley, the Rector, and asked him to look at it for me, and give me a correct copy. I don't know what the "*societas militaris*" may have been, but possibly, as the City Gaol was in the *South Gate, adjoining* the Church (both having been taken down in 1819), there may have been some sort of guard of soldiers

always on the spot. I take it that "sa*ce*llanus" must be
"*sacce*llanus," treasurer, for the word would be "capellanus"
if it meant chaplain. Mr. Bazeley tells me that he had
considerable difficulty in finding the monument, which is a
very small black marble oval tablet in the vestry, and that it
required dusting and washing before it could be deciphered,
being, moreover, in a very dark place. I append the words
and a translation, which your correspondent asks for:—

MS.
Thomæ Wight, A.M., S. Stæ* Trinitatis
    Exon Rectoris necnon Societatis militaris
    ibidem sacellani
Qui obijt 11₀ Februarij Anno Dom 1682 Aetatis 40,
    Fortis eras Probus (et quod rarum est) Fidus amico
    Doctus item sed (quod rarius est) Humilis.

Translation :—Sacred to the Memory of Thomas Wight, Master of Arts, Rector of Holy Trinity, Exeter, and also Treasurer (?) of the Military Society therein, who died 2nd of February, in the year of his age 40, and of our Lord 1682.

Brave wast thou, upright (and, what is rare) faithful to your friend. Learned also, but what is rarer, humble.

I venture on a free translation, or paraphrase :—

    Manly wast thou, Tom Wight,
    And upright to the end.
    And, as man hardly ever sees,
    Full faithful to thy friend.
    Learned beside, yet humble quite,
    Which last, man almost never sees.

While I am on the subject of the inscriptions, I should like to be allowed to add just a word with regard to the vexed question of the Sidbury epitaph, and I would suggest this, as a probable interpretation, based on the acknowledged fact that every seventh year was regarded as an "annus climactericus." The Greek word "δευτεροπρωτος" (if it can be called Greek) occurs, I believe, only once, in S. Luke vi., 1, and is there translated "the second after the first." It seems not unlikely that the author of the inscription adopted the idea of the second climacteric year after the first, as a kind of fanciful conceit to express the twenty-first year. The first such "annus" would be the seventh year of the child's age; the next would be the fourteenth, and the "second after the first" the twenty-first. I do not see that the Greek word on the

---

* S. Stæ = Sacro Sanctæ,

brass is intended to be so entirely separated in type, or in sense, from the rest, as the reproduction on p. 201 implies. Possibly a search in the registers might enable us to trace the baptism of Henry, son of Robert Parson, and so settle this knotty point. If I am right, it should be found about 1629. The words of S. Luke " ἐν sαββάτω Δευτεροπρώτω " are translated by Wyclif, 1380, "in the seconde first saboth"; by Tyndal, 1534, "on an after saboth"; Cranmer, 1539, "on an after principall saboth"; Geneva, 1557, "on the second sabbath after the first"; Rheims, 1582, "on the sabbath second-first"; Authorised, 1611, "on the second sabbath after the first'; and the Revised Version, 1884, leaves the word out altogether, except in the margin, and merely says "on a Sabbath."

190. IN answer to your query on p. 201, I venture to think both epitaphs are interesting, chiefly because of errors. " δευτερόπρώτω " is the rarest of all rare words, being found only in S. Luke vi., 1—where probably it ought not to appear in the text, but is rather a combination of two marginal glosses. The seventeenth century knew little of textual criticism; and perhaps the writer of this epitaph was struck with a sonorous Greek word, though neither he nor we can make sense of it. My suggestion is that he took it to mean 21, and so wrote: "*Here lies Henry, son of Robert Parson, who died in the year of his majority, 21.*" (The Greek was written in uncials to correspond with the Roman capitals).

The difficulty of the next inscription is surely a false concord on the second line? In this case we have no photograph, but only a copy of the lines; and there may be on the tablet itself a mark of abbreviation *(militans)* for "militantis." But the verb is properly a neuter; though, unless memory fail me, occasionally in low Latin it is active. Mr. Wright appears to have been Rector of Holy Trinity, and also head of the Guild which served a chapel there. " Militans " would equal " serving" in a religious sense, as well as a military one. If so, the translation is :—

"Sacred to the memory of Thomas Wight, M.A., Rector of Holy Trinity, Exeter, and of the Guild serving the Chapel there, who died on Feb. 11, 1682, in the 40th year of his age.

" Thou wert a strong man, tried (and, what is seldom) faithful to thy friend; learned also (but, what is rarer still) humble-minded."

E.G.P.

191. DEPORTMENT OF CONVICTS.—The subjoined extract from the *Town and Country Magazine*, of 1784 (p. 222), depicts very forcibly, one of the terrors incident to the former system of deporting convicts to distant penal settlements; and may be contrasted with the excitement that is created when, at the present time, some unfortunate fellow escapes from the prison boundaries.

"Exeter, April 15 (1784). The following letter was last evening received by express from Captain Cadman, of the Helena sloop of war, dated Torbay, April 14.

'Sir,— A ship arrived here last night from London, with convicts, who rose about ten days since on the master and crew. Sixty landed the same evening at Paignton, and escaped. The master informs me they are a desperate set of fellows, and may commit many depredations. I hope this account submitted to your attention may be the means of some (if not all) being detected. Forty attempted their escape this morning, but my boats were so fortunate to take them before they reached the shore.

I am, Sir,
Your most obedient and very humble servant,
GEORGE CADMAN.'

To the Right Worshipful the Mayor of Exeter,

Upwards of twenty were re-taken here in the course of the last night and to-day; the strictest search is still making by the constables and soldiers. Sixty that were taken in getting ashore were brought to Topsham by water this evening, under convoy of the Helena's crew, and from thence escorted to Bridewell by the military. There are about fifty left on board the ship. The whole nnmber that were on board were about a hundred and sixty." T.N.B.

192. COBLEIGH OF BRIGHTLEIGH (par. 179, p. 210).—We regret that there were two serious mistakes in the pedigrees given in our last number. In the first pedigree as printed, Isabel (the wife of John Cobleigh), is made the daughter of Robert Cornu, instead of the daughter of Thomas de Brightleigh, and consequently the point of the query is lost. In the last pedigree sketched by Mr. Hardinge F. Giffard, as being probably the correct pedigree of Cobleigh, it was pointed out that Isabel de Brightleigh, by her *second* husband, John

Cobleigh, probably had a son, John Cobleigh, who was the father of the third John Cobleigh, the husband of Jane Fortescue. As printed, John Cobleigh No. 2 appears to be the son of both John Cobleigh No. 1 and also of Robert Cornu. In the concluding paragraph, page 214, it is scarcely necessary to say that *Fitzwarnie* is a misprint for *Fitzwarine*.

EDS.

193. A LODDISWELL DEED.—By the permission of Col. Wise, the owner, with the kind assistance of Mr. H. L. Jenkins, of Clannacombe, Thurleston, we are able to give our readers a *fac simile* reproduction of a very pretty little and interesting thirteenth century deed. It is a grant of the Manor of Loddiswell, excepting the advowson of the Church and the land given to the Prior and Canons of Studley, the Augustinian house in Warwickshire, by Eva, widow of William de Cantilupe. The Cantilupes were great benefactors to Studley. Dugdale gives us (*Mon. Ang.*, vol. vi., p. 185) particulars of the gift of this lady to the Canons, granted *cir.* 46 Henry iii., the land in Loddiswell being of the value of c^s. per annum, with the homage and services of certain freeholders there, and a yearly rent of xx^s. The date of the deed we print is probably about 1265—it may have been after the gift just mentioned,—and Mr. John S. Amery points out that amongst the names in the Roll of the Guild-Merchant of Totnes, are those of Walter le Bon, and Thomas de Strete, who are witnesses. With the always readily accorded and valuable help of the Rev. Prebendary Hingeston-Randolph, we are able to give a fully extended copy of this document.

> Sciant presentes et futuri quod ego Eva de Cantilupo in Ligia viduitate mea, dedi, concessi et hac presenti carta mea confirmavi pro me et heredibus meis Domino Radulpho de Knouyle, pro homagio et servicio suo, totum Manerium meum de Lodeswelle, cum pertinenciis, salva michi et heredibus meis advocacione Ecclesie euisdem ville, et excepta terra quam dedi domino Priori et Canonicis de Stodleye, in eodem Manerio cum pertinenciis. Habendum et tenendum de me et heredibus meis sibi et heredibus suis, In feodo et hereditate, libere et quiete, bene, in pace plena, inperpetuum Reddendo inde annuatim michi et heredibus meis ipse et heredes sui sexaginta solidos ad duos anni terminos, videlicet, ad festum Sancti Michaelis triginta solidos, et ad Pascha triginta solidos, pro omni servicio exaccione et demanda michi vel heredibus meis pertinenti. Ego vero Eva de Cantilupo, et heredes mei dicto Domino Radulpho et heredibus suis totam terram predictam cum pertinenciis suis, ut

predictum est, contra omnes homines et feminas inperpetuum warantizabimus. In cuius rei testimonium presenti scripto sigillum meum apposui. Hiis testibus, Domino Willelmo, capellano meo, Roberto Wallensi, Roberto de Fremins, Waltero le Bon, Henrico de Tydeworthe, Willelmo Fychet, Thoma de Strete, et multis aliis.

Endorsed : Carta de Lodeswille, facta per Evam de Cantilupo.
Liberata per indenturam.

194. COURTENAY AND OTHER MONUMENTS IN SHEVIOCKE CHURCH.—I am indebted to the Rev. Gerald Pole-Carew, M.A., the present Rector of Sheviocke, for a memorandum of a visit made by his grandfather, Reginald Pole-Carew, to Sheviocke Church. The account, which if somewhat discursive, is very circumstantial, so we will record the facts contained in it as concisely as possible. The record is particularly interesting as showing beyond question that much heraldry existed in 1797, which had completely disappeared when I made the notes printed in my *Heraldic and Genealogical Church Notes from Cornwall*, and it is an evidence of the usefulness of such notes if carefully made.

The memorandum states that on September 7th, 1797, R. Pole-Carew went to Sheviocke and requested the Rev. Joshua Jeans, Rector of Sheviocke, to accompany him to the said church to examine the monuments, armorial bearings, and other historical remains, and particularly to ascertain who the recumbent figures in the south transept represented and also the figure under one of the windows in the north aisle.

Mr. R. Pole-Carew then states that on the monument with recumbent effigy of a lady in the south transept, the arms of Courtenay impaling Daunye or Dawney (the latter is correct) " were extremely distinct on one of those escutcheons in 1782, and are still very discernable and ascertainable on this 7 Sept., 1792." He says the escutcheon on which the Courtenay arms are, does not face the spectator approaching the monument, but must be looked for over the back of the lady's head on the pillar or stone partition which separates the figure of the lady from the knight. To this fact it probably owes its better preservation. It was then not easy to say what were on the other escutcheons, but those which were most visible had only Dawney's arms, viz. : *a bend cotised*, the colours uncertain. Mr. R. Pole-Carew states that the colours of the Courtenay coat were very plain when he first saw it in 1782 or 1783, but the blazon he gives is not correct, viz.: Dawney, *the field or. a bend cotised az.* Courtenay, *azure or argent three torteaux a label of three points*, the blazoning of the torteaux being gules, was very visible when he first saw them in 1782 or 1783, but that in 1797 the colours were gone and the outline only could be seen on the plaister. This means doubtless that the outline could be seen through the whitewash which had been added after his first visit. Mr. Pole-Carew states that no arms could be seen on the shields over the knight adjoining the lady, nor could any arms be seen on the monument with the effigy in the north aisle, but it was then partly hidden by the pews.

In the east window of the north aisle there then existed the arms of Cole impaling Kingdon, viz.: *arg. a bull pass. sa. within a bord. of the second, bezantee, imp. arg. a chev. sa. betw. three magpies ppr.* In the next window of the north aisle he says there is a large Saxon monument with these arms twice in a scroll so that one has the arms backward, that is bendways. The arms he gives as *arg. on a bend cotised sa. three roses or.* This *Saxon* monument has entirely disappeared, so that it is difficult to say what it was, but from a rough sketch of the shields it was probably a seventeenth century memorial of the Dawney family, the figure under the north wall probably represents Sir John Dawney, for his father does not appear to have possessed Sheviocke, although he held the Manor of Antony and other lands and manors in Devon and Cornwall. John Dawney was found to be his son and heir and of the age of thirty years and more. (Inq. P.M., 6 Edw., III. No. 79, 2nd memb:). This son, Sir John Dawnee, chev'ler, died 20 Edw. III. (Inq. P.M., 20 Edw. III, No. 33, 1st memb:), when he was found seized of the manors of Anton'. and Chevyoke, with other lands and manors in Devonshire, Cornwall and Somerset all enumerated, and Emelina was found to be his daughter and heir, and of the age of eighteen years and more. The returns from the escheators of each county make a long document. This daughter became the wife of Edward Courtenay, from the marriage of whose granddaughter, Joan Courtenay to Nicholas Carew, the Manors of Antony, Sheviocke, &c., came to the Carews, whose descendant and representative, the present Sir Reginald Pole-Carew, K.C.B., now possesses the estates.

Edward Courtenay survived his wife about seven years, and though there is not any evidence of his having been buried at Sheviocke, the figure adjoining his wife there can be little question represents him, and that it was placed there in his own lifetime after the death of his wife.

In the British Museum (Sloane Charters xxxiii, 13) is a grant by William de Aleyton, Lord Sheviocke, of half-an-acre of land at Lansehawyn, to Nicholas Selwyn and Matilda, his wife, reserving to himself and his heirs a ground rent and manorial rights in the same. It is witnessed by Willm. Tregrove Fulcono de Mone, Rico de Trewynnard, and others. In an Inquisition of the lands of Thomas, Earl of Lancaster, and other rebells, the Manor of Sheviocke occurs (Inq. P.M., 16 Edw. II, No. 49); so that it would seem to have been granted after that to Nicholas de Daunay (Dawney).

ARTHUR J. JEWERS.

195. CUSTOM AT ST. PETROCK'S CHURCH, EXETER.—GALLEYHAPENS.—The following paragraph is transcribed from Dr. Oliver's *Eccles. Antiq.*, I. 34.—" We find in the Fabric Roll of the Cathedral, A.D. 1415, the sum of 3s. 2d. received" in Galyhapens de Ecclesiâ Parochiali de Wodbury.' This was probably the contribution or fees paid by the girls or women of the parish who were married in the course of the year. We have met with a similar custom in the churchwardens' accounts of St. Petrock's parish, Exeter."

The custom in the latter parish is corroborated in Mr. R. Dymond's *History of St. Petrock's*, where it is recorded to have been a regular one during the 15th century; but it is invariably entered in the accounts as " Ballesylver," or some variant of this term, *e.g.*

> " For a collection made amongst the women of the parish married this year called 'balsılfer,' 5d." (29).

Dr. Oliver appears to accept this word as identical with " Galyhapens" in the above extract from his work, whereas they were widely different. Ships from Genoa landed their goods at Galley Key, London, and, according to Stow, the men who brought them " had a certaine coyne of siluer amongst themselves, which were halfe pence of Genoa, and were called Galley halfe-pence." Their introduction, together with other foreign money, such as " Dandy Prattes," " Roman

Grottoes (groats); " (*N. & Q.* 5th, Ser. II. 187), was deemed so injurious to small traders at that period, that by a statute of 1411-2, and again of 1416-7, any one found bringing them into this country, was to be " punished as a thiefe, and he that taketh or payeth such money, shall lose an hundred shillings; " but notwithstanding this heavy penalty, Stow remarks, " in my youth I have seene them passe currant." (*Survey of London* (1633), 127).

It may have been due to the deficiency of small English money, but whatever the cause, it is difficult to understand why, in 1415, base coin like Galley half-pence should be received by the Cathedral authorities. The difference between the two kinds is further accentuated by the fact that while the Woodbury money, in base coin, amounted to 3s. 2d., that received at St. Petrock's was, states Mr. Dymond, " usually less than 5d."

T.N.B.

196. WILLS OF THOMAS CHAFE AND PASCOE RISDON.

In nomine patris et filii et Spiritus Sancti. Amen. On the ffour and twentieth day of September Anno Dm one thousand six hundred forty eight I Tho. Chafe of the parish of Saint Giles in the County of Devon Gentleman able and sound of body and minde for which with my whole hart and soule I doe glorifie my good God the donor do make and ordaine in manner and forme following ffirst a poore penetent doe render and bequeath to the blessed Trinitie in Unity my Creator and Redeemer and Sanctifier my poore soule and my corruptable corps to Christian buriall in decent and silent manner some few houres before the candle doth inheritt the same office. Item I give to the poore of Saint Giles, my body being interred amongst them, twentie shillings. Item I give unto my wife a mourneninng gowne; also my will is if she so pleaseth to make use of my bedsted with the green curtains that are now about the bedstead while she lives. Item I give unto my good neece Mrs. Catherine Brookin twenty poundes. Also I give unto her good husband Mr. Thomas Brookin five pounds for a remembrance I would heartily acknowledge another neece but her impious deserts deserve nothing for present but teares and prayers that she may prove a second Mary. Item I give to my dearly beloved sisters Mrs. Dorothy Bigilston (*sic*) and Mrs. Richourd Curson twelve shillings a peece. Item I give to my loving nephew Mr Phillipp Bigilston seaven pounds. Item unto his Brother Mr. John Bigilston seaven poundes. Item to his brother Mr. Thomas Bigilston ten pounds if he be alive, if he be dead then I give the ten pounds which his mother his (*sic i.e my*) sister owes me unto her selfe and not to have the above legacies of twelve shillings and the bonds which I have for the securitie of that tenn pounds in my keeping to be delivered unto her by my executor. Item I give unto my cozen Mr. Peter Bigilston seaven pounds. Item I give unto my gratious cozen Mr. James Bigilston

(I doe wish I were of abilitie to give as he deserves) ten pounds. Item I give unto my neece Mrs. Dorothy Bigilston ten pounds. Item I give unto my nephew Mr. Thomas Curson six pounds. Item to my nephew Mr. John Curson six pounds. Item unto my nephew Mr. George Curson seaven pounds. Item I give unto my neece Mrs. Mary Serrell (*sic*) six pounds for a momento. Item I give to my virtuous neece Mrs. Margarett Yeo twenty shillings and to her good husband ten shillings I desire their noble goodness to accept of my myte. Item I give unto my loving neece Mrs. Joane Sterrill (*sic*) to bestow in a Ring she please twenty shillings. Item I give unto my nephew William Ryledon *(sic)* ten pounds. Item I give to Mr. Arthur Rolls one pound two shillings a poore index of my well wishes towards him. Item I give my antient friend Mr. Thomas Baylis one pound six shillings who I presume will respect the *donor* not the *donum* to be bestowed by my executor in a little peece of plate with my arms thereon. Item I give to my nephews wife Mrs. Catherine Chafe for a true species of my good intentions towards her and hers one pound two shillings to be bestowed in a ring and thereon a deathes head. Item I give to my hopefull Godson and my young nephew Thomas Chafe forty pounds and my plate after his fathers decease. Thus distributing what the Lord hath sent me after my great losses oppressions and sufferings witness these dismall dayes doe desire my Executor under nominated to satisfie these legacies by me given with such convenience as he can without long expectancie, further I require my executor to interr my body as neere as he can by my sister Risedon. And I doe ordaine appointe and require thirty pounds rather more then lesse to be bestowed in a monument of my effigies by my Executor of whose love herein I am not diffident who have reaped soe many gratuities formerly from me and now in present burthening his conscience for effecting it as he shall answer *coram Deo*. I desire him to inscript in my monument some memory of his good Aunt Risedon and of the family deceased there interred, also of my wief and her two children noe great onos to an ingenious generous and grateful minde. Now all the rest of my goods and lands not given or bequeathed I give and bequeath to my onely most respective nephew Thomas Chafe Esq. and Councellor at law whome I ordaine institute and nominate to be my whole and sole Exr. of this my last Will and testament written with mine own hand and soe well known that I doe not greatly repute the subscription of wittnesses to strengthen it. And this my last Will and Testament to corroboratt and to make it legall I do impresse my seale and subscribe my name the day and yeare above written. *Vale* T. Chafe *Scripsi*. Not omitting this subsequent I inioyne and desire my nephew my executor to redeliver peaceably all such mortgages as I shall be on^r of at my death to the true owners being satisfied of his conscionable due. Item *Vale*. T. C. *Laus Deo, pax hominibus.* T. Chafe de Doddescott.

Proved in London 18 Feb. 1648-9) by Thomas Chafe, Esq., the Executor. P. C. Fairfax, 25.

In the Register the name is spelt Shafe, but the original will filed has the name spelt Chafe.

In the name of God Amen. I Pascoe Risdon of Winscott in the Parish of St. Giles in the Countie of Devon widdowe in my perfecte health and strength of body and minde praise be to Almightie God for it doe make and ordaine this my last Will and Testament in manner and forme followeinge ffirst I committ my bodie to the earth whereof itt is made to have a decent and Christian buriall my soule I comend into the hands of God my maker hopeing assured he through the onelie merrits of my Saviour Jesus Christ to be made perfect of eternall glorie. Item I give and bequeath unto my Sonne and heire William Risdon whome I appointe hereafter to be my sole Executor all that the mannor of Winscott and the Barton farme and demesnes thereof with the rents services and appurtenances thereunto belonginge in the parishe of Saint Giles aforesaid and all other my lands tenements messuages dwellinge houses rents and services whatsoever in the said countie of Devon or elsewhere to have and to hould to him and his heires for ever. Item I give to my daughter in law mistress (*sic Margery in the Margin*) Risdon two stockes of Bees and my still. Item I give to my daughter Mrs. Joane Hearle all my best woollen and lynnen apparrell and my weddinge ringe. Item I give to my grandchild Joane Hearle a bearinge blanckett and all my child bed linnen. Item I give to John Maddcott godsonne unto my husband Mr. Tristram Risdon deceased five shillings. Item I give to my goddaughter Pascoe Romikly *(sic)* a yeo. Item I give goddaughter Pascoe Norman a yeo. Item I give to my servant Grace Copleston (if she be with me at the time of my death) my best old woollen and linnen apparrell and my rideing shute. Item I give to the poore of the parish of St. Giles thirtie shillings. Item I give unto the poore of Rooburrough tenn shillings. All the rest of my goods and chattels lands and tenements not given or bequeathed I give and bequeath unto my said Sonne and heire William Risdon whome I make the full and whole executor of this my last will and Testament. And I desire my loveinge nephewe Mr. Thomas Chafe and my loveing Sonne in lawe Mr. James Hearle to be overseers hereof and to be assistant unto my executor in the execution of the same and for their paines therein I give unto each of them twentie shillings. In witness whereof I have hereunto set my hand and seale and published itt to be my last Will and Testament this one and twentieth daie of Aprill And in the year of our Lord one thousand six hundred fortie six. In the presence of those whose names are here written. The signe of Pascoe Risdon. Witnesses present att the signeinge sealinge and publishinge hereof, Thos. Chafe, Leonard Pettie.

Proved in London 10 September, 1647, by William Risdon, the son and executor. P.C.C. Fines, 184.

197. JAY'S GRAVE (par. 142, p. 187).—In his notes on Local Traditions of North Bovey and Neighbourhood, the writer asks concerning Jay's Grave, which is by the side of the Ashburton and Chagford road, where the Heytree and Hedge Barton estates meet. A workman of mine, aged 74, informs us that about forty years ago, just before he came to Ashburton,

where he will have lived thirty-nine years next October, he was in the employ of Mr. James Bryant, of Hedge Barton, Manaton, when he remembers Jay's Grave being opened, in which a young unmarried woman who hung herself in Cannon Farm outbuildings, which is situated between Forder and Torhill, was said to have been buried, but no one then living at Manaton could remember the occurrence.

The grave was opened by order of Mr. James Bryant in the presence of his son-in-law, Mr. J. W. Sparrow, M.R.C.S. Bones were found, examined and declared to be those of a female, the skull was taken to Hedge Barton house, but was afterwards placed with the bones in a box and re-interred in the old grave, a small mound raised with head and foot stones erected at either end. Such is the present appearance of the grave. P.F.S.A.

198. FOREIGN CHURCHES AND THEIR PROPERTY IN DEVON.—It is always a pleasure to get something from the pen of Mr. J. Horace Round, though in the case of the book—"Calendar of Documents preserved in France illustrative of the History of Great Britain and Ireland"—he only acts as editor. But what labour and trouble this editing must have cost him! In print it looks very little—a few dates, a copious index, but that index a mine of information as to persons and places. Mr. Round limits his documents to the time before the separation of England and of Normandy, which he fixes in the year 1206.

Foreign churches had a good deal of property in Devon. The church or convent of the Holy Trinity at Caen possessed Umberleigh; St. Stephen's Caen possessed Northam; St. Michael's of Monte Tuba, Otterton, Sidmouth and Yarcombe; St. Mary's of Rouen, Ottery and Rawridge in Upottery; St. Mary's of Montebourg, Axmouth. Of all these churches the original charters existing in France are now made available for the historian. The historians of Devon should be grateful.

One point which these documents bring out is the far-reaching reality of the papal power in this county in the 12th century. A dispute arises as to a presentation to the little living of Rousdon. The matter is at once taken to the Pope, and the papal delegates of Urban III. write "to their worshipful brother and most dear friend the Bishop of Exeter" telling him how they have settled it. Another dispute arises as to the amount payable by the living of Tawstock under a charter to St. Mary Magdalen's Church at Barnstaple. It is also at once taken to Pope Clement III., and the papal delegates notify all whom it may concern how they have settled it. The Convent of Montebourg finds itself straightened in funds. Application goes to the Pope, and Innocent III. issues a decretal letter authorizing it "for the maintenance of its poor folk" to divert and apply the income of Axmouth Church, "saving the Bishop's rights, and the assignment of a sufficient maintenance to the chaplain."

If we must criticize we venture to express a regret that Mr. Round has in one or two places not grappled with the difficulty of place-names. Thus on p. 269 in a Bull of Pope Adrian IV. confirming to the Abbot and brethren of St. Michael all that they possess in England, the following names occur:—" In the diocese of Exeter, the cell of St. Michael's Mount, Cornwall; the township of Otritone with the church; Seduine and its church; the church of cudeb[eria]; Wiscumba, Estelleia, Erticomba, and the church and township called Bordelar." Here, as is usual in papal Bulls, English ames are frightfully corrupted. Seduine is of course Sedemuan or Sidmouth, and Cudeberia is, as Mr. Round points out, a corruption of Wodeberia; for Domesday printer (p. 45) tells us that St. Michael held the church of Woodbury. Erticombe is Yarcombe, one of the Domesday estates of St. Michael's; and Bordelar is Budleigh, which Testa de Nevil (No. 1,341, p. 194a) says was given by Henry I. to St. Michael's. But what are Wiscumba and Estelleia? Mr. Round gives no information. There is a Wishcombe in Southleigh, but is there any evidence that it was ever connected with Otterton or St. Michael's? May we suggest that one or both represent the Domesday Donitone which belonged to St. Michael's, which certainly lay in Axminster hundred and formed part of the present parish of Yarcombe? Can Estelleia possibly be Stoutleigh in Yarcombe?

Again the charter of Henry, Bishop of Exeter in 1205, permits the monks of St. Michael on the next vacancy to apply to their own uses the revenues of "the churches of Otri with its chapel of La Hedreland, of Sichenny, of Harticombe

combe and of Hepeford" in Devon. In this list Otri is clearly a mistake for Otritone—tho' Mr. Round does not notice it—for Ottery St. Mary belonged to Rouen; Sichenny=Sidemue or Sidmouth; Harticombe=Yarticombe or Yarcombe; and Hepeford=Harpford. But what of La Hedreland? Mr. Round suggests that it is Ladram Bay in Otterton, but an entry in Testa (No. 1,208, p. 191a) puts that out of court. In Budleigh Hundred the Abbot of St. Michael holds the " manors of Oterington, Sidemue, *Hetherland* and Wonleigh." This entry shows that the prefix *la* is merely the article and that La Hetherland or Hetherland is in the Hundred of Budleigh. It was, I believe, suggested by the late Mr. Hutchinson that it was Hetherland in Washfield, which, as a fact, is in Budleigh Hundred, and Prebendary Hingeston-Randolph (Bronescombe 481) seems inclined to favour that view. But the entry in Stafford's Register, p. 365, shows that that Hetherland was a dependent chapel of Washfield, not of Otterton, and was in the same private patronge as Washfield. It, therefore, can hardly have been Mont St. Michel's Hetherland. The taxation of Pope Nicholas in 1288 gives the temporal estates of St. Michael in Devon as " manor of Otritone, Sidemuwe, Budleigh rents and mill, Ertecombe, Hederlonde, Forsham rents, city of Exeter rents." It also shows that Hederlonde must have been a very small possession as the revenue from it was only one shilling. It is possible that Hederlonde and Wonleighe may be in the north of Sidmouth, and that the latter name may still survive in the name of the stream the Wolbrook?

In the charter of Goslin de Pomeray, p. 536, Mr. Round seems to have gone wrong in rendering Otrevum, Ottery. Ottery belonged to St. Mary of Rouen. Pomeroy, therefore, could not dispose of the tithe which was not his to give. What the Pomeroys did posses from Domesday times, and the tithe of which Goslin de Pomeroy gave to the Augustinian Abbey of St. Mary du Val in the year 1125, was Upottery. Otrevum is therefore no doubt Upottery, not Ottery St. Mary.

OSWALD J. REICHEL.

199. POT DE VIN, NEAR TOTNES.—It would be interesting to know why there is a Vineyard and Puddaven interpreted *Pot de Vin*, near Totnes. That there are other places of that

name in Devonshire is not a satisfactory explanation, nor is the fact of the fields there assuming a terraced form disposed of by saying similar indications of former cultivation are seen when descending the Dart. The fact of some chips of rude brown pottery, sometimes half-an-inch thick, having been found in one of these fields, may be placed on record.

A. H. SWINTON.

200. JONATHAN JELLETT.—Can any one give any information as to a certain Jonathan Jellett or Gillett, who sailed from Plymouth, on March 20th, 1630, on board the *Mary and John*, in company with the Rev. John Warham, a Congregational Minister, who gathered a company of people, some hundred and thirty from Devonshire, and came with them to New England.

Are the ship's archives still in existence? If so, they may say where he came from, and I should like to know if any of the family still live in Devonshire.

JAMES J. JELLETT.
St. Paul's, Minn.

201. THE LETHBROCS, LETHBROGS, OR LETHBRIDGES (par. 180, p. 214).—In continuation of the paper on Regner Lothbrog the following foot-note to the legend of "The Raven Banner," published in the *Western Miscellany*, 1849, will no doubt be interesting. The writer of the legend says as follows: " If anyone, walking through the South Street of Exeter, will take the trouble to step a few yards into St. James' Street, he may observe on the left hand a small arched door leading to the court of some almshouses. Over the door are inscribed the following words: 'Built and endow'd by Christopher Lethbridge, Esq., one of the aldermen of this city. *All things come of Thee, and of Thine own have I given Thee*, 1 Chronicles, chapter xxix, verse 14.'—1669."

This Christopher Lethbridge was Mayor of Exeter in the year of the Restoration, and founded these almshouses for the habitation of six poor people, allotting them yearly the sum of £15 12s. He is stated by Prince in his *Worthies of Devon* to have been the last male descendant of Regner Lothbroc, an opinion which seems to be confirmed by his arms, which bear in chief an eagle or raven displayed sable."

A. J. DAVY.

202. ATWELL AND MAINE FAMILIES. — Many early colonists of the present State of Maine were Devonshire men, and some effort is now being made to locate their places of birth. John Maine came to Maine between 1630 and 1640, and with him one John Atwell, who became Maine's son-in-law. They settled on Casco Bay, near the present town of York, Maine, having for neighbours, Felts, Carrals, Prebles and Corbins. Associated with them were the noted colonists, Richard Cleaves (a Devon man), Richard Martin (son of a Mayor of Plymouth), and one John Tucker (who named his home Stogumber, after his natal place in Somerset). Robert Corbin and one of the Atwells were killed by the Indians, August 11th, 1676. John Atwell is probably the man aged one year in the Visit. of Devon, 1620 (Harleian Socy., p. 12), and as such from Kenton and Mamhead. Can anyone place John Maine, his wife Elizabeth, or any of his children born in Devon. STUART C. WADE.

203. CELT FOUND NEAR THE TAMAR (par. 160, p. 195).— This is in the possession of Mr. George Lott, of the Barton, Lawhitton, near Launceston, the occupier of the farm in that parish on which the above was found.
CHRISTOPHER L. COWLAND.

END OF VOLUME I.

INDEX.

A (J. S.) on Thomas, first Lord Clifford, 81
A (M.) on Shields on Font at Dunsford, 120
A (P. F. S.) on Great Fulford, 1 ; on Emmanuel Baptisms, 17 ; on Wishing Trees, 26 ; on Bull-ring at Ashburton, 26 ; on the Voice of the Waters, 42 ; on Election Day Treating. 44 ; on Devon Muster Roll, time of Armada, 49 ; on the Grand Jury and their Port Wine, 101 ; on Rapid Travelling, 104 ; on Burleigh Dolts, 149 ; on Letter of Marque, 159 ; on Little Silver, Manadon, 219 ; on Jay's Grave, 251
Abbey of St. Saviour, 87
Abbotskerswell, 47, 70, 71
Ackland, Baldwin, 168
Adams (Maxwell) on Arms on Great Fulford House, 4 ; on the Fulford Monument, 5
Alberica, 209
Aleyton, William de, 248
Altar at Torbryan Church, 208
Amery (P. F. S.) on Rev. J. B. Swete's Tour, 205
Amery—*see* A. (P. F. S.)
Anti-Cromwellian Song, 136
Apprentices' Warning-Piece, The, 219
Apprenticeship Indenture of a Domestic Servant, 13
Armada Chest at Fulford, 4
Arms :—Arthur, 135 ; Babington, 239 ; Bampfield, 6 ; Belston, 4, 6 ; Bowth, 59 ; Bozum, 4 ; Broughton, 229 ; Burgoyne, 131 ; Chafe, 131 ; Chaltons, 5, 6 ; Cloth Workers of Exon, 190 ; Cole, 247 ; Collins, 239 ; Consul, 190 ; Coram, 226 ; Cottell, 103, 152 ; Courtenay, 6, 247 ; Davie, 231 ; Dawnay, 246, 247 ; De la Beare, 152 ; Dennis, 4, 6 ; Fitch, 234 ; Fitzurse, 4, 6 ; Fitzwarren, 144, 183 ; Fulford, 4, 6 ; Grenville, 237 ; Gould, 233 ; Gove, 229 ; Harpsfeld, 120 ; Haydon, 237, 239 ; Jervice, 230 ; Kingdon, 247 ; Malet, 131 ; Martyn, 232 ; Merefeild, 226 ; Molford, 152 ; Moreton, 4, 6 ; Morys, 188 ; Paulet, 230 ; Risdon, 131 ; Rolle, 196 ; St. Aubyn, 5, 6 ; St. George, 4, 6 ; Trent, 226 ; Trosse, 231 ; Tyrell, 239 ; Tytherleigh, 229, 239 ; Walters, 152 ; Weekes, 228, 239
Arthur Family, 135, 190
Ashburton, Bull Ring at, 26
Atwell and Maine (U.S.) Families, 256
Atwell, Elizabeth, 256 ; John, 256

B. (G. L.) on Devon Glee Club, 120
B. (J.) on Exeter Bookseller's Label, 143
"Balbesywer," 248
Bampfield, Ursula, 5
Baraberga, 209
Baring-Gould (S.) on St. Petroc, 6
Barnstaple excluded from Common Rights, 80, 119, 133 ; Swete's Description of, 171
Barnstaple Mechanics' Institute, 200
Baron, Thomas, 34
Barrow, Martha, 158
Bartlett, Elizabeth, 54, 55
Bason, Hamlet of, 136
Bayley (A. E.) on Sidbury, 132
Baylis, Thomas, 250
Beetor Cross, 65 ; reputed Gibbet at, 186
Bells rung during thunderstorm, 18, 69
Berriman, John, 5
Berry Pomeroy, Wishing Tree at, 26
Bidgood, Humphrey, 219, 220 ; Dr. John, 221
Bideford, Swete's Description of, 169
Bigilston, Dorothy, 249, 250 ; James, 249 ; John, 249 ; Peter, 249 ; Philip, 249
Bishopsteignton Church, Norman Tympanum in, 188
Blake, George, 201, 203
Bodmin, Guron's Cell at, 7 ; St. Petroc at, 10
Boger, Edmund, 14
Bon, Walter le, 245
Books noticed :— Feudal Aids, 1284-1431, 29 ; Dickinson's Lecture on Ottery Church, 64 ;

Dickinson's Lecture on Parish Registers, 64; Coleridge's History of Ottery St. Mary, 96; California Register, 96; Wade's Wade Genealogy, 127; Gaythorne's Furness Lore, 127; Note-book of Tristram Risdon, 128; Phillimore's Pedigree Work, 160; Cresswell's Teignmouth, 191; Falcon s Dartmoor Illustrations, 192; Chanter and Wainwright's Barnstaple Records, 192; Salmon's West Country Ballads, 224
Booksellers' Labels, 18, 143, 168
Bottles, Named, 72
Bounties to Seamen at Ashburton, 1793, 197
Bourchier. Lady Joan, 53; William, Earl of Bath, 52
Bowth, Bp. John, Monumental Brass of, 57
Branscombe Folk-Lore, 49
Bridford Church Screen, 137, 139, 176
Brightleigh, Elizabeth de, 211; Isabel de, 210, 212, 213, 244; John de, 210; Thomas de, 210; William, Sir William de, 210,213
Brodmor, Thomas, 63
Brook. Catherine, 249; Thomas, 249
Brushfield (T. N.) on Raleigh v. Slade, 34; on Huntsman devoured by his Hounds, 48,176; on Branscombe Folk-Lore, 49; on Ralegh Family, 63, 219; on Abbotskerswell and Kingskerswell, 70; on Silver Tazza in Colaton Raleigh Church, 73; on a former Election Custom, 79; on the Boyhood of Ralegh, 97; on Christopher Jones, 109; on Norman Tympana in Devon, 136; on Sir Walter Ralegh, 150; on a Dartmouth Bookseller's Label, 168; on Torrington, 48, 176; on David Long, 196; on Will of George Raleigh, 202; on the Apprentices' Warningpiece, 219; on Deportment of Convicts, 242; on Custom at St. Petrock's, Exeter, 248
Browning, Thomas, 229
Bruton, William, 63
Buck (J. H.) on Church Plate, 159
Buckfast Abbey, 10, 13
Buckland Brewer, Christmas Local Tune, 183

Budleigh Salterton, Residence of Sir J. E. Millais at, 97
Bull-rings, 26, 48
Burleigh Dolts, 68. 149, 197
Burnel Family, 103
Busy B. on the Cuckoo in Devon, 35

C. (W. F.) on Devon Commons, 119
Cadhay House, Ottery, 236
Calmady, Sir Shilston, 119
Calvert, Edward, 82
Canonteign. 91
Cantilupe, Eva de, 245
Carewe, Nicholas, 247
Cary of Follaton, 117
Cary Cadell, Agnes Mary, 117
Celt found near the Tamar, 195.256
Chafe, Catherine, 250; Dorothy, Will of, 165; Thomas, 81, 164, 250, 251; His Monument in St. Giles' Church, 129, 163; Will of, 249
Champernowne, Arthur, 5. 53; Gawen, 49, 52; Richard, Sir Richard, 51, 53
Chanter (J. F.) on Church Plate, 191
Charles II, Miniature of, 157
Charles, Boy on Charles Church, Plymouth, 189
Charles Church, Plymouth, 189, 201
Chichester, Elizabeth, 52; Joan, 52; John, Sir John, 91, 199
Chittlehampton Church, Cobleigh Memorials in, 212
Chronogram in T. Chafe's Epitaph, 164
Chubb, Robert, 63
Chudleigh, Christopher, 33; Sir Richard, 53; Mary, 81; Sir George, 91; William, 145
Church Plate, 102, 158. 159
Church Right and Church Charters in Devon, 39
Churchyard Cross, Plympton, 209
Civil Engineer on Effect of Strong Winds, 182
Civil War, Relics of the, 118
Cleaves, Richard, 256
Clifford, Hugh, 81; Thomas, first Lord, 81
Clocks at Exeter, 177
Cloth Workers of Exeter, 190
Coal in Devonshire, 204
Cobleigh of Bryghtleigh, 210, 244

Index.

Cobleigh, Cobblegh, Cobbleigh, Cobbleye (Anne) 211; Elizabeth, 211; Hugh, 211; Jaket, 211, 213; Joan, 211; John, 210, 211, 212, 213, 214; Margaret, 210, 211, 213; Mary, 211; Thomas, 210; Walter, 211
Cobley, Rev. —, of Ide, 49
Cocktree in South Tawton, 103, 151
Cocktree, Coketrewe Family. 103
Cockworthy, Alice, 211, 212. 213
Coke, John, 232; William, 233
Colaton Raleigh Church. Silver Tazza in, 73
Coleman (E. H.) on the Hams, 48; on Wishing Trees, 48
Coleridge (Lord) on Bernard F. Taylor, 190
Collier (W. F.) on Eggsworthy New Bridge, 196; on Charles Church, Plymouth, 201
Collins, Grace, 239
Combmartyn, Swete's Description of, 173
Common-rights in Devon, 80
Commons of Devon, 119, 133
Consul, Robert, 190
Coory (?) John, 63
Convicts, Deportment of, 242
Cook (Samuel) Three Portraits of, 161
Copleston Family, 188
Copleston, Grace, 251
Corbin, Robert, killed by Indians, 256; William, 211, 213
Cornu, Isabel, 244; John, 226; Nicholas, 210, 213; Robert, 210, 211, 212, 213; William, 210, 213
Cottell Family, 152, 158
Cottell, John, 158; Thomas, 158
Cottell (W. H.) on Arms of Cottell, 103; on Drake Monument, 158
Courtenay, Edward. 181, 247, 248; Joan, 247; Sir William, 51, 52
Courtenay Monument in Sheviock Church, 246
Courtney (W. P.) on Baron de Vastey, 118
Cowland (C. L.) Celt found near the Tamar, 256
Cranch, John, 193
Craven, William, Bookseller, Dartmouth. 168
Cross in Plympton Churchyard, 209
Crosses, Ancient, in Neighbourhood of North Bovey, 65
Crymer, Anne, 115

Cuckoo, The, 35
Curson, George, 250; John, 250; Richard, 249; Thomas, 250
Custom at St. Petrock's Church, Exeter, 248

Dartmouth Bookseller's Label, 168
Davidson (J. B.) on Hooker's Discourse of Devon, 184
Davie, Margaret, 231
Davies (W.) on Two Interesting Epitaphs. 240
Davy (A. J.) on Bell-ringing during Thunderstorms. 18; on "Yend" and "Voach," 108; on Devon Saying. 120; on Portrait of Sir Humphrey Gilbert, 132; on Verses on White Ale, 133; on Anti-Cromwellian Song, 136; on a Noted Pluralist, 198; on Coal in Devon, 204; on Christopher Lethbridge, 255
Dawney, Emelina, 247; Sir John, 247
Deer Park, License to enclose, 15
Dennis, Denys, Sir Robert, 33, 51, 52; Thomas, 1
Deportment of Convicts, 242
Deserters, 133
Devon Commons, 80, 119, 133
Devon Dialect, 43
Devon Glee Club, 29, 72, 120
Devon Muster Roll, time of Armada, 49
Devon saying "That's extra," 120
Devon Societies, 108
Devon, Earl of, Domesday Estates of, 77
Dickinson (Rev. F. B.) on Two Interesting Epitaphs, 241
Doddridge, Judge, Chronogram on his Tomb, 164
Doe (G. M.) on Bull-ring, 48; on Formation of Royal North Devon Hussars, 76; on Sir Richard Whittington and Torrington, 143, 189; on Little Silver. 210
Dolbeare Family, 103, 152
Down St. Mary Church, Norman Tympanum in, 136
Drake, Sir Francis, 117; Margaret, 202, 203; Thomas, 202
Drake Monument in Werrington Churchyard, 116, 158
Drake (Morris) on Norman Tympana in Devon, 188
Drewsteignton Cromlech, 93
Duck, Richard, 59, 63

Index.

Duke. Francis, 190; Richard, 33
Dunkeswell, St. Patrick's Well at, 13
Dunning, John, 54, 55, 56
Dunsford Church, Fulford Monument in, 5; Font in, 120
Dunsford Manor, 1
Dunsford (G. L.) on Baldwin Ackland, 168

E. (E. A. S.) on Cuckoos in Devon, 36; on Burleigh Dolts, 68
Easterbrook, Mary, 111
Editors on Swete's Tour to North Devon, 81; on Cobleigh of Brightleigh, 244
Effect of Strong Wind on Fermentation and Springs, 144, 182
Eggworthy (or Eggesford) New Bridge, 190, 196
Election Day Treating in last Century, 44
Emmanuel Registers, 46
Eolus on the Effect of Strong Wind on Fermentation and Springs, 144
Epitaphs, Two interesting, 201, 240
Every, William, 230
Exbourne Church House, Deed of Foundation, 145
Exeter Custom, A former, 79
Exeter and London Coach "The Mercury," 104
Exeter Mayor and Councillors removed, others substituted, 1687, 113
Exeter Jeu d'esprit, 116
Exeter and Common Rights, 133
Exeter Bookseller's Label, 143
Exeter Guildhall Front, 153
Exeter Clocks, 177
Exeter Cathedral Bell, "Great Peter," 178
Eyre, Beatrix, 158

F. on Samuel Farley, 195
Fairfax, Sir Thomas, 2
Fall, John, 186
Farley, Samuel. 195
Feudal Aids, 29
Fitch, Alice, 234
FitzHamon, Mabel, 190
Fitzwarren Family, 143
Fitzwarren of Toteley, 183
Fitzwarren, Alice, 189; John, 211; Thomas, 211; Sir William. 211
Font in Dunsford Church, 120
Foreign Churches and their Property in Devon, 252

Ford, Katherine St. Clair, on Ford Family, 157
Ford Family, 157, 180
Ford, Edward, 180; Francis, Sir Francis, 157, 158; Joan, 157, 180; John. 158; Thomas, 157
Fortescue, Anne Mary. 13; Hugh, 51, 52; Jane, 211, 245; Joan, 211, 213; John, 210
French Family, 162
Frithelstock Priory, 126
Ffrost, Richard, 54, 55
Fry, Nicholas, 233
Fulford, Great, Notes on, 1
Fulford, Bridget, 53; Elizabeth, 5; Francis, Sir Francis, 1, 2, 3, 5; Henry, 1; Sir John, 1, 53; Thomas, 2, 5, 51, 53; Ursula, 5; William, 5

G. (H. F.) on The Whitchurch Fee, 63
G. (S.) on Prince of Orange's Flag, 25
"Galleyhapens," 248
Gibbet, Reputed, at Beetor Cross, 186
Gibbs (Roscoe) on Bridford and Lustleigh Screens, 139
Giffard (Harding F.) on Cobleigh of Brightleigh, 210
Giffard, Sir Roger, 210, 211, 213
Gilbert, Sir Humphrey, 52; Portrait of, 132; Sir John, 52, 53; Robert, 226
Gillett—*see* Jellett
Gittisham Register, entry as to Deserters, 133
Glanfyld, George, 63
Glass Manufactory in Devon, 135
Gould Elizabeth, 233
Gove, John. 228, 229
Grand Jury and their Port Wine, 101
Great Fulford, Notes on, 1
Great Torington Bull-ring. 48
Grenville, Richard de, 190; Robert, 235
Grenville and Arthur Families, 136

H. on Hamlet of Bason. 136
H. (J.) on Barnstaple Literary Institution, 200
H. (W. T. B.) on Eggworthy Bridge, 190
Haccombe, Elys, 33
Hales, Joan, 239
Haldon Barrow, 89
Hams, The, 17, 48

Hare, Sir George Ralph, 238
Harpesfeld, Nicholas, 120
Haydon of Woodbury and Ottery, 225
Haydon. Benjamin Robert, 49
Heanton, Swete's Description of, 121
Hearle, James, 251 ; Joan, 251
Hearn (?) Nicholas, 63
Heavitree Parish Church Orders, 59
Hems (Harry) on Stanzas on Slack the Boxer, 69
Hodder, Thomasine, 202
Holman (H. Wilson) on Holman Family, 135
Holwey, ——, 211. 213 ; John, 211 ; William, 211, 213
Honeychurch, Poor Law Administration at, 54
Hooker's Discourse of Devonshire, 184
Hooker, John, 184
Howard William, clockmaker, 177
Hughes (T. Cann) on Devon Societies. 108 ; on Celt found near the Tamar, 195 ; on Rolle Family Ring, 196
Huntsman devoured by his Hounds, 48, 176
Huxtable, William, 56

ILFRACOMBE, Swete's Description of, 172
Isack, John, 59, 63

JACOBSCHERCHE, Devon, 41
Jay's Grave, 251
Jellett, Gillett, Jonathan, 255
Jellett (James) on Jon. Jellett, 255
Jerman (James) on Exeter Guildhall Front, 153
Jervice, Fredeswith, 230
Jewers (A. J.) on Jower Netherton, 79 ; on Ford Family. 180 ; on Monuments in Sheviock Church, 246
Jones, Christopher, 109 ; " Poetic Attempts," 69
Jones, John, silversmith, Exeter, 74
Jower Netherton, 79, 107
Jower, Jour, Jourie, Jury Family, 80

KARKEBK (P. Q.) on Abbotskerswell and Kingskerswell, 47 ; on Glass Manufactory in Devon. 135
Kelly, Alice, 228
Kenton Church, Dedication of, 13
Kerslake, Kastlecke, Richard, 132

King, Bp. Henry, Elegy on Sir W. Ralegh, 150
Kingskerswell, 47, 70, 71
Knight, Ruth, 13
Knighton, James, 13

L. (R.) on Regnar Lothbrog, 214
L. (W.) on Regne Lothbrog, 187 ; on Oxenham Tombstone, 194
Lang. John, 63
Langdon (F. E. W.) on Civil War Relics at Membury, 118
Laurence, Jacob, 13
Leare, Joan, 157, 180
Lee, Dorothy, 233 ; Richard, 20, 21
Lega-Weekes (Ethel) on Cocktree, 103 ; on Prisoners in Devon, 181
Leigh, John, 34, 59, 63 ; Thomas, 63 ; William, 63 ; Walter, 229
Lethbridge, Christopher, 255
Lethbridge Family, 214
Lethbridge (Frances) Memorial to in Farringdon Church, 216 ; Rev. John, 216
Lethbridge (Sir Roper) on Poor Law Administration at Honeychurch, 54 ; on " Town Living," 77 ; on Deed of Foundation of Church House, Exbourne, 145
Letter of Marque, 159
License for Papists to leave their Homes 1679, 199
Lidford and Common Rights, 133
Lightfoot, Peter, clockmaker, 177
Littlecote Family, 188
Little Silver, 189, 210 219
Local Tune of Christmas Hymn, 183
Local Traditions. North Bovey and Neighbourhood, 186
Locke, John, 159
Loddiswell Deed, A, 245
Long, David, Sheriff of Devon, 196
Lovelace. Jacob, clockmaker, 178 ; his clock at Exeter, 178
Luscombe, Catherine, 21
Lustleigh Church Screen, 113, 139
Lynton, Swete's Description of, 173

MADCOTT, John, 251
Maine (U.S.) Families, 256
Marlborough, British Camp near, 68, 149
Martin, Richard, 256
Martyn, Mary, 232 ; William, 232
Mathew, silversmith, Exeter, 191
" Matthew the Miller," 178
Medland, Margaret, 202

Meere, John, of Leigh, 59, 63
Membury, Civil War Relics at, 118
Merton, Alis. Agnes, 210, 211, 213
Millais, Sir J. E., at Budleigh Salterton, 97
Miniature of Charles II, 157
Molford,, Mulford, Family, of Devon, 119, 131, 152
Monk, William, 51, 52
Monument to Sir T. Fulford in Dunsford Church, 5
Montacute House, Somerset, 155
Mountstephen (?) William, 63
Moore. Philip, 219, 221
More, Hugh, 235
Morris Family, 188
Morris (G. T. Windyer), on Drake Monument in Werrington Church, 116; on Littlecote and other Families, 188
Morshead (John), on Yonge's Plymouth Memoirs, 87
Mulford, see Molford
Mynyfye, Roger. 63

Norman, Paschœ, 251
Norman Tympana in Devon, 136, 188
North Bovey. Ancient Crosses in neighbourhood of. 65 ; Superstitions,105; LocalTraditions, 186
Northcote (Lady Rosalind), on Pixies. 37
Noted Pluralist, a, 198
Okehampton. Swete's description of, 121
Ottery St. Mary, Charter granted and Grammar School founded, 235.
Oxenham, Elizabeth. 195 ; James. 195 ; John, 194 ; Mary. 194.
Oxenham Tombstone. 194

P. (E. G.), on two interesting Epitaphs, 241
Padstow, St. Petroc at, 8 ; St. Samson's Chapel at. 9
Palk, Walter, his Election Bill, 44 ; Sir Robert, 90
Parker, George. 15
Parkhouse, John, 132
Parkin, Isaac, silversmith, 158
Parsons, Henry, his Epitaph, 201, 241
Partridge, Samuel, 198
Paulet, Joan, 229
Peard, John, silversmith, 159, 191
Pengelly (J. Isaac), on Devon Glee Club, 29

Perdue, Thomas, bellfounder, 178
Peryam, William, 34
Pilton, Monolith at, 172
Pirates, Letter of Marque for suppression of, 159
Pixies in the Present Day, 37
Plymouth Portraits, Volume of, 161
Plympton St. Mary, Enclosure of Deer Park in, 15
Plympton St. Maurice Churchyard Cross. 209
Plympton, the Honour of, 77
Pode (J. D.) on Devon Glee Club, 72
Pollard, Anthony, 51, 52 ; Thomas, 13
Pookay, Edward, 63
Poor Law Administration at Honeychurch in 18th Century. 54
Popham, Sir John, 157
Portrait of Sir Humphrey Gilbert, 132
Pot-de-Vin. near Totnes, 154
Powl (?) William, 63
Prestwood. Susan, 232
Prince of Orange's Flag. 25
Prisoners in Devon *temp.* Ric. II., 181
Punchard, Richard, 22
Pym, John, 63
Pyne, ——, 211 ; Joanna, 213

Quisquis on Arthur Family, 135

R (G.) on Heavitree Parish Document. 59
R. (G. W.) on Dolbeare of Dolbeare, 103 ; on Walter or Walters Family, 115
R. (Q.) on two interesting Epitaphs, 201, 240
Radford (J. H.) On Edward Calvert, 82; on three Portraits of Samuel Cook, 161.
Ralegh Family, 63, 219
Raleigh of Fardel, 201
Ralegh. Raleigh. Carew. 34 ; George. 33, 201, 233 ; Mary, 203 ; Walter, Sir Walter. 34, 49, 150 ; Boyhood of, 97 ; *versus* Slade, 33
Rapid Travelling. 104
Red Deer, the last killed on Dartmoor. 3
Regne Lothbrog, Regne Lodbrog, 187, 214, 255,

Index. 263

Reichel (J. O.) on Feudal Aids, 29; on Church Right or Church Charters in Devon, 39; on Ringing of Bells during Thunderstorms, 69; on Abbotskerswell and Kingskerswell, 70; on the Whitchurch Fee, 77; on the Commons of Devon, 80; on Jower Netherton, 107; on "Town Living," 110; Notices of Books, 127; on Deserters, 133; on Cockfree, 151; on Reynell Family, 152; on Little Silver, 187; on "Squirrel" as a Fieldname, 197; on Shillingham, etc., in Devon, 209; on two interesting Epitaphs, 240; on Foreign Churches and their Property in Devon, 252.
Relics of the Civil War at Membury. 118; Renell. Reynell Family. 111, 152
Renell. Reynell, Richard, 111, 176
Reynell, Sainthill, etc., 176
Risdon Margery, 251; Pascha, 129, 251; Will of. 251; Tristram, 129, 251; William, 251
Roger the Clockmaker, 177
Rogers, Mawdlin, 202
Rogers (W. H. H.) on the Haydons of Woodbury and Ottery, 225
Rolle Family Ring. 196
Romikly Paschoe, 251
Rose, Martha, 228
Rouge-et-noir, on local Christmas tune. 183
Rowe (J. B.) on Domestic Servants' Apprentice Indenture, 13; on License to Enclose a Deer Park at Plympton, 15; on the Hams, 17; on Book Label of an Exeter Bookseller, 18; on Death of Rev. Cobley, at Ide, 49; on Bp. John Bowthe, 57; Notices of Books, 64; on Cary of Follaton, 117; on the Chafe Monument, 129, 163; on Hooker's Discourse of Devon, 184; on John Cranch, 193; on Plympton Cross, 209
Rowe, Richard, 63
Royal Oak Inn, Dunsford, 2
Royal North Devon Hussars, formation of, 76
Ryledon, William, 250

S. (H.) on Named Bottlés, 72
St. Giles-in-the-Heath, Chafe Monument at, 129
St. James' Priory, Exeter, 41; see also Trew St. Jacob
St. Mary Steps, Exeter, Clock, 178
St Marv's Priory, Totnes, 41
St. Petroc, 6; Dedications to, 12
St. Petrock's Church, Exeter, Custom at, 248
St. Petrock's, Exeter, Clock, 178
St. Saviour, Abbey of, 87
Sainthill, Dorothy, 111; Elizabeth, 111, 176; Samuel, 176; Walter, 176
Sampford, John, 153
Samways, Ann, 5
Saunders (Helen) On Mulford Family, 131
Savery, Servington, 21
Score. Edward, 143
Screen in Bridford Church, 137, 139, 176
Screen in Lustleigh Church. 113, 139
Scarle. Ebett, 240
Selwyn, Matilda, 248; Nicholas, 248
Serrell, Sterrill Joan. 250; Mary, 250
Seymour, Sir Edward, 81
Sherman, William, 235
Sheviock Church, Monuments in, 246
Shillingham, 209
Sidbury, Devon, 132; Epitaph in the Church, 201
Sidmouth, Deeds in Parish Chest, 34, 35
Skardon (T. G.) On Cottell and other Families, 152
Slack the Boxer, Stanzas on his Death, 69
Slade, Roger, 33
Snedall, Snidall, Henry, 202, 203; Hugh, 203; Walter, 203
Snell, Andrew, 54, 55; John, 176
Soper, William, 54, 55
South Molton Church, Molford Monuments in, 131
Southcote, Margaret, 231
Southwood, Clement, 239
Squirrel as a Field Name, 197
Steed. Ezekiel, 111
Sterrill—*see* Serell
Stokes, Catherine, 234
Stowford, John, 210; Jone, 213
Strete, Thomas de, 245
Strong (Herbert A.) On Devon Dialect, 43
Superstitions at North Bovey 105

Swete, Rev. John, 88 ; his Tour in North Devon, 88, 121, 169, 205
Swinton (A. H.) On Pot-de-vin near Totnes, 254
Sydenham, John, 5

T. (F.) On Emmanuel Registers, 46
T. (W. H.) On North Bovey Superstitions, 105
Tate (A. L.) On Lustleigh Church Screen, 113 ; on Bridford Church Screen, 137 ; on Altar at Torbryan. 208
Tavistock, Swete's Description of, 170
Taylor, Bernard Frederick, 190 ; James, 63
Tazza of Silver in Colaton Raleigh Church, 73
Tiverton, Swete's Description of, 207
Thornton (W. H.) On Ancient Crosses in and near North Bovey, 65 ; on Local Traditions, 186
Thunderstorms, Bells rung during, 18, 69
Torbryan Church, Altar at, 208
Torrington, 176 ; and Sir Richard Whittington, 143, 189
Totnes and Common Rights, 80, 119, 133
Totnes old Church Walk, 20, 41
Towell, John, 229
"Town Living" as the name of a Tenement, 77, 110
Tracey, Oliver de, 88
Tragedies near North Bovey, 186
Trent, Joan, 226 ; William, 235
Trevill, Joan, 239
Trewe St. Jacob, 104, 151
Trinity Church, Exeter, Epitaph in, 201, 240
Tripe, John—see Swete
Trist, Nicholas, 23
Trivet, John, 132
Trosse, Anne, 231
Troup (Frances B.) On Bounties to Seamen at Ashburton, 197
Tucker, William, 63 ; John, 256
Tympana, Norman, in Devon, 136. 188
Tytherleigh, Christian, 229

UPHAM (Reynell) On Ralegh v. Slade, 31; on Reynell, etc., Families, 111, 176 ; on Richard Renell, 112 ; on Raleigh of Fardell, 202
Upton, Anna, 158 ; Arthur, 233

VASTEY, Baron de, 118
Vilvaine, Dr. Robert, 219
"Voach," 108
Voice, The, of the Waters, 42

W. (F) On Bridford Screen, 176 ; on Fitzwarren of Toteley, 183 ; on Cloth Workers of Exon, 190 ; on Arthur Family, 190
W. (J. H) On Church Plate, 102
Wade (Stuart C.) On Molford or Mulford Family, 119 ; on Attwell and Maine (U.S.) Families, 256
Wainwright (Thos.) On the Abbey of St. Saviour. 88 ; on License for Papists to leave their homes, 199
Walter or Walters Family, 115, 152
Ward Bridge, Dartmoor, 190, 196
Ware. Elizabeth, 232
Warrant for Manning the Fleet, 1770, 24
Water throwing, an Exeter Custom, 79
Watts (John) On French Family, 162
Week Down, Crosses on, 67
Weekes, Joan, 228
Werrington Churchyard, Drake Monument in, 116, 158
Westlake, Richard, 56
Whitchurch Fee, The, 63, 77
White, John, 211
White Ale, Verses on, 133
Whittington, Sir Richard, and Torrington, 143, 189
Wight, Thomas, Epitaph on, 201, 242
Wilcocks, John, 102
Wilcox (William A.) On John Wilcocks, 102
Wilkinson (W. J. W.) Exeter Jeu d'esprit, 116
Williams, Richard, 228 ; William Peere, 238
Windeatt (Edw.) On Old Church Walk, Totnes, 20, 41
Wishing Trees, 26, 48
Withycomb Raleigh Manor, 33. 35
Woodbury Church, Haydon Aisle in, 226
Wreckage Mark, Elizabethan, 87
Wyke, William, 103

YARDE, Gilbert, 233
"Yend," 108
Yeo, Margaret, Margery, 18, 250
Yonge, Anne, 115
Yonge's Plymouth Memoirs, 87

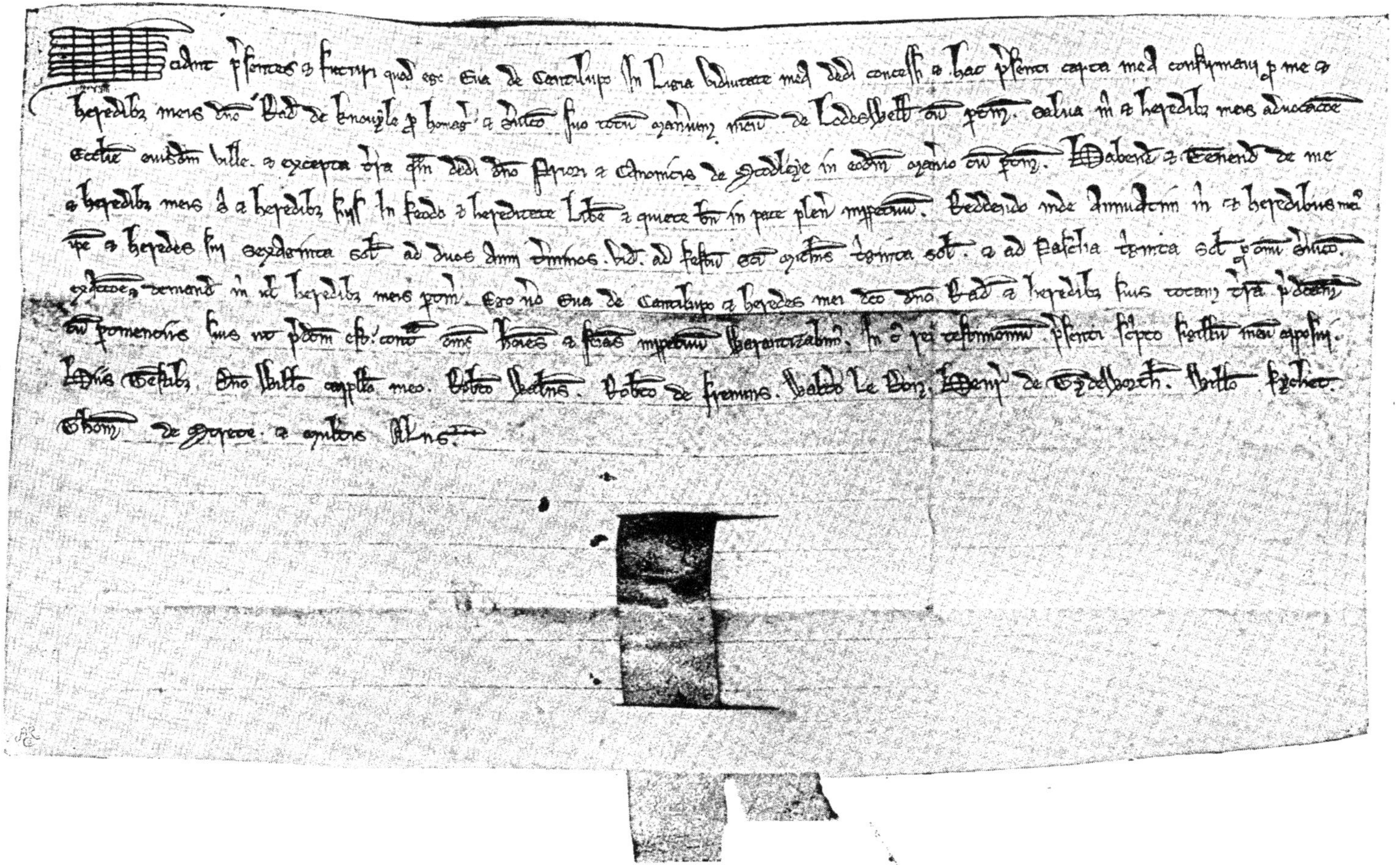

Sciant presentes et futuri quod ego Eva de Cantelupo in ligia viduitate mea dedi concessi et hac presenti carta mea confirmavi pro me et
heredibus meis domino Radulfo de Knoyle pro homagio et servicio suo totum manerium meum de Ledesbeth cum pertinentiis. salva mihi et heredibus meis advocatione
ecclesie eiusdem ville. et excepta terra quam dedi domino priori et elemosinarie de Bradleye in eodem manerio cum pertinentiis. Habendum et tenendum de me
et heredibus meis sibi et heredibus suis in feodo et hereditate libere et quiete bene in pace plenarie imperpetuum. Reddendo inde annuatim mihi et heredibus meis
ipse et heredes sui sexdecim solidos ad duos anni terminos. videlicet ad festum sancti Michaelis octo solidos. et ad Pascha octo solidos pro omni servicio
exactione et demanda mihi vel heredibus meis pertinentibus. Ego vero Eva de Cantelupo et heredes mei dicto domino Radulfo et heredibus suis totam terram predictam
cum pertinentiis suis ut predictum est contra omnes homines et feminas imperpetuum warantizabimus. In cuius rei testimonium presenti scripto sigillum meum apposui.
Hiis testibus. domino Willelmo capellano meo. Roberto Walens. Roberto de Fremins. Waltero le Boy. Henrico de Edelberch. Willelmo Fychet.
Thoma de Grovere. et multis aliis.